CATHERINE BLYTH

THE ART OF
MARRIAGE

A HANDBOOK FOR LIFE

JOHN MURRAY

First published in Great Britain in 2010 by John Murray (Publishers)
An Hachette UK Company

I

© Catherine Blyth 2010

A CIP catalogue record for this title is available from the British Library

Hardback ISBN 978-1-84854-167-2
Trade paperback ISBN 978-1-84854-168-9

Typeset in Mrs Eaves by Servis Filmsetting Ltd, Stockport, Cheshire

Printed and bound by Clays Ltd, St Ives plc

John Murray policy is to use papers that are natural, renewable and recyclable
products and made from wood grown in sustainable forests. The logging and
manufacturing processes are expected to conform to the environmental regulations
of the country of origin.

John Murray (Publishers)
338 Euston Road
London NW1 3BH

www.johnmurray.co.uk

For Sebastian

Contents

Contents

MARRY? WHY WOULD YOU WANT TO DO THAT?

He – or she – asks, 'Will you marry me?'

In the past, your range of acceptable replies was limited to 'Yes', 'No', 'When?' and 'Ask me again, later'. In the twenty-first century, this extraordinary question begs another: 'What for?'

But as you walk down the aisle, arm in arm with your new spouse, your head is more likely to be filled with gauzy notions of everlasting love than doubts as to why you have voluntarily subsumed your identities in the impersonal clichés of bride and groom. The dreams embodied in these timeless, hopeful figures are taken as read. Still, if happiness writes white, the precise instructions for how a couple will reach their chosen destination, their happy ever after, are also elusive. Marriage is a very beautiful dream, but the dull, practical job of merging two lives into one is not dwelt on in its mythology.

Not everyone is optimistic about marriage. On Christmas Day in 1685 the naval administrator Samuel Pepys noted in his diary, 'To church in the morning, and there saw a wedding in the church, which I have not seen many a day; and the young people so merry one with another, and it was strange to see what delight we married people have to see these poor fools decoyed into our condition, every man and wife gazing and smiling at them.' Some find such spectacles intolerable. Mrs Willis, who worked for my grandmother, declined an invitation to my parents' wedding: 'I never go to weddings. Poor young things, all their troubles just beginning!'

So hard was it to drag grooms to the altar in eighth-century BC Sparta that the ruler Lycurgus passed a law ordering that bachelors who were slow to marry should be excluded from summer games and shows, and in winter, be forced to patrol the forum, nude, uttering curses on their own heads that theirs was a just penalty for neglecting their civic duty. No amount of pressure from her own or other governments could persuade Elizabeth I of matrimony's merits. She told her French ambassador, 'When I think of marriage, it is as though my heart were being dragged out of my vitals.' As her father Henry VIII severed ties with her mother, Anne Boleyn, by dividing Anne's body from her head, Elizabeth's misgivings are understandable. Yet the suspicion that a wedding marks not the start but the end of a charmed period has always haunted marriage, like an unwelcome guest, lurking outside the chapel.

After all, call your wedding day the happiest of your life, and what are you really saying?

That it is all downhill from here.

Marriage is an heirloom. The first recorded exchange of wedding rings took place in Ancient Egypt in 2790 BC, but the invention of marriage must predate this occasion by many moons. It exists to yoke men and women together, to draw lines around groups of people and call them families, ensuring the production of legitimate children and the peaceful inheritance of property and other social privileges. Without marriage, each king's death would have precipitated a war of succession. Each union forged a link in a chain of being that kept humanity at peace, allowing each generation to transmit its values to the next, and society to reproduce itself more or less smoothly. Its success at this task has been such that while pyramids are ancient history, marriage is still with us. Whether it should be is another matter.

Until recently marriage was a rite of passage, the next thing to do in life, after learning how to shave or wear lipstick, and to make your living. A spoilt playgirl heaves a sigh in Hitchcock's *The Lady Vanishes* (1938):

> I've no regrets. I've been everywhere, and done everything. I've eaten caviar at Cannes, sausage rolls at

the dogs. I've played baccarat at Biarritz and darts
with the rural dean. What is there left for me but
marriage?

But do we still need to ink the ties of blood and affection in
the legal contract of marriage? Today DNA-tests confirm
which child belongs to which parent, and many social forces
that once coerced couples to the chapel have lost their bite.
Pre-marital sex, cohabitation and illegitimacy are no longer
taboo. Now that women can work, nobody need marry to
raise a family or have a home of their own.

Marriage is extraordinary. Less for the fact that it still
exists than the courage it asks. Each couple to hold hands
and swear their wedding vows takes a giant leap of faith into
the unknown future. They are seizing their one chance in
life to change the story that they tell the world, and each
other, about who they are. To make this almighty wish come
true requires more than faith: it takes art. But epidemic
levels of divorce suggest that it is an art which many fail to
master.

Marriage has never been so free, or seemingly unneces-
sary. Yet many people continue to regard a wedding as the
summit of life's achievement. The question remains: why?
What propels millions of newlyweds down aisle, into regis-
try office or up garden path, now that everybody knows that
marriage is not until death but divorce do us part?

THE MADNESS OF WEDDINGS

What does the word 'marriage' mean to you? With all the effort, and money, that we are urged to devote to it, you could be forgiven for thinking that a show-stopping Big Day and a successful marriage are one and the same thing.

In the lexicon of modern love, a wedding is a fairy-tale occasion, and fairy tales demand fancy dress, as well as a wedding theme (Rock and Roll, Guys and Dolls, or Knights in White Satin perhaps), and a multi-storey wedding cake (price: equivalent to a small second-hand car). Not to mention co-ordinated table-settings, witty canapés, imaginative music, party favours, floral sculpture, napkins tortured into swans, and food that is original yet sufficiently dull to appease the palates of toddlers and toothless Great-aunt Enid alike. Oh, and maybe a Bollywood dance routine for the bride and her maids, or real live butterflies in glass cages, to release during the champagne toast.

Or so preacheth the gospel of the wedding and bridal magazines that heave their bosoms in the news-stands at a supermarket near you. And plenty of couples seem to believe that these measures are necessary.

Today's average bride cannot feel herself camera-ready until she has tanned, dieted and shoehorned herself into a Disney gown of complexion-draining hue and weird, pâtisserie construction. Meanwhile your typical groom must witness the grisly transformation of his beloved into Bride of Visa. Suddenly he must form opinions about cutlery and flowers, and develop at least the appearance of an anxiety disorder about hitherto unsuspected aspects of hospitality, like party favours. If he tries to change the subject from wedding plans by saying, 'Whatever makes you happy, dear' Bride of Visa will snap back, 'You just don't care!' Which may strike him as ungrateful, given that he has already pillaged his savings for a gob-stopping, diamond knuckle-duster (if the engagement ring is not a knockout, people will talk). No wonder that grooms feel compelled to expunge several billion brain cells on an extravagantly drunken stag weekend paint-balling in Croatia.

What price this pomp and nincompoopery? In 2008 an average wedding cost about £23,000, raped from a parent's pension pot, a child's mortgage deposit, or both. Many couples spend far more than this. And that is not accounting for the stress and unpaid hours of planning. Laidback brides and mothers-of are lesser spotted animals and not encouraged, since the wedding industry was worth £6 billion a year to the UK economy, and an estimated $58.5 billion in the United States in 2006. Yet these astonishing figures may underestimate the true financial oomph of marriage. In the late 1990s newlyweds comprised 2 per cent of the US population yet bought 58 per cent of its knives and forks. It could be worse: in Japan, diamond companies have waged a successful advertising campaign to persuade grooms to heft up several months' salary on an engagement ring, and this is a land where traditional Shinto weddings entailed nothing fancier than drinking rice wine from a wooden bowl.

Clearly, consumer societies believe in marriage. But perhaps they do not mind so much if, by the time we reach the aisle, we are so frayed by the stress that we end up splitting sooner rather than later — and buy more cutlery, then spend another fortune on marrying somebody else. From an economic point of view, the more we marry — with bells, whistles and hand-blown glass knobs on — the better.

Not for a moment am I suggesting that the vampiric wedding industry is a conspiracy to ensure that couples cannot stand each other by the time they say 'I do'. Perish the thought that the debt hangover from the Big Day has anything to do with the fact that one in ten marriages end within five years. I will even concede that weddings are fun. I loved mine and cry at my friends'. Most people find them uplifting. Maggie Blunt, a spinster of Slough, was not jealous at her future queen's 1947 nuptials:

> Turned on wireless. A moving occasion. I do not need commentator to tell me this or doubt the cheers from the crowd broadcast. The feeling is genuine enough — a delightful sort of family feeling . . . We do love our little ceremonies. And why not? All of us are hungry for colour, romance and

adventure . . . I wept copiously into the washing up bowl as I listened.

What a nice voice the groom has. And so surprisingly English — though I don't know what I was expecting. The Princess's voice too was becomingly virginal. One wishes them a long and happy life together, to set an example to the nation of what marriage *can* be like.

We make a fuss about weddings because they are not just tokens of two people's love. Fading TV soaps boost their ratings with a hasty union because weddings tug at the very roots of the idea of society as a 'pact between the dead, living, and the yet unborn', to paraphrase the philosopher Edmund Burke. When we witness our loved ones swear their undying promises, our pleasure is deepened by the knowledge that they are following a path likely walked by their parents, and almost certainly by their grandparents.

Our styles of weddings are also symptoms of society's attitude to marriage in general, and the madness of modern nuptials suggests that our feelings about marriage are confused, verging on manic. 'The best part of my wedding?' confided several friends. 'That we had got it over with.'

A wedding is not an end, except in novels and comedies; in reality, it is a beginning. But should we be surprised if after the steeplechase to the altar, to suggest that there is any further art to married life strikes some couples as absurd? Having survived the wedding, well may they feel that their most vital marriage skills — spending, arguing, knowing when not to listen, and how to offend relatives — have been well honed. And the idea that marriage marks an end to the games of love must have been around for as long as marriage itself. 'It was a strange condition of things,' reflects David Copperfield in Dickens's great autobiographical novel, 'the honeymoon being over, and the bridesmaids gone home, when I found myself sitting down in my small house with Dora; quite thrown out of employment, as I may say, in respect of the delicious old occupation of making love!'

The fuss involved in the show business of weddings should make couples think hard about the commitment they are getting into, but there is evidence that, to the contrary, it distracts many from what married life involves, both its demands and its deeper benefits. A greater sadness is that the high price of getting hitched puts off those who could profit most from marriage. Poor, young parents in deprived areas tell sociologists that they would dearly love to marry, but are too ashamed to do so, because they cannot afford to marry 'properly'. By which they mean, like celebrities in magazines. Inflated wedding expectations can even lead others to regard marriage as one long, flat after-party. Many a divorcee can trace the first seed of doubt to the moment after the ceremony, as they walked out arm in arm, and found themselves thinking, Is this it? Because they did

not feel as happy as they expected – which is not surprising
if they were tired and stressed – they concluded that something must have been wrong.

There was a time when a couple could call themselves
hitched after nothing fancier than jumping over a broom,
hand in hand. Maybe today's couples drop more coins into
the wishing well that is a wedding because they are older and
richer when they get around to marrying than the majority
of brides and grooms in bygone days. But I suspect that
many go overboard because they are also frightened of
divorce, so hurl money at their nuptials in the hope that a
perfect day will guarantee theirs is a perfect marriage. By
similar reasoning, I heard a champagne-soused bride reas-
sure her guests, 'I said I'd never do it, but I married him,
didn't I? So he must be worth it.'

Addled as my friend's logic was, to marry today, wishful
thinking is necessary.

THE CASE AGAINST MARRIAGE

A cynic would argue that weddings have evolved into such
exotic blooms to lure us, like dazzled insects, into the
increasingly irrelevant trap of wedlock. Certainly, it is a
great irony that the more weddings cost, the less in love
society seems to be with marriage.

Each year half a million British men and women marry,
but numbers are falling, and we seem less adequately

equipped than any previous generation to turn the fairy tale of marriage into reality. At present 45 per cent of unions end before the grim reaper cuts in on their dance. Yet these baleful odds of success do not discourage everyone: 40 per cent of weddings are remarriages for at least one party, usually him, although divorce is likelier for them than for first-timers.

Rare is the groom who will confide on the eve of his vows, as did an acquaintance of mine, that he believes life-long love is neither reasonable nor possible, 'because when marriage was invented, you were dead by thirty'. But it is often said that monogamy is unnatural. Given that scientists cannot decide if ours is a tournament species, like peacocks, who compete for mates, or a pair-bonded species, like swans, who pair off for ever, let us assume that we are polygamous monogamists. In other words, that marriage is a choice, and often a difficult one to stick by.

Many believe that this choice is no longer necessary and that marriage retains its grip on our imaginations for no stranger reason than the rigor mortis of custom. To some, marriage is a discredited old bully that limits men and women and subjugates them to Church and state. Even priests have had reservations about it. In 1672 Richard Baxter, Presbyterian divine, lamented that 'if nature itself had not inclined' women to accept 'so calamitous' a life, with children causing 'tedious trouble day and night', and 'subjection to their husbands, and continual care of family affairs', these and 'much more would have utterly deterred their sex from marriage'. Until the 1870 Married Women's Property Act, a wife had no right to her property, and in legal terms existed only 'under cover' (as a subdivision) of her husband. The inequities between men and women's status were such that until 1828 a British wife who killed her husband, even in self-defence, committed petty treason, the penalty for which was, for many years, the witch's punishment, burning.

Some cannot forgive marriage its past sins. In 2008 Georgian singer Katie Melua, that rare thing, a self-made teenage girl millionaire, griped: 'Marriage . . . was invented for money and convenience. I'd like to believe in monogamy but if I have children I am never going to read them stories about finding Prince Charming because they will grow up feeling disappointed.' Others believe that the conjugal commitment is purer made outside the cobwebby institution of matrimony, unsullied by God, law or in-law. Like aviator Amelia Earhart, who on the morning of her wedding in 1931 handed her groom this billet-doux:

> You must know again my reluctance to marry, my feeling that I shatter thereby chances in work which means most to me. I feel the move just now as foolish as anything I could do. I know there may be compensations, but have no heart to look ahead . . .
>
> I shall not hold you to any medieval code of faithfulness to me, nor shall I consider myself bound to

you similarly. If we can be honest I think the diffi-
culties which arise may best be avoided should you or
I become interested deeply (or in passing) with
anyone else.

Please let us not interfere with the other's work or
play, nor let the world see our private joys or disagreements. In this connection I may have to keep
some place where I can go to be myself now and
then, for I cannot guarantee to endure at all times
the confinements of even an attractive cage.

I must extract a cruel promise, and that is you
will let me go in a year if we find no happiness
together.

I will do my best in every way and give you that part
of me you know and seem to want.

Earhart went through with it, calling theirs not a marriage
but a 'partnership' with 'dual control'.

Marriage has been accused of many crimes. The charge
sheet reads something like this: in the name of love, money,
family and social legitimacy, marriage oppresses women;
depletes men's testosterone (scientists claim true); enriches
divorce lawyers (you bet); curbs desire (up to a point);
blights ambition (debatable); and co-opts otherwise sane
individuals into signing a code of conduct bequeathed to us
by an outmoded world (why, certainly). A world in which
men were men, wives were married to their houses, and
children were God's blessing, not unlimited domestic

liabilities with grave implications for your finances, social life and career.

So marriage is, you might say, a big ask, and even the state seems disenchanted with it. Under British welfare arrangements, parents are financially better off if they live apart and do not tie the knot, and in 2003 the term 'marital status' was abolished from government-sponsored family research in the UK. Instead we get to tick a box marked 'couple parent families'. In effect, this move declared marriage to be meaningless, of no statistical significance as an influence on our lives. As a result, no longer shall we know what difference marriage makes to a British family – whether it helps couples to stay together, or has any other impact on their or their children's wellbeing.

Is marriage meaningless? Not according to the vast, well-documented difference in outcomes for families of the wed and unwed. Those who imagine that because marriage is old it is also irrelevant to modern life overlook marriage's distinguished pedigree. As history shows, wedlock can knot us into almost any sort of social and familial formation – be it nuclear, feudal, bourgeois, or pharaonic, back when claimants to Egypt's throne had to marry their sister. The custom of marriage has survived by being flexible, and by obeying the evolutionary imperative, to change, or die. One charge we can convict it of is suiting a whole host of ways of living. If marriage is guilty of anything, it is association with our past.

In 2008 one in five British spinsters were saving for a

dream wedding, although they had yet to meet their would-be groom. Yet what, in our free world, has marriage still to offer?

THE WONDERS OF WISHFUL THINKING

If marriage is a story that we tell about who we are, the reason it has been told by countless generations is that today, tomorrow and always, it answers timeless human needs. But now the terms and conditions of the story have changed: we need not marry people because our parents say so, nor must we be wed to leave home, have sex, get a job, nor are we obliged to conform to starchy roles of husband and wife, and if we want to walk away from our marriage, we can.

This means that marriage is ours to remake in our own image. Elderly as the institution is, it remains fresh, as each couple strikes their own deal, so it is also always personal. Now it can be custom-fit, marriage can be better than ever, as long as we understand what makes it an asset.

When those Ancient Egyptians traded nuptial bands, five millennia ago, they placed them on the third finger of the left hand. This finger was believed to connect to the heart by the *vena amoris* or 'vein of love'. Rings also touched on the supernatural, their eternal circle a spell against ill spirits. And then, as now, there was an element of casting a spell about marriage. As Ted Hughes wrote in 'A Pink Wool Knitted Dress', of his wedding to fellow poet Sylvia Plath:

> I stood subjected
> To a strange tense: the spellbound future

Part of marriage's enchantment is the appeal of tradition. The fact that so many people have thought it a good idea means that by casting our vote into the marriage box, we gain membership of the reassuring 'democracy of the dead'. But the real magic of marriage is the audacity of its ambition, for what men and women can be to one another. To marry is an act of hope that tells the world that you intend to share your life, that this commitment comes before all others, and that love is at its heart.

This is wishful thinking, yet surprisingly often it comes true. As agony aunt Irma Kurtz said, marriage 'is the best retirement plan'. It is the downiest of nests too, since married couples are richer. The US Health and Retirement Survey in 1992 found that unmarried women were 86 per cent poorer than wives and widows, and bachelors 61 per cent poorer than husbands and widowers. The married enjoy more and better sex (those who have it), as well as better hormonal balance, mental and physical wellbeing. Husbands outlive bachelors by seven years, wives outlive spinsters by four. Children of married parents are also more emotionally stable, educationally successful and likelier to make stable marriages themselves.

A married family is not only the most effective welfare state, but it costs taxpayers nothing. According to the institution's advocates, married people commit fewer crimes, and most husbands confine their illicit behaviour to white-collar frolics. Married fathers who live with their children provide greater support, financial and otherwise, and married people are less likely than the unmarried to boot their old parents into care homes – not because they care more, but they have more space and more flexible living arrangements. So marriage is good for society, and governments should keep faith with it.

By what mechanism does marriage have these beneficent effects? There is an element of self-selection. Happy people are likelier to marry, and optimistic expectations of marriage are found to predict the best outcomes. Conservative people also tend to keep the peace. Even so, research confirms that these factors cannot explain all of marriage's success.

What we gain by making this promise to transform the meaning of our life is a chance to transcend our limitations and become more than the sum of our parts. Gay marriage campaigner Jonathan Rauch wrote: 'No other institution has the power to turn narcissism into partnership, lust into devotion, strangers into kin. What other force can bond across clans and countries and continents and even cultures?'

At times, other people are hell, but without them life has no meaning, and if living in others' mess is occasionally maddening, so can be the loneliness of a home where the air is disturbed by only the flies and you. Sharing your life is healthy too. Scientists suggest that there are five ways to enhance wellbeing: to connect with your world; to give; to learn; to be observant and curious; and to be active. A life-long relationship demands all these, and goes further, by extending our possibilities with shared memory and com-plementary life skills, offering an endless learning curve in human sympathy. 'There are no words to express the abyss between isolation and having one ally,' observed G.K. Chesterton. 'It may be conceded to the mathematicians that four is twice two. But two is not twice one; two is two thousand times one. That is why, in spite of a hundred dis-advantages, the world will always return to monogamy.'

Need you marry to be monogamous or to have a life companion? Of course not. To champion marriage is not to call other ways of life bad. I don't believe that my friends are defective for living alone, or with a dog they adore, or with friends with whom they may or may not have sex. But I do believe that marriage, when it works, is the most reliable means of support, and I know that it is more than a piece of paper. It means something.

A wedding is not simply a 'fateful moment' when you take stock of your relationship. It is a decision, and the instant you make it, it is real. The act of marrying may not reconfigure your DNA; however, it will alter your self-image and your view of your spouse.

As literary historian Phyllis Rose observed: 'Commitment grows when you begin to use the language of commitment.' And psychologists find that although women may commit deeply to another person without ceremonies (perhaps due to the emotional weight of deciding to carry a person's child), for men in particular, marrying transforms their feelings for their loved one. For all of us, a sense of ownership increases the value we vest in something, be it a person or a possession, and this deepens our sense of duty towards it. It is also harder to flounce off — divorce being expensive, difficult, and, having sworn undying love, then to change your tune you also look a fool.

Even if you lived together before, and superficially your life remains the same, marriage alters the compass of your world. In the eyes of the law, friends and family, from now on you are side by side, in a three-legged race, before the obstacle course of life. Like an axle between wheels, marrying shifts your centre of gravity to somewhere between you two. This is your wedlock. Henceforth, your first obligation is not to yourself but to a strange new state of being, us.

What a relief. 'I am — can it be true? — no longer the most interesting thing in my life,' observed novelist Zoë Heller. 'Of all the gifts of middle-age, this release from the dank cell of self seems to me the most precious.' Marriage also offers certainty. A friend, belatedly wed after two children, wrote: 'I still struggle with the terms "husband" and "wife" . . . But I love that we have the wedding as an important and happy memory in the story of our lives and I love wearing a ring and I love having an anniversary and I love that the path, together, is chosen. Obviously, the relationship still has ups and downs but somehow it feels like they happen on firmer ground.'

In this respect marriage is a confidence trick. You are

staking a claim for how the future will be, whatever destiny flings in your path. And to feel in charge of your destiny is a great tonic. When the eighteenth-century politician Charles Fox revealed his clandestine marriage to a famous courtesan, a friend noted that Fox was full of vim, compared to his contemporaries' 'air of shattered debauchees'. Sometime Prime Minister Charles Grey observed: 'Is it not a fine thing to grow young at 50?'

Crucially, the new perspective of marriage also transforms our relation to time. Studies find that cohabiting couples tend to measure their relationship by the years they have been together, by what they have done for each other. By contrast, a wedding is a mark in time that decisively turns us to the future. Opening up this long-term horizon gives the married a huge strategic advantage in life.

Ours is an age of high-pressure jobs, short-term contracts, declining loyalty, instant rewards. But as short-termist as our culture seems, it is built on a model in which, for success, we need to defer gratification; to make plans, study for exams, invest in mortgages, climb career ladders, and play a long game. Likewise, for psychological stability, we need to feel anchored. So we are pulled in contrary directions. Understandably, many of us find it less than easy to accept setbacks, to take a gamble, to resist easy options; to summon the trust and confidence to step off a career path, take out that loan, have children or to quit and seek something better, never mind to marry. But marriage, if we trust in it, offers flexibility, motivation and a safety net.

Even setbacks may seem opportunities with a little encouragement and support. One day in 1848 Nathaniel Hawthorne came home to inform his wife that he had been fired from his job as District Surveyor for Salem, Massachusetts. 'She leaves the room; she returns with fuel and kindles a bright fire with her own hands; next she brings pen, paper, ink, and sets them beside him. Then she touches the sad man on the shoulder, and, as he turns to the beaming face, says, "Now you can write your book."' Hawthorne wrote *The Scarlet Letter*, and made his fortune.

In everyday judgements, a second opinion makes us brainier. Just as the aggregated guesswork of a crowd is wiser than any expert, so married people gain the wisdom of couples. Having another person to guide you, or to react against, can make it easier to form opinions, to discern problems, to make choices and be assured you have picked the right ones. No advice is disinterested and spouses may lack distance, but since they have almost as great a stake in our happiness as we do, we can trust their advice as we cannot that of any seemingly neutral friend. And when it comes to making the gravest decisions, the heart is the surest guide.

The support is not only external. When we feel needed, courage helps to brace us from the inside. Doughty British housewife Nella Last described her reaction after Paris had fallen to the Nazis in 1940:

I put rouge and lipstick on . . . picked some roses and got out my best embroidered tea-cloth. I cannot tell what made me do it, and there were only boiled eggs, strawberry jam and some rather indifferent cake for my 'party table'. My husband came in and we looked at one another silently, and then I said, 'Bad — very bad'. He nodded and sat down at the table, and he said, 'It's not so bad now I'm HOME,' and I saw his work-grimed finger tracing the holly-hocks embroidered in the corner of the cloth. I poured out the tea and, as I passed him, he leaned against me and looked up at me, and I saw the terror bogey looking out of his eyes. Mine had gone — please God never to come again — and I felt strong and sure. I bent and kissed him and said, 'get your tea, my dear' . . . He said, 'You never lose courage or strength, my darling . . .' To confess my terrors would have been to rob him of his faith, so I smiled and said nothing.

Marriage not only widens our world, but deepens our experience of it. The daily grind is altogether more signifi-cant than one damned thing after another, when it is shared. Telling tales to one who knows you intimately is a pleasure — even, perhaps especially, if you are recounting misfortunes. (Historian's wife Jane Carlyle put all her genius into telling her grouchy husband mock-heroic tales about her battles with neighbours over noisy cockerels.) And if sharing troubles reduces their hold over us, our joys multiply in mutual laughter.

To philosopher Søren Kierkegaard, marry without romance's 'impulse to eternity' and you had merely a marriage of convenience. I would say that marriage salves the human impulse to eternity by satisfying our deepest desire, to slow down time. Joan Didion wrote of her experience of widowhood: 'For forty years I saw myself through John's eyes. I did not age. This year for the first time since I was twenty-nine I saw myself through the eyes of others. This year for the first time since I was twenty-nine I realized that my image of myself was of someone significantly younger.'

Shared memories, special moments, knot together the years like beads on a necklace, and empower a spouse to teleport you to a happier place too. One mother wrote: 'My husband is the one and only person in the world who I can rely on to recall the dazzling highbrow conversation I *can* enter into, even though I may be discussing Johnny's runny nose or Laura's tummy-ache.'

Above all, being married means having someone to believe in you. When bits start falling off you, having that special person to boil the egg, to remind you where you left your false teeth, to laugh when you cannot touch your toes, to argue about who did what to whom, to remember how gorgeous you were, how you adored the baby who is now a selfish son, and why you, of all people, were their one and only – all this is more than a consolation. You might even have grandchildren.

It is a risk to stake your life on another person. If your marriage works out, you create a place of safety in life's voyage, but this place will exist only for you two. 'Grief feels like suspense,' C.S. Lewis wrote after his wife's death. 'Thought after thought, feeling after feeling, action after action, had H. for their object. Now their target is gone. I keep on through habit fitting an arrow to the string, then I remember and have to lay the bow down.' Lose your centre of gravity, that person, the axle between you two, and you can feel lost. But the risk is worth taking because marriage, when it works, enhances life as nothing else can.

All too easily in the daily grind we can feel victims, as if we are losing pieces of ourselves. But anything we give to marriage, if only patience, is also an investment in something better, and bigger, than us. As Epicurus, philosopher of pleasure, observed: 'The greater the difficulty, the more the glory in surmounting it.' Even sacrifices can be rewards, if they are seen as gifts to a marriage. Whatever life chucks at you, be true to each other and you may hold your head high.

Why bet that this person is the one to trust with your life? The impulse is easier to follow if it feels inexplicable, therefore unarguable. The singer Seal said of meeting his wife, Heidi Klum, who was then expecting another man's child: 'I wasn't looking to be in a relationship but we saw something in each other and that recognition transcended everything else. We were in a seemingly complex situation but we both had such clarity.' Comedian Jack Dee, on the other hand, surmised that he had found the right woman when, after he prevaricated over a date, she firmly told him to naff off (or words to that effect).

Marriage is a mystery, full of questions, because it is not his, or hers; it belongs to you two, and everybody else. Each story has at least two sides. Reconciling them is the art of marriage, and it can be done for better, or worse. The beauty is that what makes your marriage great will be for you to decide. Because every marriage shares one secret. That it is like no other.

This is why it can work for you.

IS IT FOR ME?

If in doubt, you might be comforted to learn that the greatest mind of the nineteenth century struggled. In the summer of 1838, Charles Darwin recorded his internal debate over whether to propose to his cousin Emma Wedgwood. (The spelling mistakes are his own.)

THIS IS THE QUESTION

Mary

Children — (if it Please God)
Constant companion, (& friend in old age) who will feel interested in one,— object to be beloved & played with. —better than a dog anyhow.
Home, & someone to take care of house
Charms of music & female chit-chat.

These things good for one's health. — but terrible loss of time.

My God, it is intolerable to think of spending ones whole life, like a neuter bee, working, working, & nothing after all. No, no won't do. Imagine living all one's day solitarily in smoky dirty London House. —
Only picture to yourself a nice soft wife on a sofa with good fire, & books & music perhaps —
Compare this vision with the dingy reality of Grt. Marlbro' St.

Marry — Marry — Marry Q.E.D.

Not Mary

No children, (no second life), no one to care for one in old age. —
What is the use of working without sympathy from near & dear friends —who are near & dear friends to the old, except relatives

Freedom to go where one liked —
choice of Society & little of it. —
Conversation of clever men at clubs —
Not forced to visit relatives, & to bend in every trifle. — to have the expense & anxiety of children — perhaps quarelling
Loss of time. — cannot read in the Evenings — fatness & idleness—

Anxiety & responsibility — less money for books &c — if many children forced to gain one's bread. (But then it is very bad for ones health to work too much)

Perhaps my wife wont like London; then the sentence is banishment & degradation into indolent, idle fool —

It being proved necessary to marry, Charles posed himself another question: 'When? Soon or Late.'

The Governor [his father] says soon for otherwise bad if one has children — one's character is more flexible —one's feelings more lively & if one does not marry soon, one misses so much good pure happiness. —But then if I married tomorrow: there would be an infinity of trouble & expense in getting & furnishing a house, —fighting about no Society —morning calls — awkwardness —loss of time every day. (without one's wife was an angel, & made one keep industrious). — Then how should I manage all my business if I were obliged to go every day walking with one's my wife. — Eheu!! I never should know French, — or see the Continent — or go to America, or go up in a Balloon, or take solitary trip in Wales — poor slave. — you will be worse than a negro — And then horrid poverty, (without one's wife was

better than an angel & had money) — Never mind
my boy — Cheer up — One cannot live this solitary life, with groggy old age, friendless & cold, &
childless staring one in ones face, already beginning to wrinkle. — Never mind, trust to chance
—keep a sharp look out — There is many a happy
slave —

1

HOW TO BE A HAPPY SLAVE

If there is a formula for living happily ever after, in 1990 rock star Rod Stewart thought he had it. At his wedding reception he raised a glass to wife number two, New Zealand supermodel Rachel Hunter, announcing, 'I'm as happy as a dog with two dicks.' Sadly, by 2001 not even his tail was wagging. Marriage certificates, he said dolefully, 'should be renewed annually, like dog licences'.

Stewart has since remarried, to another leggy model. His is an ingenious system for stemming time's drain on wedded bliss: find a fresh prototype blonde, and repeat those solemn vows. But although I am glad that Stewart is keeping the faith with marriage, his solution to its short-comings seems unlikely to work for everyone. Few of us can afford to fund a chorus line of divorcees, or rely on a continuous supply of nymphs to recharge our ageing libido. Yet strangely, Stewart is not the first to champion renewable nuptials. Political think tanks have also recommended that governments remodel the institution of matrimony in response to rising divorce rates and life expectancy, and that instead of for life, couples take out ten-year contracts. The advantages of this approach are clear: a short-term marriage means less complacency, less alimony and lots more excitement. The drawback of short-term unions is that they lack the foundation on which the magnificent social fiction of marriage is built.

Marriage is not real. It is a concept designed to solder people together, and a story that couples tell the world, and each other, about what their life means. Its golden rule is that you suspend disbelief and take it seriously. If to marry is an act of faith, to stay married – to keep your promises, and trust your spouse to do so too – is a matter of active belief.

Cynicism about marriage's capacity to furnish lifelong love has long been de rigueur, but it renders disenchantment nigh inevitable. The jaundiced romantic climate that prevailed among victims of arranged marriages is illuminated by French aristocrat Geneviève de Malbossière's shock, as she wrote to a friend of a mutual acquaintance:

Imagine, M. de Flavigny is still in love with his wife. What a lasting passion after ten months of marriage living together in proximity. They will be an example to posterity.

It is no use sitting back, expecting marriage to happen to you: each act is a choice, a turn in the story. As Carol Shields wrote in her novel, *Unless*: 'Happiness is a lucky pane of glass you carry in your head. It takes all your cunning just to hang on to it, and once it's smashed you have to move into a different sort of life.'

Rod Stewart is not entirely wrong then. Marriage can only provide a lucky window to the world if you understand that it is always changing, and requires constant renewal. So marriage is not a contract, nor even a dog licence, but a process, more like an obstacle race. To design it to suit us, we must understand what we ask of marriage, and what marriage asks of us.

I SHOULD HAVE MENTIONED

One might think that couples would discuss their expectations of marriage before tying the knot. In the past, betrothals were negotiated by families, and financial and living arrangements all mapped out. Today most couples freely raise personal dreams, and discuss their careers, and questions like whether they want to live abroad, yet many are shy of discussing what they hope actually to get from living

together. As a result, some are 'blind to key differences between them', said Terry Prendergast of
Marriage Care. Some wilfully keep their blinkers
on. Even a professional communicator, like journalist Kathryn Flett, can fly blind into wedlock, and
crash: 'We had talked about travelling, even about
living abroad, but there were never any specific
long-term plans, and although I assumed children
would come in to the equation at some point, that
point was not quite yet. I thought we would (should)
work hard and that then we would get somewhere —
although quite where that somewhere was, I had no
idea.'

Unvoiced expectations are the mothers of misunderstanding and disappointment. Here are the top
ten topics that couples neglect to discuss at their
peril. They would be ideal clauses for a marriage-
conserving prenuptial contract. Even if you are
married, you may be surprised by your spouse's
views on these subjects. Find out now, not in a row.

1. Parenthood: to be or not to be? (Two-thirds of
   fiancés never raise this)
2. How to rear children (including education and
   religion)
3. Debts
4. Joint bank accounts — or not
5. Pensions

6. Chores: who does what, how?
7. Time at work versus time at home
8. Time together versus time apart
9. Bad habits
10. How to communicate about difficult or sensitive subjects, like sex

1. WHAT MARRIAGE ASKS OF US, AND WHAT WE ASK OF MARRIAGE

Once, as the thirteenth-century English king Henry III put it, marriage's purpose was to obtain 'friendship between princes'. Nowadays we ask far more of marriage. Many expect lifelong lust and attraction of a relationship that is rooted in the numbing slurry of domesticity. The least romantic couple would agree that marriage is an arrangement in which two people co-ordinate paths as long as both shall live – or like. An assumption is buried in this statement, one that might baffle our ancestors. It is that marriage is about procuring happiness, and that you can find this heaven on earth by living together.

This commonplace expectation is wildly ambitious. For a start, repetition and happiness are like oil and water: hard to marry, long term. And all human beings wrestle with two conflicting urges: we want both to co-operate and to compete. So in marriage we need to balance our needs as individuals against our needs as a couple, to simplify our living arrangements, create routines, and at the same time, not go stale. This is not easy, as priorities and expectations vary so much. Some find it demeaning to take out rubbish while others believe that this is What Men Do. Some find coming home to someone who does not look up from the TV, let alone say Hi, is the abomination of desolation. Others say take a chill pill, and hands off my remote control. Who is right?

To ask this question is to misread the situation. Robert Louis Stevenson put it best: 'Marriage is one long conversation, chequered by disputes.' Conversation, from the Latin for 'changing sides', is about taking turns, reading minds and changing them. Why do some couples keep on talking while others flounder?

Twice-wed, twice-divorced film star Mae West suggested that 'separate beds, and even separate bedrooms, can be the secret of a happy marriage'. Psychologist John Gottman, who runs the world's largest marriage laboratory, reckons that the recipe for conjugal bliss hinges on the ingredients. Anthropologist Helen Fisher agreed that who you marry is the key. Her book, *Why Him? Why Her?* offers a theory of compatibility based on four personality types, similar to the Ancient Greek system of four 'humours', with each type dominated by one of four brain chemicals. They are:

- Explorers (thrill-seekers, who get off on dopamine)
- Builders (steady Eddies, who respect rules and are influenced by soothing serotonin)

- Directors (testosterone-fuelled bossyboots)
- Negotiators (easy-going, oestrogen lovers)

Fisher's extensive research suggests that explorers and builders are content only with their own kind, whereas negotiators are unhappy together, as are directors, whereas a one-director, one-negotiator pair will thrive.

This theory oversimplifies (our brain chemistry is not set in stone, but alters with circumstance). Set aside the biological hocus-pocus, however, and the implications of Fisher's ideas are fascinating. Namely, that the traits which many of us seek in lovers (wealth, height, looks) are irrelevant; true compatibility comes if couples share a dream, and have complementary attitudes towards power and risk. Hence free-spirited explorers find fulfilment only with fellow explorers, while methodical builders are annoyed by anyone less steady than themselves. But in the case of directors and negotiators, opposites attract because one party likes to lead, and the other to be led. (A good example of a negotiator-director couple is Victorian philosopher John Stuart Mill, whose brilliant mind and mild temper required the lesser intellect but intense passion of bossy wife Harriet Taylor to form opinions strong enough to turn his social insights into compelling arguments.)

So successful couples are those who not only want to head in the same direction, but also can agree on how to get there. In other words, the art of marriage is essentially management: to organize your life to foster your shared dreams. To achieve this, couples must divide labour, solve problems, manage their hopes and feelings, reach decisions and polish the lucky pane of glass in their head that keeps them happy.

There are eight key areas to manage: sex; finances; children; work; housework; in-laws; leisure; and social lives. The goal is to manage these things without getting bored.

This was a complicated business back in the days when roles and rules in marriage were preordained, back when husbands (supposedly) decided and wives (supposedly) obeyed. In 1911's *Devil's Dictionary*, divorcee and professional cynic Ambrose Bierce summarized the challenge: 'Marriage, n. The state or condition of a community consisting of a master, a mistress and two slaves, making in all, two.' This may be why, if sociologists ask couples what they argued about last, each spouse gives a different answer. Such distortions come of the fact that each spouse has two 'marriages': one is an opinion, their general view of the relationship, that pane of glass in their head, and the other is a process, their daily experience of married life – both of which continually redefine, and distort, each other. Consequently, every marriage is an ever-changing kaleidoscope of opinion. As the eighteenth-century banker Samuel Rogers said, 'It doesn't much signify whom one marries, for one is sure to find next morning that it was someone else.' But with a positive view of marriage, the everyday experience is more pleasurable.

So marrying well requires rather more than wandering

down the aisle with the right person. We must keep faith with the belief that they are the right person, and do all we can to ensure they remain so. Start falling out, and we may begin to doubt our choice. In fact, arguments are rarely just symptoms of a bad match; it has been found that destructive arguments can break any bond. Those who focus on their partner's negative behaviour inevitably create more conflict, which can sunder couples who could, with art, hope and minimal friction, be happy. On the other hand, reconciling differences effectively can turn our optimistic expectations of marriage into reality. Treat each other well, take a rosy-tinted view, and a seemingly misbegotten match will seem less so by the day.

Marriage has never been so free. As social conventions lose their grip, as women work, men stay home, couples can make their lives up as they go along, so you would think that a custom-fit marriage is within all our grasps. Unfortunately, conflict is escalating in marriage. It is not that we are more selfish than our parents were (though this is possible: anything that smacks of self-sacrifice is suspect in an aspirational society that tells us we are 'worth it'). The trouble is that men and women have never had so much to discuss, or to fall out about. Most expect equality, yet we are all different, all individuals, with our own needs, strengths and weaknesses. In the absence of established marital roles or chains of command, the dreary management tasks of dividing labour, solving problems and reaching decisions are complicated. In other words, the penalty of our new liberty is negotiation, and sadly, in bargaining, no one is equal.

Marriage has ever been a lopsided deal, requiring different services of each side. 'Lady' derives from two Saxon words, 'hloef' (a loaf) and 'digan' (to serve). A lady baked and dispensed bread, her lord supplied the ingredients, and until recently, a wife counted herself lucky if her husband did not burn the water that he boiled for the rare cup of tea, never mind changed a nappy. This legacy, and the fact that women are usually saddled with primary childcare if a marriage ends, has given husbands greater negotiating power than wives when brokering their domestic bargains. Many men also expect more thanks for doing a lot less at home because they know that their bare minimum is still greater than that of the bone-idle majority of husbands. Meanwhile many wives feel entitled to dictate how their family operates, even if husbands pay for most of it, on the grounds that they both earn money and do most chores. So the marital bargain is skewed on both sides, and potentially a recipe for misery, since in a relationship, the greatest power lies with the person who cares the least about it.

The worst of living in our aspirational world is that options multiply regrets, yet very often these options are illusory. As life goes on, with mortgages to pay, mouths to feed, children to collect from school, decisions are increasingly driven by necessity. But although much of the strain in modern marriage is due to larger social pressures, it is

felt personally. So how tempting is it to outsource responsibility for your dissatisfaction to the nearest bystander? To
think that you are miserable not because your expectations
of life are unreasonable, but because your spouse is?

There are many ways to be unhappily married. You can
grow bored or apart, be aimless, snare yourselves in self-
delusions, or turn into a bickering, two-headed monster.
In his *Journals*, the married homosexual writer John Cheever
described, 'The terrifying insularity of a married man and
woman, standing figuratively toe to toe, throwing verbal
blows at each other's eyes and genitals.' Certainly, the risk
of intimacy is that your expertise in each other's strengths
and weaknesses may one day be used as manuals for torture.
No wonder the romantic poet Heinrich Heine called matrimony 'the high sea for which no compass has yet been
invented'. Nevertheless, for many couples marriage is not
the choppy water, but the vessel to carry them through life's
voyage.

What marriage you have is up to you, your spouse, and
everybody else. Nobody decides the story, there is no final
analysis, so accepting the limits of your responsibility for
each other is crucial. It is a dreadful burden to make
someone else accountable for your joy or sorrow. It also
deprives you of one thing we all control, our attitude. The
Roman emperor Marcus Aurelius wrote: 'The things that
affect us stand outside us. Change your attitude and then,
as a ship entering harbour, you shall find calm.'

Reconcile what we want with what we can get, and with

what is best for both of us, and marriage can offer a balancing perspective, a steady horizon. A less-demanding
alternative — though I would not recommend it — is to take
short-term pleasure cruises and develop a short memory,
like Rod Stewart, who seems to think that he has been with
variants of the same female all his life. 'The most memora-
ble is always the current one. The rest just merge into a sea
of blondes.'

HOW MARRIAGE CREATES HAPPINESS

When you are happy, it is all in your mind. The
message is escorted there by brain chemicals called
neurotransmitters. Oxytocin, the cuddle chemical,
is released when we hug and touch, and bliss is signalled by the home-grown opiate, dopamine.

Like all drugs, dopamine is flawed: the more you
have, the less you feel it. This is why, although joy
has many causes, some are more enduring than
others. In most cases the effect soon wears off, since
our happiness nerves blunt with use.

That we may grow bored even by bliss is good news
for the survival of the human species. Excitement is
dangerous, as it stresses out our immune systems
and makes us take risks. But as evolution attests,
humanity's great strength has been our ability to
adapt to new conditions, and as a result, exciting

things soon cease to thrill us. This adaptability lets us sleep at night and live in precarious situations, such as under volcanoes. The downside of our species' ready habituation to new conditions is that our unslakeable thirst for happiness means that whatever we dream of, if we have the luck to grasp it, it will not deliver the joy we anticipated – or not for long. Not even winning the lottery alters a person's outlook long-term; within months, millionaire recipients of jackpots revert to their former temperament.

So dopamine is the secret of happiness, and its production depends on novelty. What is more, dopamine is released in greater quantities if we anticipate it. The longer the build-up to a pleasure, the fiercer our jolt of joy. Therefore enduring contentment, as Richard Layard remarks in his book, *Happiness*, comes of things we 'can never fully adapt to'. And since a marriage is ever changing, if we get it right, it has the rare, munificent power of bringing lasting happiness.

Studies find that married couples' contentment peaks in the first year, but most spouses remain happier, years down the line, than they were before tying the knot. Given dopamine's flighty nature, you might think that marriage's stability would erode our pleasure in it over time, and some unions do indeed survive on little more than inertia. But it need not be so. Habituation is possible only if a source of happiness never changes, and since life always throws up new challenges, we are always evolving, so the process of adaptation to a spouse never ends. The surprises, anticipation and shots of dopamine can keep on coming on the conjugal obstacle course, and with them oxytocin, to cement the bond between us; that is if we bother to nurture it, and remain interested enough in each other to notice and have fun.

By happy coincidence, purveyors of a new science, positive psychology, find that the most enjoyable activities are those that develop skills and harness strengths such as wisdom, creativity, courage, responsibility, generosity, perseverance, optimism and spirituality. Traits that make us adaptable to life, and that, conveniently, also happen to be amply exercised by marriage.

2. HOW TO DESIGN YOUR MARRIAGE FOR LIFE

Marriage is an odd contract. It is written in invisible ink so, apart from the vows, the precise nature of the commitment is vague. But one contradiction faces all couples: we seek unconditional love, yet no relationship is so conditional as marriage.

A good marriage is one that fosters conditions which

enable love and friendship. Mercifully there is no formula, as we are all unique. See how others have fared, however, and it is easier to discern the guidelines to plot a course to suit you, and recognize what challenges are not personal but universal themes in a timeless tale of what happened after a boy met a girl and they imagined that they could live happily ever after.

1. Prioritize pleasure

Working at marriage not only sounds a chore, but may defeat its purpose. Brain scans of lovers across the globe have found that love follows the same pattern from New York to Nanking. They reveal that love is born in our reward-seeking circuitry. Often infatuation fades within two years, but not always. New York's Stony Brook University gathered couples who had been together two decades or more, put them in an MRI scanner, then showed them photos of their spouse. One in ten of their brains lit up in a burst of dopamine, such as you might expect to see in someone experiencing the first heady flush of love. The amazed researchers gave their ageing Romeos and Juliets a nickname: swans.

What was the swans' secret? Most were 'calm, generous, and deeply attached'. All enjoyed 'intensive companion-ship and sexual liveliness', and their daily life was contrived to minimize conflict and stress between them. As a result, they protected the idea of marriage in their head, while doing their best to keep the everyday reality enjoyable.

2. Seek the best

To be satisfied in marriage means reconciling expectations with experience. But to be happy requires more than that our expectations fit reality. Optimism protects faith in a bond, and high hopes can come true. Dr Donald Baucom of the University of North Carolina examined married couples' expectations, and found that those who asked the most of each other were not the most disappointed, but had the best marriages. So to glaze over, or look the other way, let things slide, or expect a good-enough marriage, is to court disaster.

Even the unhappily married are not always better off alone. Most divorcees report being less happy after a break-up than before. Tellingly, the least-contented divorcees are those who had taken marriage the least seriously in the first place, and ended it out of boredom or disenchantment. As with mortgages, bad faith in marriage guarantees negative equity and collapse. But the more you give it, the more it gives you. If you trust that the future will be brighter, polish that rose-tinted pane of glass, and seek the best in each other.

Communicate great expectations of your spouse in flattery and praise and automatically you will create a positive feedback effect, as they strive to live up to their high billing.

Conversely, if a spouse senses contempt or condescension, automatically this changes a marriage for the worse, because emotions are not just information about feelings; they are also instructions that direct others' feelings. Talking lovingly creates love, but talking nasty can be far more corrosive because pain outlasts joy. Hence any criticism must be diluted. Marriage guru John Gottman prescribed a ratio of five positive messages per negative (a negative can be a sigh or roll of an eye) to keep love blooming.

3. But keep noticing

It is a mistake to rest too heavily on optimism. If we are too generous in how we interpret our beloved's conduct, or bite our tongues too often, we risk misunderstanding, even complacency. As couples adjust to each other, they form assumptions and habits — the emotional equivalent of red tape. The danger is they stop reacting, hear only what they expect to hear, or stop noticing their words' effect on their spouse. If we fail to hear the need inside what each other says, or withholds, it is easy to mistake proximity for intimacy and then become strangers without noticing.

Happy couples remain alive to each other's strangeness. They relish that there is much they do not know about each other, an awareness that keeps them alert and polite. One of John Gottman's students revealed: 'We were watching newlyweds, and what often happened with the couples who ended up in divorce is that when one partner would ask for credit, the other partner wouldn't give it. And with the happier couples, the spouse would hear it and say, "You're right." That stood out. When you nod and say "uh-huh" or "yeah", you are doing that as a sign of support.' Little words are ties that bind, generating the trust that cements marriage. As the author of 1856's *How to Woo, How to Win and How to Get Married* counselled: 'Deport yourself as if still a suitor'.

4. Embrace change

Just as marriage is still with us because it is adaptable, so successful couples adapt together. (My friend said of his divorce: 'She was unhappy, she changed. I liked the person she was before, she preferred the new one.')

Interestingly, studies find that in the couples most prone to break up men have traditional, authoritarian attitudes. Yet most likely to succeed are those with traditional, flexible wives. It would be a mistake to conclude from this that marriage only works if women are subservient. A one-director, one-negotiator couple is not, according to Helen Fisher's research, the strongest recipe for a partnership. The most compatible couples, likeliest to last, are two builders. Theirs are partnerships of co-operative equals, able and inclined to face change and build a future.

5. Suit yourself and each other

To work, marriage must balance our needs as individuals and foster our partnership. Ideally, couples cherish each other's dreams while creating a world of shared meaning. But if a marriage goes awry, it can be repaired, provided a couple renegotiate their deal to suit them both, and find a dream both will sign up to. Infidelity may be a reparable breach; but if one wants a baby and the other does not, that is another matter.

Obviously, our needs as individuals and as a couple are not always compatible. Sixty-nine per cent of couples' arguments revolve around insoluble problems, like lifestyle and personality clashes. To these conflicts, the solution is not necessarily discussion. Rather, to minimize friction: to reduce pointless battles by finding roles in marriage that balance your needs and respect your feelings. We all have emotional rules that steer our views on everything from how to scramble eggs, to whether it is a man's job to make beds. These emotional rules are laid down in childhood, by our family upbringing. Therefore, if you and your wife feel differently about cooking, it is futile to expect her to change her heart to suit you. Still, both of you are entitled to expect compromise, as by marrying you pledged to put your happiness as a couple first. This means asking for change, not laying down laws. Saying nothing and doing nothing helps nothing, however. Keep quiet about annoying habits and their capacity to aggravate may grow until finally you explode. Too often couples unwittingly let differences of opinion solidify into irreconcilable differences, or, worse, indifference. So let him cook if he wants, even if he does not do it your way. Why make her wash up if she hates it and you do not? If you both hate it, buy a dishwasher, or do it together and chat.

6. Create protected airspace

Do not stint on time to be yourself. One-hundred-year-old Doris Hutchison of Aberdeen enjoyed sixty contented years of marriage, largely because she started working outside the home at the age of fifty-seven, when her husband retired. 'It's good to have your own interests to keep you occupied,' she said. At the same time, as demands on a couple grow, so too, all too easily, their shared life slips down the priority list. I was called on a radio show by a lady from Utah whose grandparents had been happily married for seventy-five years. They attributed this to their daily routine of walking to the park, holding hands, to sit on the same bench and talk. I know of another husband and wife who each evening poured a drink, went to their bedroom, closed the door, and sat together for fifteen minutes. Some days they did more than sit, others they did nothing, or talked. This daily ritual allowed bubbling problems to surface without bursting out in a row.

7. Cultivate gratitude

Love is not selfless, it is about rewards. Fortunately, we can also derive joy from giving. A study of couples in which one spouse was taking law exams found that the support which most effectively reduced exam-takers' stress was silently given by their other half. They did not notice, consciously, the extra effort that the other was making to take up the slack around the house, and the spouse making extra efforts did not draw attention to how nice they were being. But the benefits were conspicuous in the exam-takers' calmness and exam results. This is a perfect example of marriage's long-term rewards, if you are prepared to make sacrifices and forgo instant returns.

Such rewards are possible because marriage is a gift economy in which we trade goods and services, from dinner to making love. Everything you give, put up with, can be regarded as an investment in marriage, even if your spouse does not personally deserve it, though not while they are being a pig — though provided that you see your contribution as a gift, do not begrudge giving it, and are grateful for what you get in return.

8. Make it up as you go along

Approach marriage as a three-legged obstacle race through life, and the path to success is obvious: to keep moving forward, side by side, with a sense of purpose and momentum. So dot your journey with reminders why you chose to spend your life together. Matthew Boggs, a young bachelor, traversed America in search of the key to everlasting love. His eighty-eight-year-old grandmother, happily married more than sixty-three years, offered this advice: 'You always ask couples their message for the younger generation. Here's mine: Make the most of the small moments. There's no such thing as a perfect marriage, just perfect moments. These moments, stacked side by side, fill your life. Don't take them for granted, because boy does life go by fast.'

With a little effort, anyone can define their marriage not by the lows, but the high points. The occasional nod to romance helps. In this, start as you mean to go on and make memories to treasure, or laugh about. British Prime Minister Tony Blair was not always such a great communicator. One day, as the young lawyer watched the prone form of his then girlfriend, Cherie, bent over a lavatory, which she was scrubbing, he decided to propose marriage. Stunned, Cherie agreed. Blair said great. 'Then after that,' his wife recalled, 'the wretched man said: "Let's not tell anyone yet, let's keep it to ourselves."'

TUNING TO A HAPPY FREQUENCY

'I want a divorce,' said the wife.
   'You want a big horse?' asked her deaf husband.

'Divorce,' she repeated.

'Oh yes, this borscht is excellent.' He placed a hand on hers. 'You are a marvel. No wife could be more wonderful. That is why I bought you this.' He secured a beautiful bracelet around her wrist.

This is an example of what psychologists term 'positive sentiment override', in which a person's rosy optimism lets them ride over bumps in the marital road. This convenient facility is present in abundance in happy couples. For example, negative sentiment override is what happens when you ask a spouse if he has eaten and he yells, 'If you wanted lunch you should have said!' In a state of positive sentiment override, your spouse would reply, 'Not yet, what can I make you?'

A positive sentiment override system requires a filter for nasty thoughts, to discharge largely pleasant noises to a spouse, and something called emotion work. If this term mystifies you, ask yourself, in the past six months, how often on a scale of 1 (never) to 5 (very often) have you:

- initiated talking things over?
- listened closely to your spouse's innermost thoughts and feelings?
- recognized the importance of your spouse's feelings even if you do not share them?
- offered encouragement?

- done favours for your spouse without being asked?
- showed your appreciation?
- listened closely to what your spouse wanted to say about their day?

The lower your score, the likelier that your positive sentiment override system needs to be re-tuned. The protocols read something like this:

1. Do not dump
2. Do not blame
3. Do not set secret tests for them to fail (they will)
4. Do not generalize pessimistically from behaviour (Is she a bitch or tired?)
5. Do not label (Never say, 'You never/always/should/shouldn't' or 'You are a . . .')
6. Avoid negative discussion after 10 p.m./in bed
7. Give specific thanks
8. Be aware of your partner's emotional half-life: do they cool down slower than you?
9. Be polite
10. Laugh. Often

Pious? Unrealistic? Irritating? Practise. Your halo will come by return of post.

2

HOW NOT TO OUTLAW
YOUR IN-LAWS

I turned to my mother-in-law after an altercation. 'Isn't it funny?' I said. 'You and I disagree about everything.'

'Isn't it?' she said.

'Oh well, at least we both like Sebastian.'

She looked at me. 'No. We both *love* Sebastian.'

This joke signalled a truce. But mothers-in-law are better known for their sharp words than their wits. It does not take a genius to work out why that popular houseplant with long, sword-like emerald leaves is called mother-in-law's tongue. In Brazil and Africa they use this plant to ward off the evil eye. In skilled hands, its fibres are tough enough to string a bow. But in the West it is more usually consigned to dusty windowsills. To me, this neglected plant encapsulates the fears that in-laws inspire — as well as their potential benefits, if only they are handled correctly.

In the past couples married not despite but for their in-laws. Kings hitched their sisters and daughters to rival kings in order to prevent war. Medieval betrothal contracts called a father-in-law 'socer' ('associate') because weddings did not merely bind men to women, they knitted together family fortunes. In our individualistic age, marriage is a free choice, so in-laws seem less central to it. They fall into a broader category, which includes stepchildren, ex-wives and ex-husbands, of unsought but interested third parties in a marriage. You and these bystanders are fast-tracked into each other's lives, though you may have nothing in common except this person you love. For these reasons, nowadays in-laws, exes and stepchildren are rated as marital assets less often than liabilities.

More is the pity, because in-laws, exes and stepchildren are always with us. Even if you never meet, even if they are dead, they live on in your spouse. You do not choose them. You cannot change them. But just as parenting is a skill, so is being an in-law, and it is worth mastering, as it introduces the first challenge of marriage: adjustment.

So why are in-laws difficult, and why should we care?

MONSTER IN-LAWS

If your in-laws should be outlawed, be consoled: it could be worse.

In the Middle Ages, culture clash between royal brides and grooms could cause wars, so familiarity was thought advisable, and betrothed infants were often sent abroad to grow up with their fiancés. English king Henry II took such an interest in the education of the French princess Alys, who was pledged to his son and heir, Richard, that he made her his mistress. When Henry died, Richard rejected Alys, who had borne a child to his father, causing diplomatic incidents galore until she was palmed off on the lowly Count of Ponthieu.

In many cultures, in-laws' powers are extensive and invasive. Victorian art critic John Ruskin let his parents pick and furnish his home and boss him about. Not surprisingly, his wife Euphemia, whom Ruskin had not touched since his horrified discovery of her pubic hair on their wedding night, rebelled. Phemy's papa wrote to Ruskin Sr: 'Married people are rather restive under the control and supervision of Parents, tho' proceeding from the kindest and most affectionate motives.' Ruskin Sr was unmoved. 'Had Phemy thrown herself entirely on our generosity and sought no independent authority, her Dominion over all our affections would have been greater at this day, and of all I know of my Son, her authority with him would have been great exactly in proportion as she had not sought to establish it on the exclusion of that of his parents.'

If in-law trouble is something of a tradition, the power play and tensions seem deliberately set in motion by traditional wedding rituals. Among the Karamojong of Uganda, a bride's outfit is chosen, then applied, by her mother-in-law, who takes a calabash of butter to her future daughter-in-law, bastes the girl everywhere but her legs, then dresses her buttery form in goatskin. In Potenza, Italy, a groom's mamma inspected the nuptial bedlinen the morning after, a custom enduring into the 1960s, as it did in Thessaly, Greece, where a mother-in-law held the hymen-blooded sheets up to the window for her neighbours' approval.

Traditional Moroccan Berber weddings make no bones about a bride's lowly condition. Her wedding is construed as a death, as her family wrap her in a white shroud then cart her to her husband's family home. But such measures may also aim to protect in-laws. Fear of daughters-in-law, as polluters of family life and bringers of chaos, is ancient. The first Greek bride, the mythical Pandora, is given to Prometheus by the god Zeus as a punishment. Pandora arrives decked in jewels and exuding a 'radiant charm', but her wedding present, a sealed jar, unleashed death and other evils on the world.

Over the centuries, in-laws have found various ways to make their disapproval felt. In 1435 Agnes Bernauer, a barber's daughter and bathhouse attendant, secretly wed the future king Albrecht III of Bavaria. When his father found out he organized a tournament. While sport-loving Albrecht took part, Agnes was seized, tried for witchcraft, and tossed into the Danube. Ruthless Renaissance duke Cesare Borgia adored his sister Lucrezia. To entertain her, he organized touching displays, such as firing his crossbow into yards of condemned prisoners. But when Lucrezia grew too fond of her husband, his strangulation soon followed. So perhaps the son of Marie Stopes, the twentieth-century contraception campaigner, got off lightly. When he married a short-sighted woman, his mother, also a eugenicist, committed to the 'improvement' of mankind, cut him and his defective wife out of her will.

Remote in-laws can chill. When Diane Burgdorf married Mark Thatcher, she had to address her mother-in-law as Mrs, then Lady Thatcher. Worse befell newlywed Jackie Kennedy, who sat through her in-laws' tribal councils, preparing for her husband Jack's presidential campaign, as they debated how to make a 'fox-hunting, French-speaking socialite' palatable to US voters. Jackie, said the disloyal JFK, had 'a little too much status and not enough quo'.

Other in-laws are too chummy by far. Augusta, Byron's half-sister, taught Byron's young wife, Annabella Milbanke, to treat the poet's melodramas as '*comical proceedings*'. Annabella was less thrilled by Byron's passion for Augusta, enduring hellish family visits, with him carping at her while praising his sister, or forcing each to kiss him in turn, and she came to believe that the poet had fathered Augusta's child. Overly intimate in-laws can also confuse their loyalties. One famous man is said to prowl for one-night stands with his father-in-law. But standing up to them can be dangerous. Alfred Kerr, a twentieth-century German theatre critic, declined to pull strings for his father-in-law's mistress, an aspiring actress. As a consequence, two goons were sent to beat Kerr up.

Pity families with tactless in-laws. Singer Michael Jackson's sorrows included his brother-in-law, Jack Gordon, who told newspapers that Jackson beat up his pet chimp, Bubbles, and had paid both wives to marry him. Yet the odd flakey in-law can brighten the human comedy. Thank heaven for Sarah Ferguson, Duchess of York, once spotted in Harrods, rapping a biscuit tin emblazoned with the image of her grandmother-in-law, the Queen Mother, asking, 'Are you in there, dear?'

I. WHY ALL IN-LAWS ARE WONDERFULLY WEIRD

The Bible commands a groom to 'leave his father and his mother' and 'cleave unto his wife'. Often couples interpret this to mean, 'Take a cleaver to your spouse's umbilical cord.'

Negative in-law expectations are part of the mythology of modern marriage. Mothers whisper of daughters-in-law who forbid sons to communicate with them, or who amble up on the wedding day and say, 'Now I am the most important person in his life.' Similarly, Jenny, a twenty-six-year-old London bride, received this e-mail from her mother-in-law-to-be two months before the wedding: 'What you don't realize is that my son thinks about me every day, every minute of the day, every second of every minute of the day.'

What is wrong with these women? Your enemy's enemy is your friend, but it is less logical that a beloved's family should be your enemy. You have so much in common. Surely they are assets to marriage.

Couples who manage to rub along with their in-laws gain far more than free babysitting and weird Christmas presents. Because marriage is a negotiation between two visions of a shared life, who better than your in-laws to answer that perplexing question: where on earth is your spouse coming from? They may also indicate ways to steer your beloved where you would rather go.

The first reason to treasure in-laws is that they helped to turn your spouse into the person you wanted to marry. This makes them tutors in disguise. For instance, my mother-in-law is not only witty, but expert at handling my husband. Fight her and I deny myself vital intelligence, and a potential ally. In-laws also offer object lessons in family life. Even if the lesson is a 'how not to', it is information worth having, as it is your spouse's blueprint of normal life — if only one that your spouse is reacting against.

Sadly we are often blinded to our in-laws' potential as assets. It would take an angelic disposition not to notice differences with them more than similarities, and the same is true of stepchildren. These intruders are witnesses and commentators, and can offer unwelcome insights into what our spouse's ex has to say about us. Like my friend, who when she mentioned her baby son's tetchiness, received this observation from her twelve-year-old stepson: 'Well, if you breastfed him longer, you would have a proper bond.' When you find yourself changing to accommodate these uninvited guests, then differences will grate.

To make matters worse, first impressions last and tend to be enduring, and uncomfortable. Remember when you first set foot in your in-laws' home, was the experience not like *Invasion of the Body Snatchers*, just a little? There was your lover, perfectly at ease, yet the jokes, the references, all were subtly, significantly different from when it was just you two together. But everybody in the room except you appeared to think that this behaviour was normal. And you were supposed to smile, charm, and try to win these body snatchers' approval.

This eerie experience revealed that you did not know all there was to know about your lover. It also provided proof positive that other people had a prior claim on their heart. And it unveiled a daunting prospect: how challenging it might be to fuse your blueprint of family life with your beloved's, and find a way to live happily together.

As each family has a unique micro-culture, the inevitable culture clash makes all in-laws seem wonderfully weird. But mistrust colours in-law and step-family relations from the start, as our problems with in-laws begin before we meet. Our culture is drenched in in-law phobia. As my father said, a parent's place is in the wrong, and in-laws seem to be permanently stranded in this location. A 1950s US study found complaints were entirely contradictory: in-laws were 'accused of being possessive, interfering and critical, but also aloof, distant and uninterested'. In-laws cannot win because we are primed, from birth, to expect the worst. They are the hobgoblins of marriage, filling a spot formerly occupied by wicked stepmothers in fairy tales, and it is worth remembering who planted this phobia. Your parents. That is right: when your father winced as your grandfather showed him how to clean the car, when your mother flinched in that puzzling way as darling grandmother helped to make the gravy, they were passing on a worrying message, a message that their parents once passed to them. It is this: 'When you are old and married, you will not want to see us very often. Your spouse and us, we won't get on, so keep your distance.'

This outlook helps to keep nuclear families nuclear, but it is not unique to Western societies. Mistrust of in-laws permeates every society. Anthropologist Margaret Mead wrote: 'Of all the peoples whom I have studied, from city dweller to cliff dwellers, I always find that at least fifty per cent would prefer to have at least one jungle between themselves and their mothers-in-law.'

Traditional grounds for conflict are obvious: if both mother- and daughter-in-law depend on the man of the house for their meal ticket, they are rivals. Another historic reason for disliking in-laws is that grooms paid for brides, fathers-in-law bought grooms with dowries, so families were apt to see an incoming spouse as a revenue stream, of land, money, children. Today's in-laws likewise assess our prospects as providers of homes and grandchildren, and their scrutiny is not pleasant to endure. And the nicest stepchild or in-law has an annoying capacity to divide a spouse's loyalties. However, if your insupportable in-laws fear that you will lead their child astray, or steal them away, their suspicions are well founded. A 2008 study of 6,108 child-parent relationships found that married couples had far less intense ties with their parents than divorcees or singles.

With such built-in conflicts of interest, in-law relationships seem rigged against us getting on. The tensions change over the years, as our circumstances change, and can grow fiendish when grandchildren are on the scene to trip or fight over. But one stubborn fact persists: neither you nor your in-laws chose this relationship. In this respect, it is the polar opposite of marriage, which is our one opportunity in life to decide who our family is, who we are and where we belong. To make matters worse for in-laws, we are fast-tracked into each other's lives: your mother- or father-in-law, your stepson or stepdaughter, your son- or daughter-in-law is meant to mean something to you as a matter of course, not because you get along personally, and this is supposed to happen instantly, without your having passed through any of the steps that build trust and warmth in a normal friendship.

How do you make friends with your in-laws? A design flaw in all relationships is that mutual interests also create conflict. With in-laws, a further cruelty is that common ground — children, or hobbies like cooking or gardening — which would be a foundation of friendship with anybody else, will feed tension. Usually, people bond by helping each other out. Sadly, when in-laws offer assistance it can smack of interference or criticism, especially as often we meet on that least neutral territory, in each other's homes, where the temptation to share domestic wisdom may be hard to resist. (It is because women's worlds overlap most that mother- and daughter-in-law rivalry often appears sharper than that between father- and son-in-law. Not because women are bitchier than men, honestly.)

Prickliness with in-laws is heightened by today's uncertainties over family roles. Are you a career girl or are you self-centred? As a stay-home dad, are you a new man or an irresponsible layabout? If questions about your life choices gnaw you from the inside, how easy is it to detect, in your in-law's smile, the gleam of critical teeth, biting their tongue?

Your in-laws may not mean to criticize. Then again, they might. A survey of 1,000 women found 80 per cent believed that a tidy home was a key factor in whether they liked their daughter-in-law. And your father-in-law may well wince when you hug 'his princess'. Your mother-in-law will also quite likely have an idea about how to burp 'baby'. Your brother-in-law could go in for casual character assassination over the colour of your car. People have this lamentable tendency to have opinions, and different ideas of formality, and pangs of jealousy. Family culture clashes, however trivial, often cause pain, as people care deeply about seemingly minor things. One couple, she a New Yorker, he a Scot, got it in the neck from both sets of in-laws for failing to respect family customs. The wife started serving her husband afternoon tea, as her mother-in-law had asked. Then her own mother told her off for feeding him 'candy' instead of real food.

If things go smoothly, it may yet be hard to know how

to behave with in-laws. Once the etiquette was clear: to honour thy mother- and father-in-law, as the thirteenth-century friar Gilbert of Tournai wrote, 'treating them with reverence, using respectful words and gestures; paying homage and providing help; avoiding being aggressive, even verbally, and appeasing any conflicts with sweetness and light. Respect, kindness, support: the same forms of respect [that] the fourth commandment . . . demanded for parents.' Today few of us are reverent to our own parents, never mind anyone else's, and most of us see our parents irregularly. By contrast, in the past, many families operated like businesses, and if you make cheese together, plough fields together, wash your clothes in the river together, relations with your in-laws may not be easy, but you will have something to talk about. Since our drift from communal living, once the coop is flown, adult children and parents are more often guests than featured players in each other's lives, with less and less to say to each other. As a result, our get-togethers tend to assume the vaguest purpose: to enjoy each other's company. This is tricky if we have lost touch with each other's habits and tics of personality. But a new wife or husband, daughter- or son-in-law on the scene can bring more awkward pauses — and someone to hold responsible for these and any other problems. If a son forgets a birthday, is it not convenient to blame his selfish wife?

If many in-law problems stem from social awkwardness and misunderstandings, it is also conceivable that we have reasons to resent one another. Maybe not every quirk that your in-laws installed in your beloved is so very lovable. So in-laws present handy scapegoats to blame for your differences with your spouse. Danielle, twenty-five, stuck with a slob husband Bill, griped: 'I don't understand how he can be the way he is – his mother is fanatically clean, but I guess she never made him clean up anything. How could she do that to me – that's what I wonder – because I'm paying the price.'

If your marriage flails, well may you feel that you owe your in-laws limited gratitude, given what is known about families' role in forming personality and the development of the brain. Psychologists agree that the influence of childhood attachments and family dynamics is impossible to overstate, and if that family is still around, working their dark magic on your spouse, their influence can seem toxic. If your in-laws are divorced, you can hold that against them too, as statistically divorcees' children are likelier to bolt. And if your parents-in-law treat each other oddly, you may recognize a similar emotional gulf in your own marriage. Or have a terrible vision: that one day, you will not turn into your parents, but something far worse. Your in-laws.

In a logical world, when picking a spouse, we would also matchmake our in-laws. Although a 'marriage of true minds' has long been the ideal, once this was thought impossible without a marriage of two families. In the past, courtship followed two parallel paths: boy wooed girl while families wooed each other in betrothal negotiations. If families could not reach terms, lovers could conclude they had had a narrow escape. Today, research finds that the happiest, longest-wed partners often have similar upbringings, which would not surprise seventeenth-century romantic Dorothy Osborne, who sent this love note to her inamorato, Sir William Temple:

> There are a great many ingredients must go to the making me happy in a husband; first . . . our humours must agree; and to do that he must have that kind of breeding that I have had, and used to that kind of company; that is, he must not be so much a country gentleman as to understand nothing but hawks and dogs, and be fonder of either than of his wife; nor of the next sort of them whose aim reaches no further than to be Justice of Peace, and once in his life High Sheriff, who reads no books but statutes, and studies nothing but how to make a speech interlarded with Latin.

That England was riven by Civil War, and Temple backed Parliament, and she the king, were beside the point. What counted for their compatibility was their equal nobility. (They met at her brother's trial for scratching a rude remark on a window about a prison governor. She said she wrote it, and William loved her for it.)

However bad it gets, comfort yourself in the knowledge that there is one thing worse than unfriendly in-laws:

over-friendly ones. Imagine if they were wild about you, as if they could not believe their luck to have offloaded their child on to you. Begging a disturbing question: why?

If it is too late to matchmake your in-laws, or you have fallen out, it is time to fall for them, and help them to fall for you.

2. THE TEMPTATIONS OF BAD IN-LAW RELATIONS

To get along with your in-laws, first you have to want to. Even if you set out with the best of intentions, it is not just down to you. If Picasso is to be trusted – and the Spaniard put as much art into his anecdotes as his celebrated canvases – his mother, Doña María, longed to see her son married, but was so disenchanted on first meeting her prospective daughter-in-law, Russian ballerina, Olga Kokhlova, that she exclaimed:

> You poor girl, you don't know what you're letting yourself in for. If I were a friend, I would tell you not to do it under any conditions. I don't believe any woman would be happy with my son. He's available for himself but for no one else.

In-law clashes are often characterized as between an incoming spouse and the new family. In reality, it is a triangular relationship. There are three parties: the incoming spouse, the in-laws, and the intermediary spouse whose fault all this is. In theory, tact should muffle their every move, as all have a stake in getting along. In practice, each party has motives to nurture in-law phobia.

Most obviously, the incomer. If falling out with the in-laws is, as it were, the done thing, go along with it and you spare yourself the trouble of kowtowing to oldsters who never spare a kind word for your lawn or your quiche. Incoming spouses have further incentive to nurture rivalries: to battle with in-laws, and exes and stepchildren, as ways to test their spouse's loyalty.

THE USES OF BAD IN-LAWS

Some in-laws are utter stinkers, but even they have their uses. They are just double-edged, like the leaves of that houseplant, mother-in-law's tongue. So handle with care.

Display power: Want to show your spouse how masterful you are? Crush your overbearing in-laws, like tycoon Sir James Goldsmith. When he asked a Bolivian tin magnate for his daughter's hand in marriage, the father replied, 'We come from an old Catholic family. It is not our habit to marry Jews.' 'We come from an old Jewish family,' Goldsmith retorted. 'It is not our habit to marry Red Indians.' The couple eloped.

Excuses: Do not want to see your grasping mother? Explain that your spouse won't allow it.

Distract from inconvenient truths: Feeling bad? Career not going to plan? Rubbish: you are a success. It is his vile parents, always asking what you're up to. Guilty about your messy house? No: it is your perfectionist sister-in-law, always dropping hints, thoughtlessly picking up toys.

Outsource marriage problems: Say, 'You're as bad as your mother/father,' and simultaneously you insult both parties. This gives your spouse a perfect excuse to be offended and stop listening to you. Indeed, to outsource tensions in your marriage – to accuse your father-in-law of spoiling her, blame your mother-in-law for never making him clean – is to label a conflict over the logistics of your married life as an irredeemable character flaw and therefore nothing to do with you. As an argument tactic, this has one merit: it ends discussion, and with it, any sense of responsibility for trying to change.

End marriage: Had enough? Encourage your in-laws to rescue their child from you. Thus ended the engagement of newspaper heir James Gordon Bennett Jr to nineteenth-century society girl Caroline May. Bennett staggered drunk into a party at May's parents' house, emptied his bladder into the fireplace before the cream of New York high society, and emptied the party.

Some power play is fun, but it is also dangerous. Your mother-in-law or stepson may be insufferable, but if you act up, provoke confrontation, then you wound your spouse. If your spouse puts you first, congratulations, you win. But you have injured your spouse – thereby corroding your marriage. If your spouse ignores your complaints? You feel rejected – thereby corroding your marriage. And if your spouse chooses them over you? Whoops, there goes your marriage. You have been warned.

When the in-laws wrangle and the stepchildren bait and hiss, it seems obvious that the person with the best motive to resolve the problem, the intermediary spouse, should feel galvanized to do so. They know everyone best, and they got them into this pickle, so are ideally qualified and morally bound to step up and play the role of diplomat. Or so you might think. Yet intermediary spouses have their own reasons to play dirty. Some duck their diplomatic duty out of laziness. Others enjoy watching Dad and husband vie to be alpha male. Playing mother against wife can be advantageous too. Lots of cakes, DIY and Christmas presents can be coaxed from the dark side of carefully managed in-law love triangles. The possibilities are endless. Pu Songling's seventeenth-century classic, *Strange Tales from a Chinese Studio*, has an ingenious mother-in-law helping out her sex-deprived son by procuring an erotic spell from a sorceress nun and stitching it into her frigid daughter-in-law's pillow. Sensual services extended further in Ancient Athens. The orator Andocides described how morals slipped so low during the Peloponnesian War that a citizen, Callias, took his wife's mother as his concubine. His mother-in-law duly bore a bastard baby uncle to share the playpen with her grandchildren.

Even a spouse who tries to smooth relations may struggle to surmount the challenges of integrating a spouse into a family. Juggling the roles of spouse, parent, child and sibling is seldom straightforward. Many of us revert to grumpy teenagers with our parents, as this is what we were when last we lived with them. Oliver James describes in *They F*** You Up* how families connive at this, shepherding us to act in old, familiar ways, as this is the person they know us to be, which is annoying. Meanwhile our spouse expects us to act like a spouse, and may not find our teenage self attractive. For all these reasons and more, a trip to the in-laws can damage a marriage, which explains why married adult children have weaker ties with their parents than the unmarried. Marriage is a greedy relationship that demands exclusive rights.

Avoidance is one way to avert in-law conflict. In the Congo there is a proverb: 'My mother-in-law is angry with me, but what do I care. We do not eat from the same dish.' And ignoring in-laws is considered good manners in cultures with in-law taboos. Australian Aboriginals have mother-in-law tongues, with special vocabularies for these dangerous females. It was once a crime for son- and mother-in-law to look at each other, lest the poor chap go mad and hare off into the bush. The remedy of silence has often been prescribed for daughters-in-law. A Rwandan wife who uttered (and thereby polluted) her parents-in-laws' names was compelled to drink *isubyo*, a spirit doctor potion.

If your spouse and family tug in different directions, sidestepping conflict may seem easier, but ultimately causes more trouble. My idle male friend for years refused to introduce his demanding mother to his equally demanding partner. Before the much-deferred encounter at last took place, in a move surely designed to guarantee that his fore-bodings came true – thereby sparing him any future meetings – he told his fiancée, 'My mother is strange. She hated every girlfriend and she'll hate you.' I know of another couple who spent each Christmas apart at their respective families – one loud, large, traditional, the other a quiet duo with a widowed mother – for fear of offending either. The dead-lock ended after ten years, when they had a baby. That year they stayed home, and argued with each other.

Avoiding in-laws deprives everyone of love and support, and all couples have good reason to resist the temptations of in-law phobia. Weak in-law relations weaken couples too, because family approval makes marriages more harmoni-ous. This influence, strongest in traditional societies, such as China, is tangible everywhere. Even for couples whose parents are divorced, studies confirm that being close to in-laws increases the happiness of a marriage, reducing the chance of divorce.

Happy families protect marriages because it is the universal dream of a happy family that lures people into marriage in the first place. So if your in-laws seem glum to meet you, bear in mind that your entry into their clan marks a deeper sadness. For them, it begins an intermediate stage in life, a prelude to that painful handover when children have to start looking after their parents. And this is why it is crazy to let in-law phobia spoil moments that one day, all too soon, you would pay good money to relive.

3.   HOW TO FALL FOR YOUR IN-LAWS

Bad in-law relations are not inevitable, but they are predictable, and therefore avoidable.

The main obstacle to easy relations is that in-laws and stepchildren are fast-tracked into our lives without the usual preliminary steps that build trust and intimacy in a friendship. The task, then, is to create a friendship out of a predicament.

There are four measures to a relationship's quality: how much time you spend together; how much love and acceptance is shared; how much you sympathize with each other's point of view; and how much you clash. Enhancing it depends on empathy. So do not be surprised if, for in-laws, the parental umbilicus throbs like an unanswered telephone call. Your spouse fell deaf to the ringtone in puberty, but the in-laws still thrill to the pulse of anxiety, because at any age, their child is their child. Many in-laws indulge in what psychologists call 'gatekeeping' and guard their offspring. Inevitably, it turns them into rivals, because spouses are also programmed to guard mates. But it is not in-laws' fault that they cannot retire gracefully like other caretakers, with a nice carriage clock to remind them that their days are numbered. If they loiter, make suggestions, it is probably because the fools imagine they are experts in your spouse's happiness, having studied the topic since long before dear Jack or Jill was in short trousers. Accepting this is crucial if you wish to solve the in-law problem.

The in-law problem has four layers. First, deep prejudice: we expect relations with in-laws to be strained. The answer to this problem is to expect better and to take nothing personally. Second, insecurities: when our ideas about family and married life clash with our in-laws'. Again, this is to be expected. The third layer of the problem is organizational: when and why in-laws see each other. Until in-laws are familiar with each other, infrequent, aimless visits will be tense. The answer is to plan encounters. Why not meet away from home, in neutral territory? This raises another dilemma: who initiates?

I know grandparents who are reluctant to offer to babysit, not because they are not wildly in love with their grandchild, but lest they sound needy. Meanwhile daughters- and sons-in-law moan that their parents are uninterested in their grandchild. Yet they never ask their in-laws to help out, lest they sound needy. Such comic scenarios derive from confusion over who is in charge of the relationship. In a hierarchy-averse world, we struggle to know who is the number one woman or man in a room, who picks up the bill for dinner or who wields the carving knife at Sunday lunch. But the answer is not obscure. Etiquette is situational: it depends where you are and who invited who. The law of hospitality dictates that if you invited, this is your turf, so you host and organize. If your in-laws invited you over, follow their lead.

The last layer of the in-law problem is how we act when we see each other. If in doubt, respect the host-guest principle. Turn to the one whose fault it is that you are all here. Let the wife tell her father that you are not a twenty-chilli curry man. If your father-in-law is gripped by the contents of your bikini, and your mother-in-law imagines this to be your fault, find a T-shirt.

The enduring solution to in-law triangles is to stop seeing them as a triangle and to forge direct bonds and find something else in common. To build genuine intimacy, we must proceed with caution, revealing our personalities piece by piece, and exploit the power of reciprocity.

Relationships are trading systems. Give and take not only prevents tugs of war but strengthens understanding. To give to your in-laws, do not threaten their authority. Why competitively bake cakes, or bring magnums of a vintage that is mouldering in their cellar, robbing them of opportunities to be generous to you? Take intelligently from in-laws too. So don't gag on the lasagne. Get the damned recipe. Asking a favour can create a useful sense of obligation. Borrow a book, then ask their thoughts on it. Get their help in organizing a surprise party. There are countless ways to demonstrate, to show, not tell them, that you love their precious child enough to deserve their trust.

These measures involve a psychological sleight of hand. Being under an obligation to someone compels them to treat you like a friend. Even if they do not like you, they may find they start seeing you as a friend, to make sense of their generosity. Our minds bamboozle us constantly, retrospectively imputing rational motives to our unthinking acts. How else do we spend a fortune on tat that we did not want but bought because it was in the sale, then convince ourselves it was a bargain?

The intermediary spouse ought not to neglect their role as diplomat. Diplomacy is communication. It helps each side see the other's point of view, by presenting it in terms to which each can relate. So to oil troubled waters, it is best to present in-law clashes not as personal but cultural or situational. Explain that a husband/sister is not criticizing, but a loudmouth/insecure/teasing/over-confident/drunk. Explain that in your family, bickering is simply gentle fun, even if it is not.

All in-laws should recall who truly has the upper hand. Sons- and daughters-in-law can ration visits, and they govern those insuperable instruments of in-law attraction, grandchildren. If in-laws are irredeemably prickly, do what men do if they want to shut women up: sit back and objectify them.

Never forget that these people programmed your spouse, so hold the code to mysteries. Maybe they installed buttons that it would never occur to you to press. These qualities make your in-laws ideal marriage toolkits, full of helpful hints for managing your spouse. To identify these tools, think like an anthropologist. One wife watched in awe as her mother-in-law chivvied her eternally non-committal husband (aged forty-two): 'She came in and asked, "Would you like to play a game of Boggle?" He said no. "How about a bath?" He said no, so she said, "It's either Boggle or bath." Up he jumped.' Possibly the mother-in-law inhabited a world of false imperatives but she had a sure handle on what persuasion experts call 'the architecture of choice'. The wife learned her lesson: if you want hubby to obey, present him with an either/or option.

In-laws, stepchildren, ex-husbands or -wives may be uninvited guests in marriage, but nor did they ask to come. If we treat them like rivals, however, they will be soon. So however monstrous your in-laws, do yourself a favour: let your spouse outlaw them.

A GUIDED TOUR OF IN-LAW DRAMA

Legends of bad in-laws are nothing if not repetitive. Listen to friends and the same problems arise again and again, like *Groundhog Day*, minus the jokes. All are chapters in a timeless tale of what happened when boy met girl, then met the parents — or the ex, or the stepchildren.

So why take it personally? Comedy dwells in each episode, if you know where tensions lie and how to play them. Familiarize yourself with the clichés of in-law soap opera, detach the people from their dramatic context, and you may see what, if any, mischief is at work.

Plot One: They Make Me Feel Foolish
Most of us feel daft when we are obliged to put on a show, something that is hard to avoid when we meet the parents, especially in those fraught early encounters. We chat about the weather, try not to talk with our mouths full, all the while acutely aware that this encounter is a test, and what a trial it feels. The chances are that we leave remembering not what the others said, but with our faces blazing at our remembered blunders. In truth, nobody set out to embarrass anyone. So make nice and be philosophical. Anaïs Nin observed, 'From the backstabbing co-worker to the meddling sister-in-law, you are in charge of how you react to the people and events in your life.' Nin urged us to choose happiness, but if that is too much to ask for, recall the Japanese proverb: 'Never rely on the glory of the morning nor the smiles of your mother-in-law.'

Plot Two: They Just Aren't That Into Me

This story is driven by insecurity. We crave in-laws' and stepchildren's approval, but the attention is on the spouse. As attack is the best defence, rather than hang about, hoping for a pat on the head, we may decide that we do not care a fig what they think of us and start criticizing them instead.

But while you may be certain you will be married for ever and ever, so accept these people are a big part of your life, they may have put decades into your spouse, or long for your spouse to reunite with the ex, so understandably they may take years to believe you are a fixture. After the wedding of publicist Matthew Freud to media baron's daughter Elisabeth Murdoch, his new sister-in-law Prue is said to have offered this warm welcome: 'If you hurt her, I'll kill you.' Freud replied that their brother James had just said the same thing. Now they are all very close.

Plot Three: What Am I, An Eggbox?

A friend's mother-in-law once enquired not after her health, but the health of her ovaries. Likewise, a male friend described a trip to meet the prospective in-laws in Cape Cod as being paraded 'like a prize bull'. Very many in-laws seem to regard offspring's spousal appendages as sperm donors or wombs-in-waiting. Most also cast a loss-adjuster's eye over their salary and spending, as they want to be confident that their child will be taken care of. Is that so odd? Of course, it can be counterproductive. A seventeenth-century lady said of a harassing father-in-law, no wonder 'Lady Tavistock did not breed, for the great bustle the Duke of Bedford made was enough to put anybody out'.

Plot Four: Enough Already With the Helpful Suggestions
Parents are clots. The more subtle they think they are being, the more obvious are their baroque connivings. If they meddle occasionally, or add peas to the pie, does it matter unless they poison you? Perhaps they feel a spare part. Let them be of genuine service, and show them how you want to be helped, and instantly your pointless encounter has a purpose.

Plot Five: They Always Criticize
If in-laws have different ideas about what their offspring should do with their lives, the son- or daughter-in-law may be blamed for putting ideas into their spouse's head. The best of us believe that our way is best, especially if we are old. To accept this it is worth trying to see your in-laws' criticisms as love turned inside out, or alternatively, to introduce the meddlers to a hobby.

Plot Six: They Are So Controlling
In other words they are parents. One day you will understand.

Plot Seven: I Don't Like My Spouse When They Are With Their Family

In-laws are there to remind us that our spouse is not a superhero, nor even a port for our every storm, but an aged child. This is unattractive unless you deliberately elect to marry a child woman/man. On the other hand, if a spouse uses their family to belittle or bully you, then you have something to discuss.

Plot Eight: The Siblings Are Unbearable

Naturally. They are our spouse's rivals, so ours by proxy. Still, this is no excuse to fight our spouse's battles or to stir up rivalries, however entertaining they can be to watch.

Plot Nine: They Are Toads

If our beloved does not get on with their family, naturally we side with them. If stepchildren treat you both like scum, naturally you will see them as poison. Naturally, there will follow the temptation to react or even to rile your antagonists, to show your devotion to your beloved. A friend of mine described a contretemps with her 'shocking step-monster-in-law'. They were invited to dinner and her step-monster served peas. So my friend turned to her husband and said, 'I thought you hated frozen food?' The meal was not a success. On the other hand, one bonus of the showdown is that all of them are relieved to have a reason not to repeat the encounter.

Plot Ten: I Can't Work Out What In-Laws Are For
I suggest getting to know them. But best not to live with them. Stand-up comic Josh Howie described life for his pregnant wife, cohabiting with his grand-mother to save money: 'All I have to do to make Grandma happy is acknowledge her existence with a grunt, while Monique is trapped in a Sisyphean struggle of tea-making, dinner-cooking and *Emmerdale*-watching for approval.'

HOME RULES

WHY ONLY STUPID WIVES CALL THEIR HUSBAND IDLE

When is a bowl not a bowl?

When it is a dirty breakfast bowl. When it is filled with cold water, bobbing with bloated cereal flakes, and left in a sink, beside a perfectly functional dishwasher. When you have seen this bowl each morning for ten years, been forced to plunge your fingers into that water to rinse it, then put it into the damned dishwasher, because you will be damned if you will wash the damned thing.

Such a bowl is not a bowl, but a crime against a marriage, and vivid testimony that your habitual cereal bowl perpetrator is not motivated to tidy up, for at least one of five reasons:

1. The perpetrator does not care about having a clean kitchen.
2. You have failed to train the perpetrator to meet your superior domestic standards.
3. The perpetrator does not care about your domestic standards.
4. The perpetrator knows that you will clean up eventually.
5. The perpetrator regards you as a servant.

These extreme conclusions are symptoms of an entirely avoidable mental illness, housework rage. Housework makes Hercule Poirots of all couples. Over the years, the most minor irritations come to sizzle with significance, as ants burn under a magnifying glass in the hot noon sun. In that grubby trail of footprints across our freshly mopped kitchen floor, in the cemetery of soiled socks in the corner of our bedroom, we read clues about the state of our marriage.

Some couples like to convey their messages directly. I know of a wife who tapes notes to the underside of the toilet seat, to remind her husband where to point. When the celebrated photographer Antony Armstrong-Jones fell out of love with Princess Margaret, he spelled out his feelings by littering their home with lists entitled 'Things I hate about you'. One day she opened a glove drawer to read 'You look like a Jewish manicurist'. They divorced.

More often, couples send each other signals through

housework without realising they are doing so. For instance, a spouse may not make a bed with hospital corners for the simple reason that they would not recognize a hospital corner if it jumped up and poked them in the eye, but to a spouse who knows all about hospital corners, such blindness may look very like disrespect. America's first couple almost parted company after their first daughter was born. Michelle Obama despaired at Barack's working hours, often not home until 2 a.m., and at his seeming obliviousness to mess. 'Whenever I could I pitched in,' Obama told a friend; 'all I asked for in return was a little tenderness.' Instead of love notes, he got Post-its: 'Please pick up after yourself. You left your underwear on the floor again!'

Tending a home is the most consuming activity that a couple can share aside from child-rearing, much of which, lamentably, is also housework. Yet we tend to underestimate housework's role in marriage, and few couples discuss it until they find themselves arguing about it.

In part this is because chores seem too dull to talk about. If children are labour-intensive, they are also cuddly, ever changing, and compelling topics, whereas hoovering is always hoovering, and it gives no love back. And doing housework can be less than rewarding. Not only is it never done, but it is always in our face, and observed more in the neglect than the performance. Except – and this the killer point – by the person doing it. If housework goes unappreciated it is bad, but careless talk is worse. A friend

spent days scrubbing skirting boards to surprise his wife
after a week away on business. She walked in and said,
'Chaos as usual.' He nearly hit her.

Nobody falls in love with somebody for their fine line in
ironing, because common interests are what draw us
together. However, it is differences that drive couples
apart, and housework matters because no differences create
greater gulfs than those encountered day after day, in our
common ground. This is why studies find that a sense of
fairness over chores can decide whether a union lasts. But
with judicious home rule, these boring, unavoidable,
unromantic tasks can be used to show love too.

1. WHO CARES?

'Housework has nothing to do with marriage,' said the
cleverest person I know. Her point was that housework has
to be done, whether you live alone, as a couple, or in a
commune.

But as evolution shows, habitats forge habits. Likewise,
homes shape marriages, and an odd thing happens to
housework in marriage. Unmarried couples who live
together and share chores equally tend to last longer than
those who do not. Yet in most married couples, wives do
more chores than husbands, and, according to the *Journal of
Marriage and Family*, flexible couples last longer than those
who split everything fifty-fifty. Clearly, housework and

marriage work in mysterious ways, not always in each other's favour. Why?

For all couples, housework is a logistical problem complicated by two managerial issues: who does what, and how? Dividing labours is a chore in itself, even if we try to distribute tasks fairly, since there is no such thing as equality in housework, as all of us have wildly different skills, priorities and standards. How tempting to blame a spouse for forcing chores on you, despite the fact that you would face them living alone? And how much worse if a messy spouse creates extra work?

Peculiar emotions pearl around the nitty-gritty of housework, so before drawing up a new rota, it is worth pausing to reflect on the psychological undercurrents that drive us to mop and pail.

It is easy to forget that definitions of 'clean' and 'dirty' are cultural, not absolute, not even for absolute rulers. Louis XIV, France's fabled Sun King, trailed a few noxious clouds; for him, bathing entailed putting on a new undershirt, drenched in scent. In the sixteenth century Elizabeth I was thought fastidious for dunking her vinegary carcass in water once a month, 'whether she needed to or no'.

We imagine ourselves to be cleaner than previous generations, but is this a home improvement? Aesthete Quentin Crisp never cleaned, on the grounds that it had devoured half his mother's life: 'After the first four years the dirt doesn't get any worse . . . I felt it was only by a series of unfortunate accidents that till now I had always lived in the captivity of hygiene.'

Similarly, prolific author J.G. Ballard, who raised his family single-handed, claimed, 'You can do all the housework in five minutes if you don't make a fetish of it.' And many seldom-questioned domestic rituals are, on closer examination, a bit superstitious. We pour bleach into our loo, but if it seethes with bacilli, who cares unless you drink it? Excessive cleaning may be self-defeating (antiseptic overuse is associated with rising allergies). And why chase dust? The more we chase, the more that we spread, since dust is mostly our own dead skin.

Admittedly, our mania for hygiene has some basis. By no measure are dust-mites ideal bedfellows, being unkind to respiratory tracts, and as ugly as their kin, scorpions and spiders. Nor is mess pretty. But Germaine Greer rightly argued: 'In a sane world, meaningless repetition of non-productive activity would be seen to be a variety of obsessive-compulsive disorder. People who said that they enjoyed doing housework, or needed to do it, or that doing it made them feel good would be known as addicts.'

The key phrase here is 'non-productive'. In fact, housework has a by-product: self-esteem. This is because our concerns with dirt transcend health and safety.

Cleanliness is next to godliness, an idea that derives from ancient taboos which equate purity with health and goodness, and pollution with danger and evil — taboos that live on in ads warning of demon bacteria, loitering in a loo near you. So we look down on dirt, we want spotless homes, but call cleaning demeaning, and cleaners insignificant. In other words, we call mess trivial but accord its absence vast importance. Such double standards demonstrate that home rule is about more than muck, but power and an irrational matter called honour.

Seventeenth-century diarist Samuel Pepys ran Britain's navy with aplomb yet fell helplessly 'angry with my wife for her things lying about, and in my passion kicked the little fine basket which I bought her in Holland and broke it, which troubled me after I had done it'. Pepys made a mess over her mess because we all care about housework, even if we do not care to do it ourselves. It is not only novelists who use homes as indexes of character; we all do. Our home is an extension of our self. We care for it and display it, like the sixteenth-century Italian brides whose conduct book advised showing guests around as if revealing 'your heart'. Or we hide at home, neglecting it if depressed, and its dis-repair depresses us more. Mess can upset morals too. In a Dutch experiment, money left in an untidy, graffitied environment was more likely to be stolen than money left in an orderly space.

To control our domestic habitat is also to control our-selves. Malcolm Gladwell wrote in *The Tipping Point*: 'Character . . . isn't a stable, easily identifiable set of closely related traits . . . [but] more like a bundle of habits and tendencies and interests, loosely bound together and dependent, at certain times, on circumstance and context. The reason that most of us seem to have a consistent character is that most of us are really good at controlling our environment.' No wonder if in marriage we like to control each other. Picture the face of the nineteenth-century American bride on the morning her honeymoon ended when she read these marching orders from her new husband, an army colonel:

1. You will see that meals are served on time.
2. You will not come to the table in a wrapper [dressing gown].
3. You will smile at breakfast.
4. If possible, you will serve meat four times a week.
5. You will not move the furniture without my permission.
6. You will present the household accounts to me by the fifth of each month.
7. You will examine my uniforms every Tuesday and, if they need repair, you will take the necessary action.
8. You will do no work in the evenings. You will entertain me.
9. You will not touch my desk.
10. You will remember you are not in command of anything except the cook.

But in the caring arts, husbands usually care less.

HOW WE INVENT HOUSEWORK: A BRIEF HISTORY OF SELF-HARM

The most amazing thing about housework is that it still exists. Run off your feet? Ask yourself: are you making work for yourself? Human beings have a knack of inventing new tasks as the old fall extinct.

Our ancestors often built their dwellings so housework entailed all acts necessary to maintain them, as well as craft, guile and buckets of unde-odorized sweat. Witness this 'lesson for the wife' in John Fitzherbert's 1523 manual, *The Boke of Husbandry*:

> When thou art up and ready, then first sweep thy house, dress up thy dish-board, and set all things in good order within thy house; milk thy kine, feed thy calves, strain up thy milk, take up thy children and array them, and provide for thy husband's breakfast, dinner, supper, and for thy children and servants, and take thy part with them. And to ordain corn and malt to the mill, to bake and brew withal when need is . . . Thou must make butter and cheese when thou may; serve thy swine, both morning and evening, and give thy pullen [poultry] meat in the morning, and when time of the year cometh, thou must take heed how thy hen, ducks and geese do lay,

and to gather up their eggs; and when they wax broody to set them thereas no beasts, swine or other vermin hurt them . . . And in the beginning of March, or a little before, is time for a wife to make her garden . . . And also in March is time to sow flax and hemp . . . and thereof may they make sheets, board-cloths, table-cloths, towels, shirts, smocks . . . and therefore let thy distaff be always ready for a pastime, that thou be not idle.

Idle? He pauses to concede: 'It may fortune sometimes that thou shalt have so many things to do that thou shalt not well know where is best to begin.' Then on relentlessly he goes:

It is a wife's occupation to winnow all manner of corn, to make malt, wash and wring, to make hay, to shear corn . . . to help her husband to fill the muck wain or dung cart, drive the plough, to load hay, corn and such other . . . also to go or ride to the market to sell butter, cheese, milk, eggs, capons, hens, pigs, geese, and all manner of corn. And also to buy all manner of necessary things belonging to a household.

He ends on a romantic afterthought: husband and wife must 'be true either to other'. But amazingly, Fitzherbert's list is not exhaustive. Other writers add profitable bee-keeping ('Wife,' wrote the poet Tusser, 'make thine own candle, spare penny to handle'). With the added uncertainties of weather, harvest and disease, in an age without gas, electricity, pesticides, or sewage plants, the astonishing part is how any wife found time to be anything but 'true'?

Over the centuries, international trade made housewifery no easier, as it introduced two new concepts: luxury and taste. Hannah Woolley's 1673 *Gentlewoman's Companion* tackled dilemmas as diverse as preserving cherries, curing 'one hurt with Gunpowder', and dissuading daughters from wearing beauty spots. Neither industrialization, nor developments in hygiene, nor mass production of food or clothes heralded humanity's liberation from housework. Indeed, the chains clanked louder. *Queen* magazine was launched in 1861, proclaiming, 'When we write for woman we write for home.' As furnishings and fripperies multiplied, stay-home wives became essential adjuncts to gentility. In 1851 one in four middle-class British wives did paid work. By 1911, the number had fallen to one in ten.

Imagine a Victorian angel of the house, caged in corset and crinoline, scarcely moving in her overstuffed home for fear of showering knick-knacks on to the Turkey carpet. It is as if society plotted to dollify women, as they grew less necessary at home, to stop them going out to work and stealing men's jobs. Yet not men but women did most to exalt the housewife. Such as Harriet Beecher Stowe, author of *Uncle Tom's Cabin*, the anti-slavery novel held responsible for the Civil War. ('So this is the little woman who caused the great war,' said Abraham Lincoln when they met.) In 1869 Stowe and her sister Catharine wrote another revolutionary text, *The American Woman's Home*, to champion a strange new science, home economics, and get women due respect by raising the status of housework as a topic worthy of study. Home economics duly entered the curriculum at ladies' academies.

In the twentieth century, war pushed women into factories and on to the land. But as the 1940s yielded to the 1950s, and men returned to the workforce, just as electronic domestic servants like washing machines, refrigerators and vacuum cleaners came into being, so fashion, the discoveries of microbiology and advertising drove women back to the home front, to wage a cold war against austerity and those dastardly invisible germs.

2.   CLEANLINESS NEXT TO GIRLINESS?

There is a sneering term, 'uxorious', for a man excessively fond of his wife. No such word exists for wives besotted by husbands. Indeed, far more wives than husbands tell sociologists that they are unhappily married, wives initiating three out of four divorces, although divorce leaves wives poorer.

The explanation for this madness begins at home.

It was no coincidence, wrote the Franciscan theologian St Bonaventure in the thirteenth century, that 'matrimony' suggested maternal activities while 'patrimony' referred to property. Maintaining a home and a marriage were both seen as women's business. If a man strayed, his slattern wife was to blame. Isabella Beeton's *Book of Household Management* was a rallying cry for this creed, urging threatened wives to compete with the smorgasbord of 'clubs, well-ordered taverns, and dining houses' that had arisen out of Victorian prosperity. Beeton's biographer, Kathryn Hughes, observed: 'Keeping your husband close to home by offering him delicious food, virtually invisible children, and a warm bed had been the standard formula for domestic bliss peddled in household management books almost since the genre began.'

Today women work. Much has changed at the home front, yet more has not. Anyone who imagines that the war of the sexes is over, that a new domestic order was ratified when women began wearing shoulder pads, forgets that equal opportunities commissions do not preside over decisions like who washes up, who cooks dinner. We broker these deals ourselves, day in, day out, sometimes fairly, but more often not. Old attitudes still line our minds, like old wallpaper showing through a thin emulsion of fresh social ideals.

Arlie Russell Hochschild's 1989 book, *The Second Shift*,

investigated dual-earner American couples. She found that wives did an extra month per year of housework, on top of their jobs, above what men did: an entire month of seven-day weeks. Hochschild concluded that housework was working wives' second job, their 'second shift'. Two decades later, conservative figures estimate that wives do three times as much housework as husbands. What is more, many men seem to fear housework, as if it sullies their manhood. Unemployed husbands of working wives often do less to help than their employed counterparts, grasping at the shreds of dignity afforded to the 'man of the house'.

Women also prop up macho domestic myths. In one study, American wives earning the same or more than their husbands did *extra* housework, as if to compensate for showing their menfolk up. So housework performed a sec-ondary task: buffing hubby's ego. (Is this why couples in which a wife earns 50 to 60 per cent of the family income are statistically the likeliest to divorce?)

It would be wrong to call such wives subservient, as they assert female honour too. Psychologist Dorothy Rowe speculated that women tend to be tidier than men as a legacy of the days when parents instilled aesthetics in daughters, since able housekeepers were easier to marry off. Such legacies are woven into the DNA of family life, enduring because they are passed on unconsciously, in the everyday lessons that parents teach their children about how men and women live. You might imagine that it takes a supersonic ego to pop soiled underwear into an envelope, mail it to a girl in another country and expect it back, clean and ironed, by return of post, as student Albert Einstein did. Such behaviour is not natural; it is the result of special training, of generation upon generation of sons not being asked or taught to tidy. And if a son told to do his homework but never to pick up his pants grows into an Einstein or a President, who except Mrs Einstein or Michelle Obama complains?

By contrast, a woman impregnated with her mother's domestic conscience will struggle to abort it, even if she is a captain of industry, because we still rate women by their homes in a way that we do not rate men. There are always other women, too, doing things the old way, to reproach those who do not. Like the charmer in the village where I grew up, who after a dinner thanked her businesswoman hostess by writing, in the dust on a sideboard: 'Hello Mary.'

Circumstances conspire to domesticate wives more than husbands. Many couples who divide housework fifty-fifty find that this changes at parenthood, as they fall victim to a little questioned axiom in marriage: whoever has a dash more experience in a task is, for ever after, the designated in-house expert. Mothers become storehouses of childcare information by a process that feels natural, yet is due not to their chromosomes but to the practical fact that they start out doing most childcare. A wife at home with a child necessarily has a richer apprehension of what needs doing in that home, and as she deals with it and then becomes good at it, developing routines and systems, her husband may seem increasingly incompetent, blind or selfish. Domestic historian Margaret Horsfield recounted a conversation that ended several of her relationships: 'Through gritted teeth I explain that I do not want to have to ask – can't he see they need doing? And then when he does the dishes, something is always left, some totemic offering on the countertop beside the sink, usually something out of the ordinary like the thermos, a yogurt pot, a large jug perhaps. Or the stove is unwiped, or the frying pan forgotten.'

Expertise brings pride and a sense of ownership that polarizes couples further, as to guard our territory we also cultivate ignorance of things outside it. For instance, my mother can re-cover a sofa, is as handy on computers as at the stove, yet claims, with utter conviction, 'I can't hammer in a nail straight.' Not coincidentally, my father, an accountant, poet and gardener, 'cannot' use a washing machine. The difference, as my mother points out, is that she has at least tried hammering; my father has never yet broached the washing machine.

Housework does more than keep us apart. If men care less, and women more, inequities come to seem normal. A 2008 paper, 'It's Just Easier for Me to Do It', found that wives still did 'the lion's share' of housekeeping, but, due to 'unspoken assumptions' about wives' roles, they, their husbands and children believed this lopsided arrangement to be 'fair'.

If men see home as a place of rest, and women see it as a workplace, men have less incentive to change. So a working wife in search of equality faces two extra chores: to persuade her husband to care more; and to quell any guilt that she is failing, as wife or mother, by not doing everything at home herself.

Yes, husbands and wives have richer choices than ever, but as drama buffs know, choice is the fount of conflict. What if you want a marriage and home like your parents' and to also have a stellar career? Wrinkled shirts, grimy kids or KFC dinners may tell you that you are letting yourself down, or your spouse is. Should the inconsiderate git force you to nag about the housework, this additional chore may bring you to breaking point.

HOW TO TURN A SPOUSE INTO A NAG

Nagging is a dance that psychologists term 'demand–withdrawal'. Its steps are simple.

First, the nag makes a request. The naggee says nothing.

Nag asks again. Nothing. Nag raises their voice.

And so on, until naggee grunts, leaves the room, or flicks on to another television channel.

Once nag is screaming, tearing out hair or rending garments, naggee points, laughs, or says, 'Why didn't you ask?'

3. IT'S NOT FAIR: THREE HOUSEHOLD SCAMS AND HOW TO GET AWAY WITH THEM

Why do not more couples split up over housework? Self-delusion spares much grief. If you do not feel like helping out, or you take on more than your spouse, to override your domestic differences you need a ploy. Try one of these popular family myths.

1. Selective Domestic Incompetence: The Disability Scam

Vera Brittain, an early twentieth-century feminist and radical non-domestic, went on the attack after her husband complained. 'Why should I have a sort of moral obligation to see that you eat enough? Much you would notice if my appetite showed a falling off! Why men should endow themselves with a monopoly in this kind of helplessness I really don't know!' Quite. Anyone can play the selective incompetence game. Claim that you 'cannot hammer in a nail', blame your upbringing. You could tell yourself that incompetence is endearing, like chaotic traveller Charley Boorman: 'Kinvara, my daughter, said, "Mummy, do you like it when Daddy is away, because the house is nice and clean?"' And if you are lucky, your spouse will play along, preferring to see your idleness as loveable dependence rather than selfishness, and enjoy feeling superior. Writer Charlotte Methven, whose lonely childhood made her an ace organizer, boasted that her husband, who had a happy family, 'is incapable of finding two matching socks'.

Selective incompetence is often accompanied by selective hearing. Many 'misunderstandings', writes linguist Deborah Cameron, 'are tactical rather than real. Pretending not to understand what someone wants you to do is one way to avoid doing it. This may be what is really going on when a man claims not to have recognized a woman's "could you empty the trash" or "the groceries are in the car" as a request.'

There is a flaw in the disability scam: if you have passed a driving test, held down a job, can you convincingly maintain that cooking is beyond you? To distract your spouse from this risky line of enquiry, concoct a sob story, a nasty childhood incident involving a pet and a toaster perhaps. Another line of defence is to develop an area of domestic expertise without which your spouse is helpless, or to master something esoteric like sock sorting – never ironing or anything of general use. The risk is that you become a luxury they can do without. Friends, especially mothers, confide that life is simpler when Daddy is away.

2. Myth of the Mother Goddess: The Flattery Scam

There are women, whose only experience of employment was choosing their wedding list, who give monologues on how tiring it is planning school barbecues. Guilt is their mantra. Millionaire chef Jamie Oliver's wife, Jools, is 'up at six every day because I want to make the girls porridge before they go to school, and because I need the time to do the stuff I think I should do because I don't have a job'. Aptly, porridge is slang for prison. Oliver has enlisted in the cult of the mother goddess.

The mother goddess is a one-woman miracle, proof against cough, cold, sleep deprivation and all known stains. Husbands marvel, 'I don't know how she does it,' but if she starts to explain they change the subject. Yet some burdened wives actually resent their husband mucking in — for stealing their martyred halo: 'A real low point was when I came home and found him making pastry. Pastry! From scratch . . . Being bloody marvellous at everything, making it all look easy, was my speciality.'

Sadly, the cult of the mother goddess puts husbands and wives into a feudal relationship. It can also alienate friends, thanks to women's gift for seeing each other's choices as reproaches to their own. Working wives envy goddesses their job-free lives, as they dash home to find their kids scoffing junk, and in the meantime, goddesses suffer to justify their jobless existence. The question for both types of wife is whether their high standards are self-defeating? Bear in mind that we prefer our partners with a few imperfections, as who enjoys feeling inferior?

3. Calling Hobbies 'Housework': The Leisure Mis-selling Scam

Hobbies are not housework. Not gardening, woodwork, fishing, shooting, brewing, not even most DIY (also known, falsely, as 'I do it for you'). To perpetrate this scam, give a spouse a reason to swallow it. Align your hobby with their interests. Grow organic veg on a faraway allotment, for instance.

Note: You can reverse the hobby-as-housework scam, and pretend that chores are hobbies. This is particularly useful with food. We must eat, and good food is life's one guaranteed pleasure. But without interest − from cook and eaters − the unavoidable task of producing it is a bore, unless a cook turns it into a hobby. Like Nigella Lawson, fabled domestic goddess: 'My children treat me as if I'm trying to poison them. "What have you put in this?" Every forkful is scrutinised . . . [My husband] Charles's greatest joke is, "There is nothing you can cook me that can compete with some Weetabix and milk, and you must admit it."'

If you dislike chores, do yourself a favour and help your spouse to help you. Just because it is not your favourite meal, this is no excuse to stare at your plate or sniff a bowl then say, 'What is it?', a compliment popular only in the land of nincompoops. Do not sniff the milk carton. Instead, laugh at the smeared plate, the carbonized sausage. Burnish that mother-goddess myth, praise that wobbly lawn-mowing. Do not joke as my grandfather, a roast beef man, did about his new wife's experiments in cookery, 'Why is it that everything I get in this house is either a burned offering or a bloody sacrifice?'

4. HOW TO MAKE HOUSEWORK WORK FOR YOU

In a dream marriage, chores would be shared pleasures, but this is hard when they are rarely choices made voluntarily. Few of us have the luxury of believing, like pop star Kylie Minogue, that cleaning cupboards is 'therapy'. However much we cherish life's small ceremonies, over the years, delicious meals, shining floors, tend to be taken for granted. And if we feel let down, the rage may fester, as people are more sensitive to insults than to joys. If it takes five compliments to make up for an insult, a few crusty dishes easily cancel out a pile of ironing.

To work out the true division of domestic labour in your marriage, plot the footsteps each of you takes around the house each day, count the steps, and where they head, then compare notes. Is it time to broker a new domestic bargain?

Before setting to, note that the value of an hour's housework is not fixed. It depends what a spouse can be persuaded it is worth. These negotiations tend to take place by clumsy trial and error, as frustrated wives find that they have less bargaining power. Indeed unequal situations can seem fair because equality is not the same as fairness. The former depends on parity, whereas fairness is a perception: it depends on what we *feel* to be fair. And fairness matters more to happiness in marriage than equality. Israeli researchers found that if couples expect the same of housework, it has no influence on their marital contentment, no matter that wives do everything. If couples have different expectations of housework, however, or keep accounts, swapping chore for chore, they may lose trust and break up.

Luckily, marriage makes it easier to take a long view, to give extra now in the knowledge that next year (in theory) something else can be taken back. At each life shift, priorities shift, which eases bargaining by making new marital trade-offs possible. For instance, a survey of 628 German couples found that among the childless, the fewer chores a husband did, the greater the chance of divorce. But among parents, idle men made divorce no likelier, and did not lower a couple's probability of having a second child. Instead, the odds of a second child rose with a father's hours of childcare. Clearly, when mothers rated husbands' domestic input, for them, an hour the father spent with his baby counted for far more than an hour ironing.

When striking a housework bargain, the happiest objective is to keep a home homely. To achieve this it is better to seek not equality but equivalence in effort, and to accept that long hours at an office also earn extra slack at home. Anyone assessing what division of labour is fair for them should be aware that the following inequities warp perceptions:

- Husbands who stay at home are still thought extraordinary, often seen as saintly for sacrificing their manhood on the altar of their wife's ambition.

- Wives' hours of housework are valued less than husbands', because in a Catch 22, women put more in. Women are also still expected to see paid employment as a privilege, and paid less per hour than men — a further reason why their hours at home are undervalued.

- Men see their salary as housework, especially if they spend more on the home than their less well-paid wife. Even if she does more housework while putting in the same hours at work, he may, say, 'I put a roof over your head.'

- Men routinely overestimate their household input, say sociologists; women seldom do.

- Some husbands feel that if they do a quarter of the housework, their wives should count themselves lucky since both know that by current averages if she shops around, she is unlikely to find a husband who does more.

Any husband tempted to abuse these insights, beware: say that you are 'helping out' while doing bugger all and you may hear from lawyers.

Overburdened houseworkers, before calling your spouse lazy, reflect. This gives your formerly beloved two choices: to obey you and lose face, or do nothing and defy you. Which option would you choose? Remember that the danger of assuming your point of view is right is that you may not spot that an issue, such as buying a dog, which for you is practical, is for your spouse emotional, and as a result you will end up arguing about entirely different things. (Your lack of respect for their emotional needs.) Better than right is to be reasonable and accept that whoever cares most is de facto housekeeper. The other has a duty to help, but also a right not to be nagged.

HOW TO REBRAND CHORES

To retrain a reluctant spouse, emulate the genius of Dyson vacuum cleaners, which is less their technology than the fact that they look like intriguing macho toys. If Dyson can make hoovering cool, you can rebrand chores. Sell them as:

Easy: They are, mostly. You could share the stirring tale of reformed idler, novelist Andrew Martin: 'The iron, I discovered, was kept near the washing machine, and when I squared up to this contraption I saw it was not quite so complicated as I had always suspected.' To support this impression of ease, only delegate responsibilities within your spouse's ability. If truly manipulative, you could praise your beloved for doing things they have not quite done.

Pleasing: Repetitive tasks soothe, and there is always satisfaction in a job well done. Many wives resent being expected to praise husbands for tasks that they perform as a matter of routine, but husbands also resent not being praised. It would be better if everyone was more grateful. Some housework is creative, and all of us take pride in improving skills, so why not connect chores with things that your spouse treasures? Suggest using their analytical skills on how to hoover faster. If technology is involved, ask them to buy the best, studying the form as they might a racehorse.

An investment in marriage: Wash up, prepare a meal or shop together and you have an opportunity to chat and stay in touch.

A way to get something else: Reveal that better educated couples share domestic burdens equally — a form of self-interest, since happy couples enjoy more sex, and hospitable spouses help careers.

The lesser evil: Ask a spouse either to grout the bathroom or peel potatoes, and suddenly peeling will seem an easy option.

In reality, no domestic conflict is you versus her or him. It is a shared problem: you two versus chaos. If you can turn housework into an ever-changing field of pleasure, and have meaningful discussions about what to eat for supper instead of yelling about who forgot to buy it, you are a better man than me. In the meantime, do not imagine that your way is best. If your erstwhile idler starts having ideas about how to do things, is that not the general idea?

4

PLAY IN MARRIAGE

WHY GIRLS DON'T WANT TO HAVE FUN,
BUT MUST

Why did the superstar Madonna and film director Guy Ritchie break up? The question is worth asking, because the Ritchies endured extreme marital conditions, and weathered the storms of life at the sharp end of human aspirations. Theirs is a parable of modern marriage.

Was it divorce by personal trainer? (Madonna's whipping girl believed a two-hour workout, six days a week, to be a form of time-travel: 'I want to keep her body looking like it's twenty years old.')

Lack of time? (Fifteen per cent of your waking hours, sweating, is a big bite out of life.)

Age? (Turning fifty hit Madonna hard. According to

anonymous friends, Guy, unlike her personal trainer, 'never said the right things to get her over that hurdle'.)

Clashing sense of humour? (And he mocked her jokes. Allegedly.)

Rival tastes? (Madonna banned newspapers, sausages, sugar, cow's milk, ice cream, cheese, cake, and television, and would stalk out in a huff at the merest whiff of steak pie. And Guy bought a pub, at which, perhaps not coincidentally, such vices are available, along with lots of hearty blokes to hang out with.)

Or their volcanic tempers? ('Relationships are about eating humble pie,' said Guy before things fell apart. Just not steak pie, it seems.)

The Ritchies' greatest problem was pleasure. Or rather, lack thereof. Work stole time from their relationship and riddled it with insecurities – with his fraught film career, and the exorbitant efforts required to maintain brand Madonna. Nobody works as hard as my missus, said Guy, repeatedly. Why did anyone assume he meant this as a compliment?

In a workaholic culture, where time-poverty is a badge of success, not even superstars can supersede the limits of the human heart. It is inconvenient that, for all the miracles of modern technology, which extend our memories, lengthen our lives and widen our worlds, there remain only twenty-four hours in a day. The price of success, then, is that the cost of love rises.

Even though love is a gift, not a commodity, it must, as

economist Avner Offer observed, compete 'in the market for time and attention'. Hence affluenza pushes up the price of love. The more interests a couple has, the more opportunities, occupations, they must sacrifice for each moment that they spend together – and the more pressure there is on them to enjoy their precious time. But pressure is not enjoyable. Ironically, they will also expect a premium return on their diminishing hours of companionship – another pressure. Worse, the greater the relative cost to us of each hour spent on our marriage, as opposed to on our hallowed career the likelier that we will resent anything less than perfection. Therefore, if after months of grinding work, a hotly anticipated holiday does not pan out as we dreamed, the shortfall can feel disastrous.

In the case of the Ritchies, ironically for professional entertainers, amusing each other seemed to be hard work. In their final two years together, said reports, one activity that the unhappy pair continued to share was 'romantic' meals. At which Madonna apparently ate nothing and talked God, while Guy looked less than fascinated. Next, perhaps terminally, the doomed couple began to work on their union, resorting to desperate measures like whisper therapy, hissing random words like 'brilliant' and 'stunning' at each other. In an odd fiftieth birthday tribute, Guy described his life with Madonna as 'invigorating': 'There seems to be no end to the desire to be creative.' Two weeks later they split. Asked if she would marry again, Madonna replied, 'I'd rather get run over by a train.'

Madonna is extraordinary. She need not sing another note, never mind wash a dish, yet on she slaves. And in her talent for grinding work from life's joys, she was a stereo-typical wife.

1.   WHAT ARE YOU PLAYING AT?

Marriage guru John Gottman argues that a good marriage hinges on harmonious chemistry:

> Make marriage work by doing the right thing at the right time[?] I don't believe [in] that . . . For example, does his face naturally brighten when she walks into a room? When he reads something inter-esting, is he thinking, 'I'd like to get her view on this'? Or are all these things an afterthought – an applied social skill? When we study couples who truly 'master' marriage, we notice that, for example, her sense of humor is delightful to him and eases his heart, even though they're discussing a difficult, long-standing issue . . . None of this works unless it is genuine. His interest in her and the effect of her anger or humor on his heart rate and endocrine secretions are all determined by the fit between them . . . by the chemistry.

But chemistry does not fix a marriage's destiny: rather, it expresses its present condition. Not only is it always in flux, but also subject to external influence. Women living under the same roof, for instance, fall into the same menstrual cycle because bodies' chemistry is mutually influential (via secretions such as sweat, scent, pheromones). Likewise, in marriage our emotional, social and physiological chemistry may become synchronized because we live cosily together. Alternatively, they may fall out of sync, particularly if we respond in mutually incompatible ways to stress, and argue, sending our cortisol levels rocketing. And any couple flounders if they are together so seldom that they forget what turns each other on.

To fall back on artificially 'applied social skills', or desperate measures such as the Ritchies' whisper therapy, is not the shortest route by which a marriage can be rescued. For a start, it is artificial, and John Gottman is right, delight cannot be faked. However, we can rig our living conditions to improve the chemistry of our marriage.

Take that potent romantic ingredient, a sense of humour. You can boost yours right now without a single joke. Research finds that you are likelier to laugh, the nearer you stand to another person. The larger the group, the more you will giggle. You will laugh harder still if you touch each other, if only a pat on the back. Why? Because humans are social animals to our core.

Happy couples' hearts still skip the same odd beat at the same odd things. Not purely due to luck, but to sharing a life that enables trivial, serendipitous, priceless events like laughing at the same daft thing at the same time. While playfulness gives love its elastic, its lack creates tension. Look at Guy and Madonna, cursed with so few of what you or I call chores, yet seemingly so joyless (not even eating ice cream). Madonna ruled the roost, became servant to her inflexible regime, then felt lonely. Meanwhile Guy let her rule, then fled to the pub. Their divorce seemed inevitable, but it could have been avoidable, if they only had fun.

Would it not be lovely to experience the bliss found by eighteenth-century farmer, Hector St John de Crèvecoeur, despite a surname that means something like broken-hearted:

> When I went to work . . . my wife would often come with her knitting in her hand, and sit under the shady trees, praising the straightness of my furrows, and the docility of my horses; this swelled my heart and made everything light and pleasant, and I regretted that I had not married before . . . When I contemplate my wife, by my fireside, while she either spins, knits, darns or suckles our child, I cannot describe the various emotions of love, of gratitude, of conscious pride, which thrill in my heart.

Today life is fragmented. Many are too busy trying to balance work and life to reflect on their blessings. But this balancing act is doomed. Life is not the opposite of work: life is work. It comprises tough tasks, like earning money and chores, and the supposedly lighter ones of leisure, family, friends, love. All can assume the guise of problems, under pressure. Acquiring friends can be a status game, as can maintaining a nice home. As for ensuring that a child is well-fed yet lean; smart yet rounded; obedient yet spirited; focused yet relaxed — well, how many circles can you square without cutting corners, feeling guilty, driving your spouse to the pub, or tucking into a tub of inorganic, triple-choc fudge sundae?

Madonna and Guy Ritchie's lives seemd to follow a familiar pattern of mismanagement and disintegration. In two-job households, most couples divide so much labour — housework, paid work, childcare — that their lives grow parallel, and increasingly apart. Unfortunately, the longer a couple has been together, the more it matters to waste time together and refresh their marriage. But as years pass, prioritizing time-wasting is harder to justify amid pressure to earn or mind children. So as play and spontaneity matter more, most couples share less leisure, and, with it, less sex. That we expect leisure to heal not harm compounds the disappointment if a holiday does not live up to expectations, which is likelier than not if we are frazzled by the time we actually take the time to take it.

Few couples give leisure serious thought since its whole point would seem to be fun. Yet we do take leisure seriously, from the chants in the football stadium to the contests to grow the biggest turnip at the village fête. The danger of not discussing it is that you may assume that your spouse loves visiting mouldy churches because you do, or mistake a frown of concentration over a golf ball for hostility, and fall into a resentful silence that they in turn mistake for contentment. How many marriages start to sour in moments when one spouse is looking away and the other longs to speak? Drip by drip, trivial everyday, misunderstandings turn into gulfs.

A further problem of leisure is that husbands and wives experience life's strains differently. However much free time women have, research finds that they feel rushed, whereas men feel entitled to relax. And the guilt gap between men and women is widening. A study of thousands of diaries from 1975 and 1998 found that women's free time diminished over these decades, but men's stayed the same. Worse, men and women's perceptions of leisure grew further apart. In 1975, if a woman had extra time off, she felt slightly less rushed. By 1998, no amount of additional free time eased her sense of pressure. Yet in 1998, as in 1975, men saw free time as their time. They felt free.

STICKS, STONES AND HOBBIES

In the late 1980s marriage researcher Arlie Russell Hochschild found 'no working mothers who maintained hobbies', unlike their husbands. In contrast to women, men have a tradition of hobbies, leisure they 'earn' by their wages. Male hierarchies equate idleness with status. 'Angling is the most popular sport in Britain,' wrote Germaine Greer, 'because it is an excuse to do absolutely nothing for days on end.'

Some sad cases fake hobbies. Gordon Brown, when scheming to be British Prime Minister, sought to soften his public image by inviting journalists round to watch England play football in the World Cup (Brown is, do not forget, Scottish). He sipped lo-cal, lo-carb lager, and won nothing but scorn from his ungrateful guests.

This was slightly unfair since hobbies often involve self-advertising. (And Scotland were not in the championship.) According to Darwinian thought, music, art and sport initially evolved as ways to attract mates. The curious thing is that once we have mated, spouses tend to use hobbies to repel their mate, and anyone else bothersome. Victorian adventurer and *Kama Sutra* translator Sir Richard Burton stalked into one of his wife's tea parties, tossed a manuscript on a table, and left without a word. The ladies raced to see what his latest work was about. The title read *A History of Farting*. Spouses' hobbies are often suspected as excuses for opting out. Kate Mostel said of her husband, comic legend, Zero: 'He seals himself up in his room. He does puzzles, reads art books . . . Now that we are rich, he has a room of his own, and once he shuts the door, that's the last I hear from him. I just heard of a refrigerator that talks. That's what I need. I will go to the refrigerator and say how are you, and it will answer me.'

Many couples accept the view that hobbies are What Men Do while wives Get On With It. Some women also appear fearful of conceding that they have time to spare, lest they meet the suspicion which greeted Alice Munro, now among Canada's most celebrated authors, in 1968, when, aged thirty-seven and a the mother of three, she published her first book. The local newspaper headline read like an accusation: 'Housewife finds time to write.'

We all need an escape, whether in the heady creosote of a shed, or at an interior design class. Eleanor Coppola seems to have learned too late that her husband, the film director, Francis, expected a traditional Italian-style wife devoted to him, first, last and always. However, her confidence grew and she began hosting art events, once giving a home tour to museum directors. Aware that most had come out of voyeuristic curiosity, Eleanor replaced the display case exhibits of Francis's Oscar statuettes with new trophies: the mocking mini-Oscar pendants, which at that time the Academy awarded to Oscar winners' wives, to wear around their necks and promote their husbands' glory. In the kitchen guests were instructed to peel a potato and then read a quote by Joseph Beuys: 'Peeling a potato can be a work of art if it is a conscious act.'

2. THE GUILT-AND-PLAY GAP

The guilt-and-play gap between husbands and wives niggles at first. In time, if couples fail to recognize that they have different priorities, or if leisure conflicts touch on unresolved questions, such as how much they see the children, and then you add a dash of competition, thwarted ambition or a husband who is paid twice what his wife is for putting in the same hours' work, then his decision to spend Saturday night playing darts in the Nag and Goat can be construed as an act of marital treachery. However, it is also treacherous to show no interest whatsoever in a husband's prize turnips.

In his 1526 conjugal manual *Institution of Marriage*, wily monk-philosopher Erasmus warned husbands who are 'morose and stern' at home but 'merry' everywhere else that they encouraged their wives 'to seek amusement' elsewhere. He also chastised a 'wife who is happy when her husband is sad' as 'not only unsuitable but hostile'. In other words, in marriage, joy cannot guarantee joy. Harmony is the balance to aim for, as the relationship between leisure and marital happiness is not direct.

All couples need to play apart at times. Moaning to mates, going for a run, defuses stress, refreshes, and creates something new to talk about when you come home. But playing apart also threatens marriage, if it distracts or creates temptation. Instead of running to the pub husbands might do better to teach their wives to relax. Unfortunately for men, while most have greater leisure than wives, it is wives' enthusiasms that decide whether leisure is a bone of contention. Husbands' feelings on the subject are weirdly irrelevant.

Few couples pursue activities together which only one spouse enjoys, but research finds that if they do, it is four times likelier to be an activity that she enjoys and he does not. Yet a husband's happiness is unaffected. On the other hand, if couples jointly pursue an activity that only he likes, both will feel unhappy. And if he should go off to pursue an activity alone that she enjoys too, his marital contentment drops, yet even though she is missing out, her marital contentment is unaffected. What is more, a husband who sneaks off to do something that his wife disapproves of will be more miserable than one hanging out with his wife, doing something that she likes but he does not.

So husbands who please themselves are unhappy, despite getting their own way. And if football does not put a smile on her face, I am afraid, gentlemen, you will enjoy it less than you thought. Even if wives skimp on leisure, it is their pleasure say the experts, that has most influence on a couple's happiness.

Is this wives' reward or punishment for doing more heavy lifting in marriage? Who knows? Maybe women always struggled to be fun. Why else did medieval weddings require brides to swear two extra vows: 'To be cheerful and obedient, in bed and at board.' If guilt is a feminine virtue, it is partly a legacy of religious blame on naughty Eve, which for centuries was used to justify caging women in domesticity. What is disturbing is how many wives today continue to let guilt lock them in a work/life prison, wives who compete over how stressed they are.

The way out is not to blame men but to question the merit of all this work, then go out and do something less boring instead.

Everyone agrees that communication is the top ingredient for a happy marriage. Wives put leisure second, husbands sex. But the more leisure couples share, the more sex they have. And as well as communication, leisure and sex foster self-esteem and a sense of equality. To prove the point, a paper followed 147 dual-earning couples into parenthood. Wives who shared more leisure with their husbands before the birth of a child reported greater love, less conflict, a year later. Whereas husbands who pursued independent social lives prior to their baby's arrival, reported less love, greater strife, a year later. Overall, researchers conclude that wives' early contentment decides whether a couple shares leisure in a marriage's later years. On the upside, couples who make an effort to play together do get happier.

Today's couples may have to work harder than earlier generations to see each other's point of view, to understand why he can veg out while she lies awake, listing tasks for the weekend. But if husbands' and wives' positions are not always compatible, reconciling them is easier if both accept that men and women have different ideas about where work ends and play begins, and strive to push joy up the list of priorities.

To seek pleasure keeps us alive to the moment and each other, and sharpens the mind too. In *The Pleasure Center*, Professor Morten Kringelbach described how joy, like pain, is a neurological on/off switch, guiding our impulses, actions and decisions.

Play and sex, pleasure and leisure. It is a virtuous merry-go-round of love. So step on it.

3.   HOW TO FIND THE PLEASURE IN LEISURE

A young man asked Albert Einstein what is 'the best formula for success in life'. Einstein smiled. A long minute passed before he replied.

'If A is success, I should say the formula is $A = X+Y+Z$, X being work and Y being play.'

'And what is Z?' asked his disciple.

'That,' said Einstein, 'is keeping your mouth shut.'

If success means hiding your failures, maybe he was on to something. Because as far as marriage went, Einstein's method was ruthlessly to sever X (his working self) from Y (his playful home body). He dreamed of galaxies while his second wife doted on him as if he were an aged tot. But the formula flopped on his smart first wife, who helped do his maths until he saw her as 'an employee I cannot sack', then changed his mind and dumped her and their attention-grabbing sons.

It is as well that Einstein stuck to theories of relativity

rather than marital relations. Although he presented work as the opposite of play, play is no more the opposite of work than life is. It is the attitude you bring to an activity as much as the activity itself: the difference between telling children that they are mucking about with paint and crayons, and telling them that they will be rewarded with a certificate if they do well. An experiment tested this hypothesis and found that those children offered a certificate for their artistic achievement were far less enthusiastic the next time the paint and crayons came out. The moral of the story is that bribes are the surest means to kill pleasure, and the last way to get anyone, child or husband, to do what you want, since the fact that you are offering a bribe instantly informs them that they are being had — that this fun thing you are proposing to them is actually no fun at all. (This is why parents should never say, 'Greens are good for you.')

To prevent hobbies becoming the third person in a relationship, embrace them or you may end up surrounded by incomplete 'projects' when your spouse's passion wanes. Or be left standing on the sidelines, like valiant Kate Middleton, girlfriend of Prince William, second in line to Britain's throne. During a polo match she was discovered alone in a hot tent, watching the action on TV. She was there, she explained, because she was allergic to horses. 'I have to pay attention to every second. I'll be discussing the game in minute detail later.'

More companionable are shared hobbies, such as pursued by visionary artist William Blake and his wife Catherine.

One sunny day in the 1790s their friend and patron, one Mr Butts, found them in a summerhouse, liberated from '"those troublesome disguises" which have prevailed since the Fall. "Come in!" cried Blake; "it's only Adam and Eve, you know!" Husband and wife had been reciting passages from *Paradise Lost*, in character, and the garden of Hercules Buildings had to represent the Garden of Eden.'

With leisure, as with housework, to get others involved make a game of it and structure tasks to be rewarding. As we have seen, wellbeing is enhanced in five ways: by connecting with the world and people around us; by being active; by being curious; by learning; and by giving. In theory, you would not just stop to smell the roses, but grow them, memorize their Latin names, pick them, then go for a stroll, chatting to passers-by, until you met one you liked enough to give them a posy.

Like junk food, junk joys grow addictive by scratching an itch they cannot sate. But certain traits make pleasure longer lasting, by tapping our brain's reward circuits. For maximally fruitful pursuits, then seek those that cultivate self-esteem, social confidence, your sense of control and optimism.

'Happiness is when what you think, what you say, and what you do are in harmony,' observed Mahatma Gandhi. Similarly, the esteemed connoisseur of pleasure, Hungarian psychologist Mihaly Csikszentmihalyi, explained enjoyment as a state of 'flow', in which a person's skill and motivation are in perfect balance with a challenge, allowing them to lose themselves in the task. If leisure is to afford deep pleasure, it is best enjoyed in conditions that aid flow, featuring:

- Clear, realistic goals, with defined expectations and rules for achieving them
- Focus — concentrate hard on a limited area
- Unselfconsciousness — being so absorbed you lose sense of time, or self
- Feedback — indications as to whether you are succeeding or failing as you go along
- A challenge to match, not overreach your skills — stretching you, not setting you up for failure
- A sense of control over a situation or activity
- Intrinsically rewarding actions — the more incidental goals, the greater your motivation

How to satisfy these conditions? Sports, games, strolls, playing music, rituals, cooking meals, all provide defined objectives and rewards, and challenges to keep refining skills. Whereas leisure that is shapeless or passive, or enjoyed slumped in a chair, is necessarily less satisfying because less demanding.

The wider lesson is that to deepen our pleasure in marriage we must constantly create incentives, offer praise, and not forget that shared laughter or the sense that we have been generous, and given a gift that was gratefully received, satisfies more than any bribe can.

What play is not is cramming weekends with supernumerary, improving activities, then getting exhausted, stuck in traffic, or cross.

If it makes you smile — enough to look up to see if your spouse is smiling too — it works.

FRIENDS WITH BENEFITS

Where does hospitality end and friendship begin? Thirteenth-century Italian teenager Marco Polo was hard pressed to answer, travelling around the Chinese province Tangut, where husbands customarily vacated the home when guests came to stay. In his memoir, Polo explained: 'The stranger stays with his wife in the house and does as he likes and lies with her in a bed just as if she were his wife, and they continue in great enjoyment. All the men of this city and province are thus cuckolded by their wives; but they are not the least ashamed of it. And the women are beautiful and vivacious and always ready to oblige.' Were they in Rome, you can be sure that Tangut's open-hearted citizens would have expected Polo to do the same for them.

Trading favours is the essence of friendship. All relationships depend on two things: mutual interest; and give and take. Hence Aristotle identified three types of friend: those who do jobs for you; friends for pleasure and shared pursuits; and soulmates. Marriage is a friendship too (with extra favours exchanged in bed); however, sociologists confirm that married couples struggle if they keep tabs on the services each renders and always expect something in return. By contrast, friendships founder if we fail to give and take. As a result, it is easy to tell if a friend is good or bad: if they are not there for you, but you are for them.

Good friends are also friends to marriage, as they transform our lives in subtle ways. It is because friendship is so fluid a trading system that fashion trends, manners, health, even moods, pass through social networks across several degrees of separation. This is why when Harvard researchers studied 4,739 people, they found that a happy partner increases happiness by 8 per cent. It sounds good until you learn that 'a friend who becomes happy and lives within a mile increases your likelihood of happiness by 25%'. For these reasons, fourteenth-century bishop-philosopher Albert of Saxony argued that 'concord or discord within a couple' are immediately echoed by friends, and that benevolent attention to a spouse's friends and relatives increases love and unity all around.

Good friends hold up mirrors to our lives, and let us escape ourselves in vicarious armchair or barstool adventures as we listen to their stories. We also compare marital notes with them. But perhaps friends' greatest service to marriage is to provide alibis for time apart from a spouse. If you want help in sticking to a resolution about food, exercise or drink, why nag your spouse to do it? Friends' power of influence suggests that you would do better to join a like-minded group. Friends also supplement deficits in a spouse. If they are not a great thinker, talker, walker or tiddlywinks champion, a friend can plug the gap. Agony aunt Sally Brampton wrote that the couple with the 'best marriage I have seen' liked each other and laughed a lot — aided by skilful misery diversion. The wife said of a row with her mother: 'I was so angry when I put down the phone, I had to call a friend and unload before he came home so I didn't dump it all over him.'

If good friends offer holidays from ourselves, bad ones make us unhappy with our lot. Sadly, competition creeps into all trading systems, so clichés about neighbours striving to keep up with the Joneses are true because friends are each other's pacemakers. Either they feel in each other's league or someone feels furious. Suddenly to be conspicuously happier, or wealthier, than friends can cause great affront. Journalist Nigella Lawson had the impertinence to do both, becoming wildly famous, then marrying art dealer Charles Saatchi. Acquaintances who once enjoyed cosy Lawson kitchen suppers in down-at-heel London suburb Shepherd's Bush, told the newspapers that since her move to millionaires' row, Lawson had become a 'bird in a gilded cage'. She denied it: 'Charles and I were simply in the honeymoon phase while our contemporaries are past disillusionment. You have to re-find a way of being with your friends. If all they want to do is moan about their husbands, they don't want you in a good mood.'

Friendship also threatens marriage if spouses do not agree on the limits of their generosity. A London lawyer's wife offered her single, childless friend the services of her husband as sperm donor. A turkey baster was used, and lo, a child was born. Surprise, surprise, feelings changed, and lo, the husband and the friend began an affair. Now they all holiday together. The wife claims she is quite content, unlike poor Mathilde Verlaine, wife to nineteenth-century symbolist poet Paul, who welcomed her husband's drunken friend, the teen prodigy Arthur Rimbaud. Rimbaud repaid Mathilde by trashing his room, mutilating an antique crucifix, a family heirloom, sunbathing nude in front of the house, and patting his head theatrically as they went on family walks to encourage his head lice to hop on to the heads of passers-by. To cap it all, Rimbaud and Paul then began an affair, consecrating their love in a co-authored sonnet in praise of the arsehole.

There is no set rule as to whether friends are

better for marriage if they are enjoyed together rather than apart. In Ancient Rome, the Greek historian Plutarch was stunned to find himself at a ritzy dinner party where not only men and women but husbands and wives were socializing — with each other. French moralist La Rochefoucauld echoed Plutarch's perplexity on visiting London in 1784. Here, husband and wife are always together, they belong to the same society . . . they do all their visiting together. It would be more ridiculous in England to do otherwise than it would be in Paris to go around always with one's wife. They give the impression of the most perfect harmony.' And indeed, studies find that couples who socialize together, at least some of the time, are happier. Infidelity researchers report that 'weaker network ties' in marriage — that is, separate social and family lives — often predict a partner shall stray. An Australian review of 9,147 first marriages that broke down found wives to be far pickier about social networks than husbands, and more inclined 'to initiate separation' if they find their husbands antisocial.

As friends have a lesser stake in our happiness than a spouse, so may mislead or make mischief, a further merit of rating friends by the favours they do (or not) is that it is easier to discern bloodsuckers in our midst.

So beware friends who offer pity instead of hope,

or advice that is unsought. Beware those who dislike or alienate your spouse. Cécilia, the second wife of French President Nicolas Sarkozy, saw his minister Rachida Dati as 'my little sister'. But when Dati called one morning, Sarkozy's third wife Carla picked up the phone: 'Now Nicolas is married you mustn't ring so early.' Dati was duly fired.

Be prepared to fight. Clementine, Winston Churchill's wife, was appalled by her husband's awe for seadog Admiral Jackie Fisher, whom she described as a 'malevolent engine' and 'fiend'. The men fell out, but when it looked like their friendship would resume, she snarled at Fisher: 'Keep your hands off my husband. You have all but ruined him once. Leave him alone now.'

And watch those supposed friends who seek more than your amity, and have designs on your life. Single white female Lady Bess Foster, best friend to eighteenth-century social leader Georgiana, Duchess of Devonshire, moved in, swiftly taking over Georgiana's house, husband, and producing two children. Novelist Elizabeth Jane Howard began an affair with her best friend's husband, poet laureate Cecil Day-Lewis, when Howard's goddaughter Tamasin Day-Lewis was a baby. Five decades later, the betrayed wife and best friend, actress Jill Balcon, commented: 'It comes back and hits me, often at night. I'm so appalled, even all these years on. I

think: How could they? . . . When she first told me
that it was her who stopped it, that he didn't want to,
well, that was even worse, in a way. I don't know it's
the truth because I can't ask him.' Yet when Day-
Lewis was dying, Balcon moved him in with Howard,
as there was a nurse he could share, and Howard
lived fifteen minutes from a film studio where
Balcon was working. With this huge favour, Howard
could repay her debt to their friendship. But clearly,
Balcon's grudge was never written off.

5

DESIRE

WHERE IT COMES FROM, WHERE IT GOES AND
HOW TO GET IT BACK

I used to imagine that marriage was invented to let people have sex in peace. But if you read statistics on waning marital libidos, you might suppose marriage's true purpose is to put us off. And there are grounds to believe this was the intention among upright religious types.

The twelfth-century French theologian Alain of Lille repeated the denunciations of St. Jerome when he damned an 'extreme *amator* of his wife' as an 'adulterer'. André the Chaplain's 1190 smash-hit, *About Love*, called love and marriage 'completely incompatible': 'Love comes from the devil; it violates God's will; it harms one's neighbours, it destroys marriages, damages friendships, and pollutes the soul and body; it is a state of servitude . . . leads to murder, adultery, perjury, theft, false witness, incest, and idolatry; it stains women, makes lovers idle, and leads to war.'

Both these sages were celibate, which may explain why the idea of sex made them shudder like a salted slug. But it is not hard to understand why many cultures saw unruly desire as a threat to social stability, to be contained by wedlock and passion-killing notions like sin and shame.

Marriage came into being to solve the problem of desire, to license men and women to have sex, and ensure that any resulting children were taken care of. The key issue was how to dampen desire. Lusty spouses were disdained everywhere. Well into the nineteenth century, respectable married couples in Fiji had to nip to the forest for secret nookie. Meanwhile, in West Africa, any pair caught at it outside the house became slaves to whoever found them, until a ransom was paid.

Up to a point, the prudes were right. Sex cannot be the main bond of marriage; friendship is what keeps us side by side on the obstacle race. As society grows increasingly liberal, the problem of desire in marriage changes. If desire pulls couples together and drives them forward, what happens when it stalls? Today the great challenge is not to contain but to sustain desire, to help keep a marriage alive.

It is no mystery why sex is humanity's favourite waste of time. 'Our passions,' pronounced the Scottish philosopher, David Hume, 'are the only causes of our labour.' Sex helps us to forget our cares, keeps us healthy, happy and gives us kids. If we fall out, sex can make it up. If we stop fancying each other, sex can warm us up. Cheaper than a night out, and far more fun than the gym, this marvellous restorative can soften the hardest case of marriage. If we have it.

The good news is that marital sex beats any transient liaison for emotional and physical satisfaction. Studies find that only one category of person relishes it more than husbands and wives: an engaged woman, awaiting her big day. The bad news is that as the years roll by, misunderstandings mount, couples cease to be startled by their fortune in being together, and some stop having sex at all. More is the pity. Because although sex does not automatically make a marriage happy, the most contented couples also have well-matched libidos, whether they make love twice a day, week or year.

Monogamy has always been a taxing ideal, as its aims are slightly contradictory — both to steady weather-vane lust and to keep it alive. But now that we live so long, and divorce is so easy, and sex so freely available, desire must be stronger, and stretch further, and last longer than ever. The difficulty is threefold: couples must want the same thing, and carry on wanting it, ideally, with each other. So this chapter is not about morality, or what bit of anatomy slots best where, but why and what we desire, and what to do if it fades.

1. THE TROUBLE WITH SEX

Everyone is fascinated by the pleasures of the bedroom, and longs to know whether twice a day, week or month is normal, because we all wish to be normal. Most of us would quite like to know how to be good at sex too. Sadly, as hard as Sigmund Freud and friends have scratched their heads, firm answers to these questions remain elusive.

The trouble with sex is that it seems to be everywhere, yet it is nowhere. Nobody can put their finger on precisely where people end and this thing called sex begins. 'There is a bit of testicle at the bottom of our most sublime sentiments and most refined tenderness,' wrote Denis Diderot in 1760, ignoring the ovary, a typical man of his time. No mindless human endeavour has inspired more poetry, philosophy or nonsense than sex, since we can vest almost any significance in it, so often overthink it. And the joy of sex is that there are no laws; this universal experience is always personal, subject to opportunity, energy, taste, technique and erectile function. Strictly speaking, as D.H. Lawrence's wife Frieda observed, sex does not exist: 'When people talk about sex, I don't know what they mean — as if sex hopped about by itself like a frog, as if it had no relation to the rest of living.'

What can be said with certainty is that sex is the source of life. To some, it is also the meaning of life, while to others, it is positively beastly. In 1985, the comic actor Stephen Fry, who is perhaps not the marrying kind, said, 'Sex does not enrich or deepen a relationship — it permanently cheapens and destabilises it.' If he spoke from fear, to fear sex makes sense, since in many respects sex is rash. It lays us open to many risks. Only when ill or in labour are we so vulnerable as when making the beast with two backs. There is the potential embarrassment, pregnancy, disease, as well as the unnerving reminder that we are animals. Do 'free will' and a puckish libido mix? As a randy acquaintance lamented, gazing at his crotch, 'It is like being chained to a maniac.'

This 'maniac' exists because through evolution, in the interests of procreation, mankind's desire for sex has grown strong. It needs to be to override our self-protective instincts, our revulsion of others' bodies, saliva and other odoriferous effluvia. Sex offers significant rewards too: love, orgasms, children (a reward if wanted). Still, desire has quite a task to master us, to make us forget ourselves and our fears, and its ability to strike us unawares is an essential weapon in its armoury. But that we so little understand where desire comes from also makes our libidos vulnerable.

One problem of sustaining desire is the pressure to perform. To slip off self-consciousness, into our animal skin, and melt into the moment are wonders of love. Yet increasingly sex is presented as a sport. Instead of goals to score, success is rated in orgasms. In this climate it is hardly surprising that a 2008 survey found one in four sixteen- to sixty-five-year-olds were 'racked by feelings of inadequacy'

in bed – a self-centred outlook that surely guarantees dissatisfaction for someone.

A further difficulty of sex in marriage, in any culture,
for any couple, is that the novelty wears off, and if we have
a bad time, desire may abdicate its throne. When the fastidious Prince Regent, later George IV, first met his bride
Caroline of Brunswick, who had a limited acquaintance
with soap, he turned to the envoy who had brought her and
said, 'I am not well; pray get me a glass of brandy.' The
envoy queried, 'Sir, had you not better have a glass of
water?' George swore, then said, 'No.' After somehow
consummating the union, he told a friend: 'She showed
. . . such marks of filth both in the fore and hind part of
her . . . that she turned my stomach and from that moment
I made a vow never to touch her again.'

Desire can also inspire us to act on wishes that we might
prefer to ignore, thanks to lust's inconvenient habit of
bursting out where it is not (consciously) wanted. For
instance, a depressed friend amazed herself by suddenly
sleeping with a different man, every day, for a week. Decades
later she remains at a loss to explain why. But, tellingly, she
was glad of the excuse to end her unhappy marriage.

Even if we know what we want in the bedroom, to get
what we want, our desires must complement our beloved's.
Alas, no two sexual fantasies are the same, as couples therapist Brett Kahr found on collecting 19,000 in the biggest
ever survey of its kind. However, everyone laughs in recognition at the two stories Kahr liked best:

Reuben: My favourite sexual fantasy? Wife turning into a 6-pack and pizza after sex.
Miriam: WHEN MY PARTNER MANAGES TO LAST FOR MORE THAN TWO MINUTES.

The fantasy that tickled me was Coral's: 'Sex with my husband like it was before we were married.' Between them, Reuben, Miriam and Coral capture the chief troubles of marital sex: boredom, selfishness and the fact that most couples' libidos fall out of sync from time to time. Sex trouble is almost inevitable, however well balanced we are initially, because with age men's testosterone declines, whereas two-thirds of middle-aged women experience no drop-off in desire, as oestrogen levels fall at menopause, which makes women's latent testosterone relatively stronger.

How can passions last if, in purely libidinous terms, the ideal hetero match is a teenage boy and forty-year-old woman – (think Hamlet and Oedipus and their mums)? The surprise is that there are any sexually satisfied married couples. Still, many claim to have equal libidos and to enjoy consistently good sex. Are they liars or lucky? Perhaps both. One way or another, by accident or design, they have created a life together that fosters enduring lust.

The universal sexual fantasy is for desire to be simple. Instead, married couples have four options: to reconcile their desires; to cheat; to like what they get; or to lump it.

Like my friend's grandmother, who finally spoke out, aged eighty-five, as her son drove her home after a spell in hospital. 'Please,' she begged, 'ask your father to lay off. He still wants his daily jump, but I can't cope any more.' The father, a stroke survivor, was in his nineties, so it took the son a moment to fathom what she meant. When he realized he nearly drove off the road.

Sadly, the grandfather's secret has gone to his grave. But there are other clues to the mysteries of enduring lust, and how they might work for you.

WHY SEX IS GOOD: THE CHEMISTRY OF SEX AND SENSUALITY

If marriage is a battle to maintain our territorial feelings for our spouse, sex is its chemical weapon.

What is in a kiss? Aside from what you ate earlier, there are muscles, aromas, tongues, lips. A kiss is spiked with intoxicating hormones. Men's saliva is rich in testosterone, triggering sexual craving, and vasopressin, which feeds a feeling of attachment to the one we kiss. Lips also contain multitudes of nerve cells, causing intense sensations that are swiftly chaperoned to the brain (these nerve cells are connected to five of the twelve cranial nerves).

As well as bringing our bodies into closer proximity, a kiss derives much of its erotic power from the blob of cartilage above the mouth, the nose. Scent and sensuality enjoy an intense relationship thanks to

5 million receptors that hang from the roof of the nasal cavity like ripe fruit, nerve cells that have a hotline to the limbic system, which is the most ancient part of the brain, and seat to our most primitive emotions — fear, rage, hate, bliss, lust — as well as long-term memory. Hence aromas have such a grip on us, from Marcel Proust's transporting sniff of madeleines to that unforgettable first whiff of a bacon sandwich. And aromas have such a pull on our emotions that while most of us would say we dislike the smell of sweat, experiments find that if you sniff a T-shirt that has been worn once by a person of the sex to which you are attracted, you may not consciously smell the sweat, but if you then look at photographs of potential sexual partners, you will find them more attractive than if you inhaled from a clean shirt.

As a health plan, sex has many benefits. It improves the skin, muscle tone and sense of smell, reduces risk of heart disease, relieves pain and wards off colds. Hugging, touching, the sense of being loved, stroking the genitals, nibbling nipples, orgasms: all release vasopressin, endorphins and oxytocin, which aids bonding by soothing the amygdala, the brain's fear centre. Sex also wards off depression, thanks to semen's load of dopamine and norepinephrine, which lower stress and increase energy, optimism, focus and motivation. Semen also releases hormones to help regulate ovulation. So the classic line about the sour wench who would cheer up if given a good seeing-to may have an element of truth. Sex is the ultimate hormone replacement therapy.

The downside of all this hormone-fuelled bonding is the aftermath, the 'little death' that male poets wrote about ('*la mort*' that shadowed '*l'amour*') — that sadness as we come down from orgasm, as our oxytocin levels droop, and we face the fact that we are still just two people, trying to connect. But like any drug, the more sex we have, the more we crave. Each bout ups testosterone, which boosts dopamine, the love drug, and puts a smile on our face. Better still, when we smile, others smile back too. What is more, as we smile, our facial muscles send a message via the nerves to the smiler's brain, instructing them to prepare for pleasure which brings us back to where we started.

2.   WHERE DOES DESIRE GO?

Some stop at nothing to meet their spouse's desires. Ghislaine Amar succumbed to knife and hammer: 'At first he said there was nothing wrong with my nose but eventually he came clean. He was diplomatic but honest, and told me he could make my nose look perfect for our wedding photos. I wasn't nervous about Roger [her husband] operating on me.' Whether you see plastic surgery as self-maintenance or self-mutilation, what is truly shocking about Mrs Amar's new nose is less that Mr Amar made it himself (the cheapskate) than that he thought her less than perfect as she was – and had the gall to tell her.

To criticize your spouse's appearance may be in the interests of keeping your marriage afloat, but it breaches our notions that love is about acceptance, and may also be counterproductive. How many men smiled when they heard that fitness fanatic, Nicolas Sarkozy, 54, President of France, had swooned and suffered a heart scare, thanks to the punishing regime he had taken up to satisfy his young supermodel wife, Carla, after she demanded he lose nine pounds and two trouser sizes. Her stipulations were deemed unseemly, and not the sort of hen-pecking that a head of state should put up with. 'He looks more like a Tour de France rider than a president,' griped another MP.

The only time you need to think about desire in marriage is when it starts to slide. Unfortunately, the more desire worries us, the less inclined we are to talk about it openly. Although marriage is the apogee of intimacy, to seek what you want in bed can be easier with a casual lover, because if you offend your spouse you have more to lose. Indeed, for some couples, to suggest that desire needs a helping hand is taboo.

For a start, marriage is meant to complete us, so to admit any flaw threatens the romantic fairy tale of marriage. In this, wife and husband are immune to shallow impulse. They are two halves of a Platonic whole, their spouse's one and only, loved for themselves, not because they remind their beloved of Greta Garbo or George Clooney. It is also the case that marriage is about love more than lust, so conjugal desire is composed of more complicated ingredients than lust with a stranger.

Desire alters as we move through love's three dimensions, from lust to attraction to attachment. In the heady early days, we strive to attract our beloved, and seem worthy to their family and friends. Then as we fall in love, joy comes in letting go, as the world shrinks to a little room where only we two matter, and we give not a fig if our darling sees our shiny, unwashed Sunday morning face. This confidence feels a proof our love is true. Indeed, as traditionally love is madness, a tidy suitor is suspect. (Rosalind mocks her lover in Shakespeare's *As You Like It*: 'Your hose should be ungartered, your bonnet unbanded, your sleeve unbuttoned, your shoe untied, and everything about you demonstrating a careless desolation. But . . . you are rather point-device in your accoutrements, as loving yourself than seeming the lover of any other.') So making an effort to be desirable to your spouse can seem unromantic.

Due to these complexities, desire in marriage can break down in rather intractable ways, but because the stakes are so high, saying nothing about unsatisfactory sex can seem more prudent than saying something, upsetting a spouse, and making the rest of your life together worse. It could be tempting to settle for less, like the mother of triplets, who rolled her eyes when asked about the children's impact on her sex life: 'We do not like to dwell.'

Couples are also disinclined to discuss desire because good sex is the opposite of self-conscious, so analysing it seems about as joyful as dissecting butterflies. What is worse, couples are so sensitive to any implied sexual criticism that obvious measures to improve a flagging sex life, such as introducing sex toys or pornography, can have the opposite effect of that intended. Use pornography from the start of a relationship, as part of the fun, and it will be part of the fun. Bring it in later, however, in order to pep things up, and one or both of you may see the pornography as an interloper in the bedroom, or an implied criticism.

Sadly, for all couples there comes a moment when sex is a dilemma. When you find yourselves arguing about who did not wash up, and little by little, lust's soufflé sinks in the cool air of Getting On With It. At this point, some fear that they have married the wrong person. But this is not a time to retreat to the baked-bean-sequinned defeat of a tracksuit. Love is not dead; rather, its three dimensions have been absorbed, and the long game of marriage has begun.

You could resort to fantasy to vary your sexual diet without breaking your wedding vows. Research suggests that 90 per cent of spouses' minds drift to another, absent body during sex. But if you want desire to last, it is best to raise your consciousness about why it goes walkabout.

First, it is worth appreciating the range of factors that influence desire. While in one-night stands desire springs from lust, in marriage it must be rooted in trust, and trust that desire is mutual. Everyone's wish is to be their beloved's desire. (Princess Diana justified her affair with bodyguard Sergeant Barry Mannakee thus: 'He'd tell me I looked good, something my husband no longer did.')

So in marriage, a sexual problem can have many origins, and, conversely, any problem that is sexual in origin will have emotional ramifications. There is such a thing as 'psychic desertion' in marriage. Maybe you are obsessed with work, kids, golf. But fixations rob the mental space that must be mortgaged to eroticism. And since so many stresses and strains find expression in our sex life, many see sex as the index of our relationship. This has the unhelpful consequence of heaping more pressure on us to perform. Yes, good sex can help a couple to override many of their differences. Even sexless unions can be happy, provided the lack of desire is mutual.

But more usually desires are unequal, and if sex stops, one spouse feels short-changed and the other guilty. Indeed, a valid grounds for divorce has long been the inability of one partner to perform their conjugal duty. In 1613, the 'beautiful but frail countess of Essex' and her husband, Robert Devereux, parted for this reason. The most upstanding citizens have sued their spouses for non-delivery of sexual services. In 1811, prurient readers could enjoy *A Full Account of the Curious and Interesting Proceedings, Instituted in Doctors' Commons, By Rachael Dick Against her Husband, The Rev. William Dick, Of West Cowes, in the Isle of Wight, for a Nullity of Marriage, on the Ground of Impotency,* published by Plummer and Brewis of 'Love

Lane'. After five years, 'unable longer to live with her husband under such teasing circumstances, which had had a considerable effect upon her health', Mrs Dick went to court with the support of her father, the Reverend Gill, who employed her husband as curate. But Mr. Dick did not get his comeuppance as the suit was dismissed as unprovable.

Even if couples do not let sex put them asunder, all too often, if it falters, they conclude that 'we' are malfunctioning too, avoid discussing it, then misdiagnose the problem. A non-sexual problem, like exhaustion, work stress or money worry, can turn into a sexual one, then linger long after the original problem is solved.

As I surveyed couples for this book, the saddest revelation was of an undeclared sexual cold war. Respondents in the second and third decade of coupledom, who still cared for and respected each other, confided that one or other's sex drive had gone missing in inaction, and the chill was spreading. Some feared that their union was doomed, and to compound their sense of impotence, many felt that desire should spark naturally, and was only authentic if it was spontaneous. All feared that asking for more would seem like bullying.

Such reluctance is understandable, but can be misplaced. If sexual malaise is an open secret that is never faced, countless betrayals can be introduced into the marriage bed, from a turned back, to sleeping with another person. Once blame enters a sexual equation, it all goes wrong.

Some couples communicate their desires obliquely. A thirty-something father of two, married eleven years, said of his wife, 'She understands that she's got to make more of an effort to want to have sex than I do . . . I don't think that she has sex more frequently when she doesn't want to as much as she more frequently makes a concerted effort to want to.' His wife had a slightly different view: 'It was like, "Hey, it has been almost a week, woman." He wouldn't say it like that but yeah, he would make his needs known.' Which sounds bad. On the other hand, to ignore a spouse's need of pleasure smacks of contempt. A wife lamented in Britain's 'Little Kinsey' sex survey of 1949: 'If only [my husband] made love to me instead of using me like a chamber pot.'

Self-censorship is another solution to mismatched libidos. Anne Douglas cordoned off her feelings to cope with her rampant husband, the *Spartacus* film star Kirk:

> I have often thought — and feared — that one day he will get up in the morning and say to me, 'Now look, it was very nice and lovely, and you are a darling lady, but I am leaving tomorrow.' . . . I have a lot of little rooms and doors that are only opened to me. I know it makes me difficult, but . . . I had to make up my mind very quickly about [jealousy]. Either I was going to be in a constant state of trauma, or I had to ignore that kind of attention.

As a result of suppressing her jealousy, she felt less desire, and less anything.

Do not talk about sex and we may kill desire. Talk about it insensitively and we may kill desire. Try to like — or lump — what we get, and we may feel worse. Cheat, and we become a cheat. None of these solutions resuscitates a libido, and no amount of sex talk can bring the one thing that assures a sexually satisfactory marriage: equally matched libidos. To balance them and recharge desire, we need not necessarily discuss sex, but open our minds to the idea that marriage is sex work. Sex work does not mean bullying or even withholding. See desire in the round, as an expression of all aspects of your life together, and you can change the conditions of your life to bring your desires in line with each other. More or less.

GIRL LOVE VERSUS BOY LUST: A BRIEF TOUR OF SEXUAL NONSENSE

There are many superstitions about sex, thanks to the mystery of desire. Many of these superstitions are unhelpful if we want to make our sex life better.

The central puzzle of human sex is that humans can copulate whenever they like, regardless of whether females are fertile and babies can result. Our species is unusual but not alone in this: dolphins, chimps and bonobos fool around for fun too. So you might think that the solution to this puzzle is obvious: that we have sex for fun, for procreation and also for benefits that come of a rewarding, ongoing relation-ship with our sexual partner.

Yet many misinterpret sex as the great gender divider. Scientists routinely assert that women are in it for babies, and men for the hell of it – an opinion as condescending as that of the German thinker Nietzche's in *Thus Spoke Zarathustra*: 'Everything about woman is a riddle, and everything about woman has one solution: *pregnancy*.' Indeed, the suggestion that women might want sex for fun is so alien to some that evolutionary psychologists have devoted reams and reams of nonsense to explaining the 'mystery' of the female orgasm. But is the female orgasm any more mysterious than the male orgasm? As we know, pleasure exists to reward pain, so logically, surely women need a bigger reward for sex than men, as women face the greater penalty of falling pregnant. An orgasm seems little recompense for the agony of childbirth.

Our sexual misconceptions feed more sexual nonsense. In reality, neither are all women baby cravers nor are all men studs. Men have plenty of motivation to procreate. So there are two vital dif-ferences in what sex means to each gender: the logistical headache, motherhood, and the shame that is still heaped on women (not men) who sleep around. These factors incline females of the species to be pickier than males about who they sleep with.

To believe that women want sex less than men do can be convenient, in societies without reliable contraception, or where women cannot work so must marry to make a living, and cannot do so unless they are chaste; however, to see sex as something that men 'naturally' want more than women — something that men take and women give, in order to get men's love — is less convenient in cultures free of such restrictions.

Research indicates that around two-thirds of married heterosexuals in the West imagine that men and women's desires are very different. But to make life really difficult, thanks to sexual liberation, they also hold a contradictory view: that sex is vital to marital happiness. Consequently, many couples both feel that it is unnatural to desire the same kind of sex, and also fear that their marriage is screwed unless they desire the same kind of sex. This contrary outlook makes it even harder for couples to enjoy the one thing that assures desire mends rather than maims a marriage: equally matched libidos.

'Women's lack of sexual interest is often explained as a biological difference between the sexes, [but] men's lack of interest in sex is typically chalked up as a physiological problem,' found one report. Often both husband and wife believed something was 'wrong' if she initiated sex more. Even husbands who say they feel ugly, rejected or that they long for their wife to initiate sex more will often quickly add that they do not want her to 'take over' (and seem a slut). Meanwhile wives say that they yearn for their husband to dominate, 'in a gentle sort of way'. As a baffled sex researcher concluded, today's ideal wife is a 'sexually experienced virgin'. An ideal husband is tender, but 'a man' not a 'wimp'. Yes, it would seem that despite the best efforts of feminism and Hugh Hefner, the twenty-first-century heterosexual psyche remains as schizophrenic as that which monk-philosopher Erasmus deplored in 1526's *Institution of Marriage*:

> I wish that, among Christians, the lustful husband were not praised to the skies . . . We must remind the bride not to instigate their lovemaking herself, as this may diminish his affection for her; on the other hand, she must not show herself too unwilling or forbidding when he suggests it. The first attitude, for some reason, makes a woman cheap and less attractive to a man, the second changes love into hatred. A respectable married woman will not be provocative, a chaste woman will know how to refuse gently, but only a false wife will persist in her protests.

All clear? To judge the success of this advice, it is worth noting that Erasmus dedicated his treatise to Catherine of Aragon, the first, if longest lasting, of Henry VIII's six wives.

3.   HOW TO BRING DESIRE BACK

What is the secret of sustainable desire?

Like all activities, for sex to happen there must be
energy, opportunity and inclination. If your life does not
allow scope for sex, you need to change the terms and conditions to let sex back in. Passions cannot fly if a mind is
elsewhere, and not even a spontaneous quickie will tran-
spire unless there is time and a place for it, and it is a
priority for both parties. That is to say, desire is a management issue like anything else in marriage, and comes down
to priorities.

How revealing to hear a husband gripe: 'She makes lists.
Things to buy. Things to do. People to call. If it's not on
the list, it doesn't get done. Once, to be funny, I put "sex"
on the list. Mistake. Now it has to be on the list or it doesn't
get done.' It is comically reminiscent of wives' complaints
about how husbands force on them the extra housework
chore of nagging them to do it.

Another man, Jason, carped: 'Dishes, even dishes
or laundry, that kind of stuff, was already a priority
first before any leisure time at all or sex, or whatever.'
Amusingly, researchers noted: 'Our analysis strongly suggests that Maria puts domestic obligations ahead of sexual
activity because she bears the brunt of the household
labour — both in terms of getting it done and in terms of
an awareness that it needs to get done — along with holding
down a full-time job. Jason describes his occasional

efforts to do the dishes [when home all day] as "helping out".'

In short, what very many couples continue to attribute to women 'naturally' desiring less sex than men is due not to a biological difference between the sexes, but a purely physical one: namely, while lusty husband whines, his listless wife is exhausted.

Tragically, as most husbands feel more responsible for managing the sexual side of marriage, because sex is a macho priority, than for the domestic chores side of marriage, because they see home as a feminine priority, few husbands perceive that the greatest aphrodisiac – the thing that would make their wife feel loved, respected and less tired – would be to help her out.

One man believed, 'You can't engineer [sex]. You know, you can't say, "Okay, here is what we are going to do. You are going to put this on and I am going to dress this way."' So what did he do? Cook most of the meals and lavish his wife with affection. He saw sex as beyond social engineering – and yet he engineered his behaviour to get it.

The conclusion to draw is not that sex is a marital service. However, this is what some advocate:

> If your husband comes home at 6:00, bathe at 5:00. In preparing for your six o'clock date, lie back and let go of the tensions of the day. Think about that special man who's on his way home to you . . . Rather than make your husband play hide-and-seek when

he comes home tired, greet him at the door when he arrives. Make homecoming a happy time. Waltzing to the door in a cloud of powder and cologne is a great confidence builder. Not only can you respond to his advances, you will want to . . . For an experiment, I put on pink baby-doll pajamas and white boots after my bubble bath. I must admit that I looked foolish and felt even more so. When I opened the door that night to greet Charlie, I was unprepared for his reaction. My quiet, reserved, non-excitable husband took one look, dropped his briefcase on the doorstep, and chased me around the dining room table. We were in stitches by the time he caught me, and breathless with that old feeling of romance . . . Our little girls stood flat against the wall watching our escapade, giggling with delight. We all had a marvellous evening together, and Charlie forgot to mention the problems of the day.

Believe it or not, this parable of marital redemption comes from a right-wing Christian riposte to feminism, Marabel Morgan's 10-million selling *The Total Woman* (1973). But how many wives today are home in time to loll in the bath before dressing up — supposing that they would want to? And how many husbands are home in time to enjoy the show?

If Morgan's take on sexual liberation seems ridiculous, it also sounds more fun, for all the family, than the remedy prescribed to wives in 2007's *Babyproofing Your Marriage*. In this, the authors assume that women want anything but sex. But they commend that a (domestically) frustrated wife should seek to become her husband's 'goddess' by the simple expedient of offering him regular oral sex. For this service, she is rewarded with a happy hubby, ready to whip off those dirty nappies with a smile. It would seem that, somewhere between 1973 and 2007, any overloaded wife who had surrendered herself to the dream of 'having it all' had also mislaid her libido, and ceased to want anything more than an unbroken night's sleep and a man who washed up. Sex had become less a performance than a box to be ticked.

Scheduling sex may not be sexy, but can be necessary in a crowded life, and anticipation also has its upside. What is troubling, and horribly familiar, in both Marabel Morgan's and the Babyproofers' tales of sexual redemption, is the assumption that marital sex problems are a wife's problem, and hers to resolve. Nonetheless it is worth making the effort. To see sex as the canary in the marital coal mine, as a sign that 'we' are falling apart, can save a relationship, provided that it is seen as 'our' problem, and both try to revive it.

The wildest sex in the world cannot make up for an unfair marriage, nor can it make a lopsided life fair. But desire is a feedback system. Through words, caresses, gestures we invite esteem to be returned, so if we rebalance an unfair marriage, with effort and patience, the sex will pick up.

You may be wondering about hormones. Can we really help it if we lose interest in sex?

It is a common mistake to oversimplify the relationship between body chemistry, sex and marriage. Biology is not destiny, and hormones do not create feelings; rather, they amplify them. For instance, men with high levels of testosterone are more inclined than their less testosterone-charged fellows to commit adultery or be violent — but only if these men are overwhelmed by other demands at work and home. However, if high-testosterone husbands are relaxed at work and home, their sex lives and marriages are better than others'.

This illustrates how hormones' influence on us varies by our life situation. And if we alter our situation, our hormones change too. A man's testosterone declines as he grows attached to his family, and babies are real ball-snatchers. Just holding a baby, no matter if it is not his, will send his testosterone plummeting. All the same if he then has sex, it will shoot back up.

However much we feel the vehicles of drives and instincts that are beyond our control, our choices direct our desires, so any spouse who objects to being forced to beg for, or rebuff sex, may wish to reconsider. Like it or lump it, love is a trading game. So why bully or nag when you can seduce? Why not mop the dirty floor that your spouse is fretting about? If you are not in the mood, before showing them a cold shoulder, why not demonstrate that there are other ways they can show you love?

There is no law against having sex when you do not feel rampant. Surprising things can happen. Acting up sexually fires a libido, if it is done for pleasure. It is such tender considerations that make marriage into what Charles Kingsley called

> the life-long miracle,
> The self-begetting wonder, daily fresh.

All of which is a very long way of saying that the secret of enduring lust is love.

6

TEN WAYS TO FUEL LONG-HAUL DESIRE

Not all aspects of desire are at our command. Only you can say what drew you to your loved one. Perhaps it was a mystery, even to you. But if you still fancy each other, it is because you still arouse that most vital erogenous organ, the brain.

Lust begins in imagination, and is magnified by tension, so there are plenty of things that can be done to help matters along. There are radical measures. Sex tips from the fourth- to sixth-century BC classic the *Kama Sutra* include enlarging an unsatisfactory *lingam* (penis) by abrading it with 'the bristles of certain insects that live in trees', then stretching it through a hole in a cot.

A gentler approach is described by the master of literary

suspense, Robert Louis Stevenson: 'Men and women contend for each other in the lists of love, like rival mesmerists; the active and adroit decide their challenges in the sports of the body; and the sedentary sit down to chess and conversation.' It sounds a performance because it is. But games can grow more interesting in marriage if we pay attention, adapt as life changes, and accept desire's ebb and flow as part of the ever-stimulating marital challenge: to reconcile two frail human beings' dreams and needs.

Here are some lessons from couples who learned to keep on wanting.

1. BE RELEVANT

It is hard to desire something useless, unless it comes in a Tiffany bag and is encrusted with diamonds. This principle is often forgotten by spouses.

Too many female friends, mostly mothers, wonder, aloud, within their husbands' earshot: 'What is he for?' But just as many husbands come home from a twelve-hour day to hear their wife bleat about her 'sacrifices', while the television drones, the microwave pings, and children scream, and feel confused. That is to say, any spouse who is not appreciative or an asset will cease to be of interest.

2. DIAGNOSE DISCONTENTS

We often misdiagnose, as sexual, problems that are symptoms of unrelated concerns, like stress at work. If our spouse is hurt, we may feel, as husbands routinely inform mistresses, that they do not understand us. Why? Because they cannot read our mind, and we did not speak up. Too much contentment can stale into disenchantment as a friend discovered. He and his wife religiously maintained Friday date nights, Saturday bar nights, through the arrival of two children, until he found himself having the same conversations, playing the same games, week in, week out, and lost his appetite for all of them. So he changed job, moved city, and now they are doing fine.

Before feeling hurt or frigid, diagnose that headache. Is a drooping manhood due to drink, fatigue or perhaps nature's favourite contraceptive, unsleeping children? Babies are delicious, cuddly larvae, but for many parents, especially mothers, this intoxicating new sensual connection can for a while displace sexual desire.

3. BE INTERESTING

For desire to last, above all we must not be boring. Boredom comes of two things: too much of something, or too little. Apply this lesson in all areas of life, and sex will pick up.

Fantasy may remake the stale or familiar. Henry VIII won

the heart of Anne Boleyn by playing a game in which he was her 'very loyal servant' (the game was up once they married, she failed to serve up an heir, and Henry trumped up charges of her adultery in order to execute her). But it is dangerous if fantasy competes with reality. A husband griped: 'In bed I'm her high school teacher, captain of the football team, her boss, the bad boy, a waiter, a lifeguard, a telephone repairman, a cop. Once in a while I'd like to be me.'

Desire swells when we are desired, and we can pump ourselves up. Shared physical activity releases hormones to set up a sexual mood. Experiments find that danger, even so little as the fear caused by walking along a wobbly bridge, will sharpen the senses, increasing arousal, making others seem more attractive. Share an exciting experience and the attraction is even higher. Do something new as a couple and a further delight is that we uncover new sides of each other too. So break routines, slough off dead habit, and ban dull topics of conversation.

4. PAY THE RIGHT KIND OF ATTENTION

Even those of us with a low opinion of ourselves prefer our spouse to hold a high one. According to a study: 'Regardless of self-esteem and depression, [subjects] were more maritally satisfied when their partners viewed them positively.' Yes, we want our spouse to see us not as we are but as a love god – and to say so.

Like any missile, the more targeted a love-bomb, the more effective. The poet Edmund Spenser excelled in these marriage verses, praising his bride's breast:

> like to a bowl of cream uncrudded . . .
> all her body like a palace fair,
> Ascending up with many a stately stair.

Judicious anti-compliments can flatter too. The self-assurance of writer Andrew Upton, who is often cropped from photos with his film star wife Cate Blanchett, is honoured in her nickname for him, 'The Hand'. However, in general, the better you know someone, the higher praise should be. Our number one is always the most beautiful in the world, because they are the centre of our world, not Brad and Angelina's.

But no amount of honeyed words means anything unless you show that you are listening. Listening is not a state of passivity; it is an activity, and must be seen as well as heard, in encouraging remarks, enthusiastic nods, interruptions, and replies above and beyond 'Yes, dear'.

5. LOOK GOOD TO SPOUSE AND OTHERS

In medieval Welsh law it was taken for granted that keeping up appearances was part of the conjugal contract. If a husband had leprosy, foul breath, or failed to have sex, his wife could walk away, her head held high, and in such divorces, she did not even lose her dowry. Such stringent requirements were acceptable because vanity is a social service, and, like it or not, it is easier to be the apple of a spouse's eye if others think that you are a peach. This may be shallow, but it is not dumb. The most educated people care most about having an attractive spouse. To feel desirable feels good too. Admittedly, it is an effort, typically seen as women's business. 'Dear girls,' cautioned Annie Swan in 1893's *Courtship and Marriage, and the gentle art of homemaking*, 'you can afford a great deal less to be careless after marriage . . . you have now to keep the husband you have won. Men like what is bright and cheerful, and pleasant to behold.'

But wives like looking too, so no sane spouse neglects appearances. Even media mogul Rupert Murdoch dyes his hair in fetching hues of aubergine and apricot. When his eldest daughter told him to visit a professional hairdresser, apparently this provoked the reply, 'You need a facelift.'

It is possible to go far in marriage not knowing what a spouse likes about your appearance, if they never compliment you or you never listen. In which case, prick up your ears, and flatter them assiduously, demonstrating the educational power of praise. Or ask what they like. You may be surprised. A wife told therapist Brett Kahr that she got wet 'when my husband dresses as a gorilla'.

6. RATION INTIMACY

How did Gunther von Hagens, the anatomist known as Dr
Death for the flayed human cadavers that he displays at his
Body Worlds shows, attract a glamorous wife, twenty years
his junior, when they met, back when she was a student and
he a professor, over congealing viscera in a dissecting lab?
'One of his colleagues at the university told me that he was a
maniac and warned me not to have anything to do with him.
But to me, he was this completely unique person. I was fascinated by the fact that he was so obsessed, so driven.'

Desire exists in the space between wanting and having, so
the forbidden is always fascinating, as is anything that
inspires curiosity and comes in limited supply. But since we
all walk on a 'hedonic treadmill' we adapt to good things,
eventually taking them for granted, so in marriage our
sexual curiosity about each other tends to fall away. For
instance, roaming naked is delightfully Adam and Eveish,
but has the unintended consequence that spouses will be
less startled by a stray glimpse of each other's unforbidden
fruits. To sustain an erotic charge, then, it helps to create a
little ersatz fascination.

Why not ration intimacy? The Anglo-Saxon Church
forbade marital sex on Sundays, Wednesdays, Fridays, fast
days and religious festivals. What fun it must have been to
break such rules. In her 1821 *Manual for the Mistress of the
Household*, Madame Pariset counsels separate bed- and sitting
rooms. This sounds lonely, and expensive, but every couple

can afford to be selective about how they invade each other's privacy. I read of a wife who dressed up for weekly, booze-sodden orgies with her husband of ten years. They were not shy. Yet she had never heard him fart.

7. JUST DO IT

IVF clinics attribute growing demand for fertility treatment to hectic lifestyles. It seems many couples neglect small cere-monies like going to bed together. All should heed the earliest recorded marriage guidance, deployed by twelfth-century Pope Eugenius III on Louis VII of France and Eleanor of Aquitaine, who came to him seeking an annulment. Instead, the Pope led them to a silk-lined chamber and commanded them to make good use of the magnificent bed. When they left, she was pregnant. But the truce did not last, because, she protested, she had 'married a monk, not a king'.

8. SHARPEN YOUR EROTIC FOCUS

Therapist Paula Hall had brisk words for a bored wife: 'It doesn't matter if he doesn't turn you on, as long as he doesn't turn you off . . . you've got to learn to stoke your own flame and no one can do that for you.' Do not see yourself as sexual and you will be less attuned to your desires. But make an effort to notice flickers of lust and you can amplify these feelings. To tune in to your spouse, advised call-girl turned author Tracy Quan, 'The golden rule is, empathy: what do they feel like right now?'

9.   PLAY UP

If Eros is dozing, entertain Byron's suggestion in *Don Juan*: 'Merely innocent flirtation, Not quite adultery, but adulter-ation.' To flirt with others is good but with a spouse, better. For those out of practice, psychologist Helen Fisher identi-fied the steps in the universal call sign, the 'come hither':

> The woman smiles at her admirer and lifts her eye-brows in a swift, jerky motion as she opens her eyes wide . . . Then she drops her eyelids, tilts her head down and to the side, and looks away. Frequently she also covers her face with her hands, giggling nerv-ously . . . cocks her head and looks up shyly at her suitor. A female possum does this too, turning toward her suitor, cocking her snouty jaw, and looking straight into his eyes.

Men thrust their chest, women wiggle 'like jell-o on springs' (à la Marilyn Monroe in *Some Like It Hot*), and both genders fiddle with their hair. Such bodypopping tells its target three things: 'Look at me; I am worth looking at; but I am not dangerous.' Then it is time to sweet-talk, in a low, mellifluous voice, with more eye contact, as your bodily posture and gestures synchronize.

Just gazing into someone's eyes is hypnotic. First the eyes moisten, then the pupils expand like ink on a blotter, which unleashes an entirely legal adrenaline, dopamine and phenylethylamine rush to send the brain spinning. This means that anyone can use eye contact to alter a mood — for better or worse. Two studies found that people 'induced to avoid another's eyes . . . do indeed feel guilty'. By contrast, four other experiments discovered that when two heterosexual strangers, one of each sex, exchanged the 'long, unbroken gaze' that usually only lovers share, both experienced 'increased feelings of attraction'. In short, with care, anyone can be stared out of a temper and helped to slip into something more comfortable.

10. BE ROMANTIC

Romance is make-believe. The original romances were epic stories of knights, monsters and unattainable princesses, and games of adulterous courtly love played by rich, bored aristocrats in medieval France. But as divorce got easier, and maintaining desire grew more important to marriage, so did romance. Some find courtly behaviour, with men opening doors and women acting girly, a bit devious — suspicions confirmed in James Magner's 1947 *Art of Happy Marriage*:

> The considerate husband will keep in mind that his
> wife is a living, throbbing human being, not merely

a galley slave to do his bidding. He will remember anniversaries, bring home candy and flowers occasionally, and take his wife out to dinner and the theater. He will notice and praise her hats and clothes and tell her how beautiful she looks . . . Upon leaving for work and on his return he will kiss his wife, and not rush out and in like one who has no obligations of affection. He will frequently take his wife in his arms, as he did in days of courtship, and tell her that he loves her, that she will always be the woman of his dreams.

The reward for making a wife's 'happiness and loveliness' his chief concern? 'She shall devote her life as a living flame to enkindle and illumine his.' She gets chocolate; he gets to be god. Nice.

This cynical view should deter nobody from romance. Creating special moments gives relationships purpose and momentum, reminding couples that they are still two people who chose each other, for then, now and always. Cautious romantics may adopt the pro-forma romantic script of hearts, chocolates and flowers, but personal rituals speak to the heart. Seek spontaneity, off-beat bliss, and by all means have a song that is yours, but also dedicate a little time to doing nothing, together.

Store romantic memories, discuss and polish them, and you gain a powerful means to exorcize bad feelings. Romance, like love, grows stronger the more you let it mean.

THE BEST SEX ADVICE IN THE WORLD?

Having researched the topic widely, I have had my mind boggled. By the sensual *sententia* of the ages, by the unsavoury promises of men promoting vaginal deodorants, and by the peculiar contraptions, such as eighteenth-century quack Dr James Graham's Grand Celestial bed (surrounded by magnets and mirrors), to which amorous couples have resorted. But having weighed this advice, and found most of it wanting, there is one aphrodisiac suggestion that I could not resist sharing from 1758's *The Pleasures of Matrimony*.

Couples who cannot take it lying down, or standing up, need only eat 'Oysters, Cock-stones, Craw-Fish, Lobsters, Perriwinkles . . . [and] the Kidneys of a littl Crocodile'. If this recondite provender is not to your taste, or you want to conceive a child, try the following plan:

> I knew a young marry'd Couple (quoth another) that were just in your Case; and the Physician told me himself, he gave the Husband this Advice, which was to absent himself out of Town for fifteen Days, and the Sixteenth Day to get on Horseback, and so order it, as after an easy Journey of Ten or Twelve Miles, to come Home just in the Evening. At the same Time, he also

gave Directions, That his Wife should provide him for Supper a Leg of Mutton boiled with a Salad of Garden Rocket, a Capon roasted, and a Glass of good Red Wine. Moreover, that he should place himself at Supper right against his Wife, bare-necked, and bare-breasted.

Three Hours after Supper, he bid the Gentleman go to Bed, lie close to his Wife, and sleep out his first Sleep; after that, to enter into amorous Discourse with his Wife, as awake as himself; and when he had so heightened his Discourse, to fall to his Work . . . [And] the next Morning to take a lusty Beverage of Yolks of Eggs, Sugar, Saffron, Cinnamon, and strong Wine; by which you may find that the French Men and Women in Provence know what's good for themselves. This Course of Life will cause a Man's Wife to embrace him like an Angel, and to shew him a Thousand other Friendly Entertainments beyond Imagination: 'Twill be always in the Evening, 'My Dear, come to Bed; and in the Morning, Love, lie a little longer.'

7

THE WISDOM OF ADULTERY?

What is infidelity? If you think that the answer is obvious, you may be surprised to learn that the terms and conditions of marital loyalty vary from place to place, person to person, and are rewritten throughout life.

Adultery has a spiritual dimension: as an infidel betrays God, so infidelity betrays the faith between a couple. But the concept came into being long before Judaism, Islam or Christianity. In Virgil's *Aeneid* adulterers' noses are cut off, a punishment that was still practised in medieval Europe. Evidently the concept of infidelity served practical as much as spiritual concerns. 'Why is what was cuckoldry in the 17th century called adultery in the 19th?' demanded the rampant

Three Musketeers author, Alexandre Dumas, pining for the days when a man could buckle his swash with honour.

> In the seventeenth century there were rights of primogeniture . . . the eldest son inherited a father's name, his title and his fortune; his other sons became knights, soldiers, or priests. To these other sons, he gave to the first a Maltese Cross, to the second a leather helmet, and to the third an ecclesiastical collar . . . What did he care who sired the knight, the soldier or the priest? . . . Things have certainly changed now, damn it all.

Under new laws, each child was entitled to an equal share of inheritance. As a result husbands feared any cuckoo in their nest, and society clamped down on wives who swived.

That was then. Today we have reliable contraception, DNA-paternity testing, internet and the liar's friend, the mobile phone, so slipping the marital leash has never been less hassle. Does hostility to adultery still make sense? Or are we cutting off our noses to spite our faces? Statistics estimate that 60 per cent of husbands and 40 per cent of wives stray. In this light, monogamy seems a fragile dream, yet we cling to it. A 2006 Gallup poll found that more Americans were upset by adultery than polygamy or human cloning. It was unclear what bothered them most: the duplicity, sexual incontinence or injury to the hallowed dream of marriage.

Sceptics argue that monogamy is not only unrealistic but

unnatural, and itself a form of bad faith, introducing falsehood and corroding the trust that joins couples. In *Lust in Translation*, a study of infidelity around the world, Pamela Druckerman compared Anglo-Saxon attitudes unfavourably to the French, who see affairs as 'part of the fairy tale of a marriage' not a complete rupture with it. This is debatable. France's 1810 Penal Code let husbands sleep around, but cuckolds could send both wife and lover to gaol. Alternatively, under article 324 they could kill them if caught 'in flagrante delicto in the conjugal dwelling'. In effect, crimes of passion (lawyers call it the 'nagging and shagging' defence) were licensed honour killings.

But Druckerman raises good points about the dangers of knee-jerk intolerance of adultery:

> I spoke to [British and American] women who, on discovering that their husbands had cheated, immediately packed a bag and left, because that's 'what you do'. Not because that is what they wanted to do — they just thought that was the rule. They didn't even seem to realise there were other options . . . There's an idea that the only way to heal is with total transparency, by revealing exactly what was involved, blow job by blow job, and I've seen no evidence that this openness helps anyone. And I mean, this can go on and on and on — 80-year-old women who have the moral high ground on their marriage, because of a one-night stand their husband had 40 years earlier.

She did not condone infidelity. Rather, she objected to unthinking responses to it, in particular an absurdity that she kept encountering, when adulterers, mortified by their failure to live up to the fairy tale of marriage, sought to repair their self-image by marrying a lover instead of accepting the ignoble fact that frankly, they just fancied a fuck. In so doing, many chucked a better marriage.

Lust is not love. So you have to wonder: is monogamy to be respected at all costs, or is it perhaps an aspiration — as a politician might say, something you can work with?

I. THE VALUES OF ADULTERY

What would you put up with? A roaming eye, stray hand, idle snog, or regular weekend trips to Bruges, *in camera* on some very important business, therefore unreachable by phone or e-mail?

When the Italian Prime Minister's wife, Mrs Berlusconi, learned of Silvio's unofficial visit to a girl's eighteenth birthday party, she cried foul on national media. When Elin Woods found out about Tiger's wild side, there was a nasty altercation between a departing car's window and a golf club. But none beat the pluck of Monsieur Descharmes, a middle-aged Parisian who in 1826 decided to follow his twenty-five-year-old wife and a shop assistant, Beauval. The *Gazette des tribunaux* revealed: 'He shaved off his black mutton-chop whiskers, replacing them with enormous mustachios. Large eyeglasses covered his eyes, and green Polish-style trousers were substituted for his usual overalls. To complete his disguise, a half-opened sleeve with his arm in a sling made from a black scarf gave him the air of a recently wounded soldier.'

He caught the lovers in the act and each was sentenced to three months in jail. His wife served half her sentence then Descharmes went back to court, citing article 337 of the Code: 'The husband has the right to annul this judgment by consenting to take back his wife.' Poor Beauval stayed in gaol.

Many a man has been slain in a duel over an injured husband's honour. But attitudes towards adultery vary. The eighteenth-century Empress Maria Theresa of Austria was so implacable in her determination to root out licentiousness that she employed spies, called Commissioners of Chastity, to monitor pretty girls and lock up errant wives, much to the chagrin of her humiliated cuckold subjects. By contrast, in sixteenth-century France, among the victims of ill-matched arranged marriages, novel solutions were not uncommon. According to Casanova, 'Two of the greatest noblemen of France [the ducs de Bouflers and Luxembourg] once calmly exchanged their wives and had children who bore the name not of their real father but of their mother's husband.'

In Japan, extramarital sex is not construed as an infidelity if you pay for it. Forty per cent of Russians believe that affairs are not always wrong, and Muscovites supposedly

suspend their wedding vows at beach clubs. In China, there
was a time when a man convicted of consorting with another's wife could be flogged, but concubines were perfectly
acceptable. But few wives have prosecuted their husbands
for infidelity, since most cultures do not consider that a
husband could be guilty of such a crime.

According to the Italian legal code of 1930, the adultery
of a wife (called '*adulterio*'), is punishable in any case, but
that of a husband (called '*concubinato*') only if he keeps his
mistress at home or elsewhere 'notoriously'. This anomaly
is due to the fact that while women's code of honour places
chastity at the top of the list, a man's honour traditionally
depends on the more flexible virtues of valiance and viril-
ity, and the chastity of his women. Hence husbands, fathers
and brothers execute honour crimes. There is still a
popular view that a sexually unfaithful wife and mother is
a greater traitor to her family than a slipshod dad. One
winces to read of Winston Churchill, realizing as a child
that his gorgeous, inattentive mother indulged in extra-
curricular activities after he spotted that she had gone out
with a hole in the stocking of one leg, but returned with the
hole on the other.

Yet there have been proud cuckolds. An 1806 traveller
reported on native Missouri tribes:

Among the Ricaras, it is a great breach of good behaviour for a woman to grant her favours without the
consent of her husband or brother. But, on the other

hand, the husbands and brothers are delighted to be able to offer this little courtesy to their friends . . . a negro in our party made a great impression on a people who had never seen a man of that colour before. He was soon the favourite of the fair sex, and we observed that, far from displaying jealousy, the husbands were delighted when he visited their homes. The whole situation was enlivened by the fact that in such ramshackle huts as theirs everything was open to view.

In cultures where marriage was primarily about maintaining patrimony, not love, infidelity was often a rich wife's compensation for enduring a dull marriage that had been arranged by her family for dynastic purposes. After producing an heir or two, a wife was entitled to employ a special friend or walker – in Spain, called an *estrecho* or *cortejo*, in France, *un petit-maître*, and in eighteenth- and nineteenth-century Italy, a *cicisbeo* or *cavalier servente*. The terms of the job for a *cicisbeo* do not sound too onerous: so long as he was a 'young cadet' – that is, a younger son who was too poor to marry himself – and so long as he respected the rule that he appear always his mistress's servant (if she were to 'enter or make use of the carriage of the *cavalier* . . . it would be presumed that she was in the service of the *cavalier*, and this would be an offence to the laws of conventional etiquette'). In Edwardian England, upper-class youths were expected to begin their romantic career in training with older women, who had done their spousal duty and produced an heir and a spare. The etiquette was that 'such affinities were open', observed historian Richard Davenport-Hines. 'There could be nothing secret, for that would have suggested scandal.'

The idea that the sin of adultery is a relative value, diminishing with age, is more than a cultural convention. In 2000 a sociologist, Chen Liu, made a cost-benefit analysis of adultery. He used a theoretical model to predict that a husband's motivation to stay faithful would rise in the early years of a marriage, as the benefits of marital sex increased with the couple's loyalty, expertise and love, peaking around two decades. But the probability of him straying would rise once the marriage was twenty years old, as the benefits of sex with his wife came to be outweighed by boredom, diminished sexual opportunity and the urge to sow his oats while he still could. By contrast, a wife would be less likely to commit adultery, the longer she had been married. Liu's predictions turned out to be an eerie match to known statistics. This is because the risks of fidelity change over the life course, and differently for men and women. Studies find that women, as they age, have fewer opportunities or incentives to stray, even though many grow increasingly desirous of sex. Whereas ageing men, whose libidos are waning, nevertheless become increasingly inclined to take risks – in part because older wives have less chance of remarrying, so are less inclined to divorce their husbands if they catch them out.

Ironically, while older generations call the young

immoral, their attitudes to monogamy are looser. According to a 2007 British survey, only 12 per cent of 18–29-year-olds had oral sex outside a steady relationship, rising to 20 per cent of 30–50-year-olds. And 30 per cent of those aged 50-plus had had vaginal sex with someone who was not their partner. Another poll found that 83 per cent of 18–34-year-olds considered kissing an infidelity, dropping to 49 per cent among over-55s. Of those who admitted infidelity, 54 per cent of 18–34-year-olds expressed regret. Only 34 per cent of over-55-year-olds did.

So are the older wiser? What is fidelity good for?

When we stand before a congregation and pledge to be there for each other, come what may, our vow to worship no other body is a warrant of good faith that is vital to marriage's grand leap into the unknown.

Trust matters more to marriage than friendship, because marriage is so often about forgoing immediate gains for long-term rewards, and it takes a lot of give and take to put up with the same person for decades when you live together. To stand by a troubled spouse, who offers no immediate return in interest, is easier if you know that they are faithful to you. This exclusive deal means that they will stick around and one day do the same for you, reducing the chance that your loyalty will not be repaid, or that as you grow grey and wrinkly you will be undercut by ruthless young competitors. The value of wedding vows is not just proof that our spouse loved us enough to marry us; having sworn, in public, to be true, to betray this commitment is more shaming than for unmarried couples who live together. Our self-image is bound up in our word.

What matters about infidelity to the preservation of a marriage is whether it shatters the rose-tinted pane of glass in couples' minds; the forgiving perspective that lets them surmount obstacles and believe that in future life will improve. But need emotional loyalty be fused with physical? Given reliable contraception et cetera, can we not separate the two forms of fidelity, and act on a passing fancy, without invalidating the time, love and money that we have invested in our marriage?

There are arguments for infidelity. Danger is a great aphrodisiac, and without adultery, we would not have films like *Casablanca* or novels like *Madame Bovary*; the arts would be dull indeed. It is also tempting to believe that the mind, heart and body can be detached from one another. But the concept of fidelity is not simply an analogy between mind and body. Our physical actions alter our feelings, so even empty sex presents a threat to a relationship, since nobody can guarantee that what starts as a passing fling will not come to mean more. Thanks to the hormones released in sex, where lust leads, territorial feelings often follow. Love and sex, mind and body, are as interchangeable as ever.

There are further drawbacks of affairs of the heart and other parts. Infidelity is costly. Forget the lawyers; there are the logistics and painful emotions, as Aesop hinted in a cautionary tale of a middle-aged man who kept two mistresses, one older, one younger, to benefit from both experience and the juices of youth. As he slept by the older mistress, she, ashamed, plucked out his black hairs. But the younger, revolted by his age, plucked out the white. Soon he was bald.

The moral of this story remains true. Over a Sunday lunch a friend and her sister were discussing the extraordinary demands of their brother's mistress. Their husbands sat in silence, periodically being snapped at for not carving the meat correctly, not passing the salt, not keeping track of the children, or for belching.

'I don't know how his wife puts up with it,' said my friend.

The husbands shook their heads. 'What I don't get,' said one, 'is how your brother can do it?'

'Exactly,' said the other. 'He has a wife. Why would you want another one at your throat?'

REASONABLE GROUNDS FOR ADULTERY? GREAT RUSES, EXCUSES AND ABUSES

Corporate raider James Goldsmith said that when a man marries his mistress, he creates a vacancy. There have been many less famous but no less striking justifications for unshackling the conjugal ball and chain. Sensuality for one. An acquaintance said of her liability to leap into bed, 'It's like chocolate, one taste and you can't get enough.' Nisa, a woman of

Africa's !Kung hunter-gatherers, took an eminently practical view: 'One man gives you only one kind of food to eat. But when you have lovers, one brings you something and another brings you something else. One comes at night with meat, another with money, another with beads.'

For the purposes of seduction, my favourite excuse was uttered by a publisher who assailed an author thus: 'My mistress doesn't understand me.' My second-favourite came from a London film critic, greeting his commissioning editor, whom he was meeting for lunch for the first time, with this alluring gambit: 'I'm famously adulterous.' Thereafter he ceased to be a film critic. More successful was Kimberly Fortier, at the time publisher of the *Spectator* magazine, dining with then British Home Secretary, David Blunkett. She proceeded to eat Mr Blunkett, said a fellow diner, commencing with this corny *amuse-bouche*: 'I've always wanted to make love to a blind man.'

Some regard adultery as verging on ethical. Dictionary author Samuel Johnson's stalker, James Boswell, knew how to mince words too. 'Fully sens-ible of my happiness in being married to so excellent a woman', he felt no compunction in adoring other 'amiable' creatures as well: 'I can unite little fond-nesses with perfect conjugal love. Concubinage is almost universal. If it was *morally* wrong, why was it permitted to the pious men under the Old

Testament? Why did our Saviour never say a word against it?'

Some excuse infidelity on ethnic grounds. The Baron de Belabre, a diplomat, was surprised that his British wife divorced him, as their granddaughter Fiona MacCarthy wrote: 'My mother was apt to be impatient with my grandmother's intolerance of his vicissitudes, maintaining that she ought to have accepted he was French.' To others, adultery is self-advertising. A friend expressed sympathy when his pal revealed that his mistress was pregnant. 'It's wonderful,' he countered, proudly adding that he was buying her a house. 'It shows the world how wealthy I am.'

No excuse to a betrayed spouse is quite so foot-shooting as 'It meant nothing' (if so, why bother doing it in the first place?) One man told his wife that he was forced into a peccadillo during a weekend away on business, on the grounds that the other woman had threatened to ring her boyfriend if he did not stay the night. But few excuses beat the cheek of British admiral Jackie Fisher, who learned his best nautical lessons by copying his hero, Horatio Nelson. Fisher told his wife that, without his illicit passion for Emma Hamilton, Nelson would never have achieved greatness. So on purely professional grounds, Fisher was obliged to screw his mistress, who happened to be Nina, Duchess of Hamilton.

2. HOW TO HAVE A GOOD AFFAIR

An affair can conceivably help a marriage. Even couples who theoretically believe that monogamy is a deal-breaker may survive betrayal, if they decide that their union matters more. This is why, if there were such a thing as a good affair, it would be one with rules, rules that both protagonists had thought through in relation to their marriage.

Sadly, few people approach affairs with clarity. As infidelity is taboo, often a selfish, self-defeating or desperate measure, people prefer not to think it through, but to act on impulse, as this feels less premeditated and it flatters us to see adultery as something that we cannot help but do. But if we set such scruples aside, what would a rational affair look like?

First, both participants would know the purpose of the affair before it started. The clearer about where they are coming from, the less likely they are to end up somewhere unintended, like married to that bimbo from the office.

Motives for affairs vary hugely, and are usually mixed. Some are all about a marriage: to test it; to punish or to avoid being trampled by a domineering spouse; to remind your spouse that you exist; or to give them an excuse to leave you, sparing yourself the trouble of doing it. Some couples use infidelity to pep up their marriage, like 1930s colonists June Mosley and John Carberry, of Kenya's notorious Happy Valley, who both slept around, but adored each other and relished the drama (once he pursued her and a lover across the plains in his plane, delightedly bombarding their car with rocks). Some use infidelity to improve their marriage, not always intentionally. Alma Mahler was a talented composer and beauty but her husband Gustav, twenty years her senior, married her on condition that she abandon all interests but him. He also banned birthdays, Christmas, anniversaries, and for lovemaking, preferred to steal into her bed while she slept, taking her unawares. Unsurprisingly, Alma was often ill, retreating to spas for 'the cure'. In one, she found it, in the form of young architect Walter Gropius. A week after her return Gustav received a letter from Gropius, asking his permission to marry Alma, as if she were his daughter, not wife. From then on, he encouraged Alma's compositions.

Plenty of affairs are not about the marriage. If you run into somebody else's arms, this may be a bona fide, falling-in-love affair. But there is always another motive: the person you are running away from. More often than not, that person is you.

If some affairs are for variety or drama, others are cries for help: to escape problems; to prove that one is still attractive; to re-enact a trauma. Many are fumbled gropes after unfulfilled dreams. Author Louise Desalvo found that adulterers often chose lovers who resembled the person that they wished to be: 'A man, who longed to travel alone, had a lover who lived three hours away. A woman, who wanted to become a famous biographer, became the lover of the world's foremost authority on her subject. Another woman yearned to be a painter; her lover was a street musician.' Other common affair triggers include: danger; the arrival of a baby; mid-life crisis, feeling old or ugly; a parent's death; the departure of children from the marital home; unemployment; any time of change, as a chapter in life closes.

In a rational affair, once participants understood their underlying motives, they might stop, reflect, and conclude that there are safer ways than adultery to satisfy them. But if an affair still appealed, the next step would be to decide what the affair meant in relation to the marriage.

There are four ways to see it: as separate from your marriage; as a complement to or compensation for shortcomings in your marriage; as a part of marriage; or, as a strategic device, to change or end your marriage.

Once these purposes were clear, participants might pause, reflect and conclude there are safer ways to gratify their ends. To improve their sex life with their spouse, perhaps, or to work on their marital communication. But if both thought it wise to press on, they would then need to decide the rules, and be relied on to respect them. The *Kama Sutra* recommends that men choose carefully, listing forty-one varieties of 'women who are easily gained over':

1. Women who stand at the door of their houses
2. Women who are always looking out on the street
3. Women who sit conversing in their neighbour's house

6. A woman who looks sideways at you

9. A woman who has nobody to look after her, or keep her in check

14. A woman who is apparently very affectionate with her husband

15. The wife of an actor

27. A woman whose husband is devoted to travelling

28. The wife of a jeweller

41. An old woman

The bystander spouse would also need to be relied on to be either blind or compliant. Sometimes it is possible to tell the truth. Some actively want their spouse to sleep around. A rash groom of my acquaintance crowed to friends and enemies alike that he had discovered the secret of happy monogamy: to hire whores for threesomes. However, his marriage ended within months, amid cruel speculation that the wife was a lesbian but had mistaken him for a millionaire, and that he, an aspiring politician, had laboured under similar financial illusions about her.

There are spouses who desire their beloved's happiness in a way that transcends convention. The most moving letter I have read was written in the Second World War, from my grandmother to my grandfather. They were in their twenties and separated, she at home with two infants while he risked his life daily, flying over enemy lines for the air force. If he wanted a lover, she wrote, he must not deprive himself. I never met them, so to see these words,

knowing that they would survive the war by five years, only
to perish in a car crash, makes it hard not to sentimental-
ize; however, my grandmother's love was saccharine-free.
There was a rider to her kind offer: if he gave her the clap,
she would kill him.

On the other hand, any spouse who seeks their wife or
husband's permission to be unfaithful will sound very like
they are making a threat. Even spouses with clear terms of
infidelity conduct go awry. I know a South American
woman whose mother informed her, on the eve of her
wedding, that her husband would be unfaithful. This was to
be expected, said the mother, and was no excuse to leave
him — unless, that is, he put it in her face. So the wife set
this rule and her husband agreed to it, until he fell in love
with his mistress. That was the end of their two-decade
marriage.

If you cannot resist the temptations of infidelity, practise to deceive. There is no such thing as a good deception:
however, an effective one entails tact, no complicated lies,
no taunting clues, and no insultingly transparent excuses.
How many times can an adulterer miss the last train, or get
snowed in at the airport? For some spouses, apparently
these are regular events, but no one is fooled.

Whatever the rational adulterer does, be kind to all concerned, never lean on friends for alibis or overlook the
risks: a sizeable bill in pain, boiled bunnies, and/or
alimony.

My personal view? Don't do it. You may not wreck the

fairy tale, but, as Aesop warned, you could well wind up bald.

3. HOW TO BE AN INNOCENT BYSTANDER

It is possible to stay married to an irredeemably goatish partner. Many couples spend decades living in an un-acknowledged *ménage à trois*. The third party's face may change but the marital dynamic remains the same.

Uncommon arrangements vary hugely. Some couples develop an interesting new social life. Tyre magnate Leopoldo Pirelli brought wife and mistress to meet the octogenarian Queen Mother at the opening of the Pirelli Garden at the Victoria and Albert Museum. Novelist Georges Simenon's second wife, Denise, accompanied him to brothels and advised him on his pick of the girls.

The most common dynamic in such ménages is that couples get locked into a push-me-pull-you dance of resentment and self-justification: out of guilt, the one who strays becomes sweeter to their betrayed spouse; meanwhile the betrayed spouse knows the reason behind the smiles, extra sex and bunches of flowers, so is anything but happy to see their spouse so joyful. Consequently, the betrayed spouse grows nastier, helping the betrayer to see their infidelity as justified. We owe ourselves happiness, after all.

Those stuck with a treacherous spouse, my commiserations. It was not your choice, but at least you can control your reaction to it.

You might choose to dismiss it as a passing whim. A survey of 70,288 people found that half of wives and husbands had cheated, but that most affairs ended within six months. You could feign ignorance, as the Vicomtesse de G__ advised in 1823's *Art of Being Loved by One's Husband*: 'She should increase her care and consideration . . . [and] let a tear furtively escape her eye, and, when her husband draws near, she should quickly wipe it away.' Or be stoical. Actress Joanne Woodward helped to burnish the image of her fabled ideal marriage to randy Paul Newman, despite his causing her grave offence by denying an affair, of which she knew, with the demeaning quip, 'Why go out for hamburger when you have steak at home?' (Oddly, many men imagine that this metaphor was flattering.)

A lot of innocent bystanders develop a system for rating their spouse's affairs by degree of seriousness. Ideally, they are confident of their charms, and see their tolerance as sophisticated: 'Of course he had other women. What would I expect? As long as they weren't serious, I was fine . . . Bailey never put it in my face. What you didn't know couldn't hurt you. At the end of the day, he belonged to me.' This was Marie Helvin, a model with a robust ego ('cheating is never to do with how attractive you are'), on photographer David Bailey. What concerned her were the affairs' degree of threat to the union – whether 'he belonged to me' – and their decorum – whether he 'put it in my face'. Until one day he did and they split. Even so, looking back decades later, Helvin seemed proud of her ex-husband's priapic antics, as if they proved what a catch he was. Caught being the operative verb. In a deliciously catty remark, Helvin contrasted Bailey with the goatish rock star Mick Jagger, the ex of her ex-friend, Jerry Hall: 'Well, [Bailey's] not attractive any more – my God, he's fat and bloated. But when we were married, he was a god. Models pursued him. I can't imagine one incident – unlike Mick [Jagger], who was always actively pursuing whoever – when Bailey had to do anything.' In Helvin's moral universe, as in many other betrayed spouses', there is such a thing as first- or second-degree adultery. Similarly, eighteenth-century political hostess Caroline Fox tolerated her husband Henry's wanderings – much as they 'vexed' her – so long as he confined himself to the lower orders and servant girls. Caroline's sister, Emily, Countess of Kildare, took a more relaxed view, writing in 1751: 'my turn for getting a lover will come in good time,' as if she were writing of a game of pass the parcel.

Those who are not so free and breezy, and want to recover their marriage by editing adultery from its future, face a more demanding task. If there were an affair repair kit, its ingredients would be for reconstituting trust: forgiveness, patience, time. A reformed adulterer would reprise the trials of courtship, doing everything possible to prove their worth, honesty, consistency and commitment. Of course, courtship is harder if you are older, sadder and uglier, or a spouse is hurt and doubtful. Therapy can make it easier to listen and care again. But no amount of talk is a surrogate for the desire to repair a marriage. To succeed, a betrayed spouse has to take an active part.

To make sense of an affair, both must establish its cause and accept that affairs rarely occur in happy marriages. If either feels a victim of the affair, and does not assume equal responsibility for repairing the relationship, there may be no marriage to save. It is better to look at how lives were organized. What gap did the affair fill? Some lifestyles almost guarantee infidelity – for example, long periods apart, lots of travel, or overloads of adulation. If to marry a rock star is a misfortune, to marry two is culpable, as Pattie Boyd, betrayed first by George Harrison, then Eric Clapton, conceded: 'I didn't put my foot down. I didn't feel that I had the right to. It takes two to tango, and I suppose in a way I colluded with the effect of their huge fame.'

Reach a position in which both spouses accept their part in a marital detour, if only by failing to keep up to date with each other's dreams, and there is a starting point for recovery. This may well mean that adulterers' spouses have to change: to be more generous, forgiving; to have more sex, share more leisure, and heap praise on whatever their spouse contributes to their lives together, however small. The one who strayed would extend these indulgences to their betrayed spouse too.

Life might be easier if we could do as the Inuits once did, routinely swapping spouses, as men moved around, following the hunting and fishing grounds. Occasionally cuckolds grew fed up. In which case, they challenged their wifes' lover not to a duel but a public song contest. However, I doubt these marriages were duets of equal parts.

8

THE JOY OF CHILDREN

'I want to marry a womb,' announced Napoleon Bonaparte, on ditching his ageing wife Josephine for a younger model. A harsh choice, but in Bonaparte's day not so controversial. The marriage business has long been about making babies. In 1662's *Book of Common Prayer*, the wedding ceremony lists 'procreation' as the first purpose of matrimony.

Few grooms today would say that they want to marry a brood mare. Most hope for a soulmate. Yet the majority of married couples also hope to go forth and multiply, parenthood being the closest that most of us will come to an answer to that ticklish question, What is the meaning of life? But are the ambitions to be soulmate and co-parent natural bedfellows?

Children, once the light of life, are increasingly presented as problems to be solved. With all the hothousing, manuals and panic about declining standards, being a parent has never looked so complicated. Sociologists routinely portray children as weapons of marital destruction. A 2000 report on China remarks in passing, 'As in the West, children are associated with lower marriage quality.' Likewise, a review of 97 studies, encompassing 47,692 people, in the *Journal of Marriage and Family* concluded that marriage with children was unhappier than without them. But it seems odd that marriage's chief selling point should also be a major drawback.

Meet a first-time parent, with their shattered air of one who fell asleep on a bus and awoke on a spaceship heading for Pluto, then look at the smiling infant in their arms, replete with milk and warmth, and you may well agree with the French novelist Colette, that children are 'happy, unconscious little vampires who drain the maternal heart'. On the other hand, Colette largely ignored her daughter, so perhaps is not the best authority on the subject. And if you bump into that first-time parent a few years later, they may emit a rosy glow, as if possessed of an intoxicating secret, known only to a select group of two: the delirious love of a parent for their child.

Parenthood is transformative. According to tests on primates, mothers not only become braver, but also have better spatial awareness than the childless. So it would be strange if parenthood did not change our marriages too.

What intrigues me is the possibility that negative assumptions are wrong. That parenthood and marriage are not innately rivals, and that a child can change its parents' relationship for the better. If those parents believe that their child's best interest is to put their marriage first.

I.   SUFFER THE LITTLE CHILDREN?

The usual parental concern is what can we do for our kids. But what can children do for us?

For a start, they are fun. Stovepipe-hatted human dynamo Isambard Kingdom Brunel, who was to Victorian engineering what Dickens was to the novel, was not too busy to hurtle upstairs from his basement office to his children's nursery several times a day, and whisk his brood outside to play with kites, or to perform magic tricks for them, such as swallowing gold sovereigns, then producing them from his ear. Unfortunately, once he swallowed one. It stuck in his trachea for weeks until he devised a board to which he was strapped and rotated at speed until the coin popped out.

We love children because they are cute, and loving them makes us better people. 'After babies, everything else seems trivial,' confide parents — out of their employers' earshot. But children renew life's purpose, even those long hours you put in at a job you hate, to supply their ever-expanding feet with new shoes. To live up to the parental commitment

is life-enhancing. Studies of thousands of deprived families found that despite poverty and limited opportunities,
doting fathers' wellbeing shoots up, with knock-on benefits
for mothers, not to mention their children, their neigh-
bourhoods and society at large. A child's love is a potent
antidote to misery too, as Judith O'Reilly wrote in *Wife in the
North*: 'There are some days so bad that the only thing which
could redeem them is a proposal of marriage. Today was
one of them. As I hunkered down by my pyjama-clad four-
year-old to start cleaning his teeth, he gazed intensely into
my eyes. "When I'm big, I want to marry you." He paused.
"If you're still alive."'

Anyone who has gazed into the eyes of a tiny person, and
seen reflected in them the world reborn, shiny and new,
has felt a child's power to put a shine on the everyday
miracle of existence. Only David Attenborough or a toddler
can make rain seem a wonder worth beholding. How much
more beguiling, then, to participate in the conspiracy of
optimism that is providing a good childhood, and together
to watch this child, who is dearer to you than life,
blossom?

If children slow down time, giving each passing day
greater weight and sharper colour, they also endow the
march of our finite days with an added poignancy. At every
birthday, we celebrate their next step towards adulthood,
and away from us. Children enrich feelings for a spouse
too. A husband or wife who is the father or mother of your
child inevitably finds extra space in the heart. 'You go

gooey about your other half,' say some. 'You think, We made this person.'

But although parenthood is an immense undertaking, and an intense shared interest, it does not always draw couples close. A friend, besotted with both his wife and month-old firstborn, confessed: 'Last night I dreamed I was so desperate for attention that I found a nappy, sat down and, with a heavy heart, pinned it on.' There is no escaping the drawbacks of caring for creatures who need so much care, in a world that cares for them so much less than you do.

The negative picture looks something like this.

Take one happy couple. Then detonate their union with an object of invincible selfishness, a baby. Now watch the bewildered pair bid a sad farewell to something that until this moment they were too naïve to cherish: unbroken sleep. And say hello to a lava of ugly, noisy, toe-stubbing plastic toys on what used to be their floor.

Next, in what psychologists agree to be the period of greatest stress to any marriage, in any land, the frazzled couple become strange to themselves, and each other, as they absorb the shock of parental love, and the screams that accompany those silvery peals of infant laughter.

Thus begins the transition from wife to mother and husband to father. Slowly the couple master their task – to maintain their baby's digestive system, with much spooning and wiping – and come to learn that they are slaves to the whim of this creature, which has no idea what it wants, other than their attention, and whose care instructions are delivered not in a manual but an unfamiliar language of gurgles and grizzling – plus the unsought advice of grand-parents, friends and those bossyboots who prowl our streets disguised as sweet old ladies.

This culture shock would be tough on even ten hours' sleep. Worse, in the first twelve months after a child is born, sex for the average couple drops by more than 40 per cent, with one in four managing only a monthly tumble. To drive them on, the couple have their love for this tyrannical being, which occasionally smiles and smells (at the top end) like sweet butter. A further incentive is that if they perform their tasks well, the tyrant will sleep. Then, for a limited period only, so may they. As a mother summed up early parenthood to me: 'When they're babies (and asleep), you yearn and yearn for them to wake up and when they do, you yearn and yearn for them to go back to sleep again.'

This period does not last for ever, but as children grow up, parenthood grows no simpler. By the time that parents are competent in one set of skills, their child has already entered a new phase, with a whole new host of demands to second-guess. These demands intensify as society gets in on the child-rearing act, and imposes state-sanctioned health, literacy and numeracy standards, then dastardly school exams.

The challenge lasts about two decades. If parents succeed, their reward is to watch their offspring fly the coop, in search of their own soulmate, to commence the whole sorry cycle again. This moment is supposed to herald a period of mourning for the empty nest. But a greater trauma may be turning around to find the unfamiliar person with whom they are left to share the wreckage.

I have never met a parent who would unwish their children, or who says that anything in life can compare with parenthood's heartsong. Nor have I met one who has found it easy on their relationship. Few couples would put 'our marriage' on the long list of sacrifices they have made for their children, but there may be a case for saying that the best thing your children could do for your marriage is not to be born. Indeed, the ungrateful lunks may remind you that they never asked to be, during the epic yodel of woe that is the teenage years.

Parents' sacrifices are nothing new. Eighteenth-century clergyman John Townsend bemoaned 'fond and anxious parents, who have sacrificed your ease, your rest, your worldly property, your health, your all, for the comfort and prosperity of your offspring'. A common mistake, often overlooked, is that when falling hostage to feeding and sleep schedules, to school timetables, to unending shopping, bathing, laundry and bills, parents frequently let one item slip down the duty list: to maintain their bond. Worse for them is that their children miss out too. At all ages, the warmth between children and parents reflects the warmth of their parents' marriage. Economist Avner Offer:

Poor marital quality, as well as declines in marital quality over time, were associated with problematic relationships with mothers and fathers . . . [and] lower marital quality among married offspring . . . Affluence, marital breakdown, and mental disorder have risen together, especially since the 1970s. The case for roping them together arises from attachment theory, i.e. from the view that an inadequate infancy leads to a deficient adulthood.

You need not be a Mr and Mrs Mozart, devoted to advancing your child prodigy, to find that parenthood divides you, or changes your relationship beyond recognition. But if many parents sacrifice their marriage on the altar of what they imagine to be their children's needs, they are apt to forget that this was their choice.

To have a child is to introduce a witness into your life, one who will reflect and distort your best and worst traits, as well as reshape your marriage. So is it not obvious that, as Richard Layard and Judith Dunn observed in 2009's controversial Children's Society Report, 'A Good Childhood': 'If parents gave more priority to maintaining their feelings towards each other, this would do more for their children than much of the rest of what they do for their children?'

2. HOW PARENTHOOD REMAKES MARRIAGE

There is no such thing as an ideal parent. The same protests reverberate down the centuries: too much is asked of a
mother, of a father, and too little credit or reward is given
to either for their tender cares.

Men have always been chastised for not providing
enough, or for providing the wrong thing. Norfolk gentlewoman Margaret Paston, twenty-two, wrote to her husband
in 1444: 'As for caps that you sent me for the children, they
be too little for them. I pray you buy them finer caps and
larger than those were.' And nobody can make up their
minds if mothers should go to work, or it is responsible to
have two or two dozen kids. The latter depends on supply
and demand. Florence, ravaged by plague, issued statutes
in 1433 commanding wives to lie back, 'replenish this free
city', thinking themselves 'little sacks, to hold the natural
seed which their husbands implant in them, so that children will be born'.

In other words, each culture remakes parents and children in its own image. *Mrs Beeton's Book of Household Management*,
the 1861 middle-class Bible, outlined what is tantamount
to a manifesto for today's creed regarding a good childhood as a reconstituted Eden: 'It ought, therefore, to enter
into the domestic policy of every parent, to make her children feel that home is the happiest place in the world; that
to imbue them with this delicious home-feeling is one of
the choicest gifts a parent can bestow.' However, in war-

faring ancient Sparta, unquestioning obedience was the virtue of the day, so the Spartan definition of a good mother was one prepared to abandon an imperfect baby to the hillside, and its definition of a good child one who dutifully offered sexual services to any adult in seniority.

There are few transcendent truths in parenthood other than that it bends parents' lives beyond recognition. But to protect marriage, it is worth examining the major stresses that children place on their parents' relationship.

1. Lopsided significance

Compared with the duty of looking after a child, tending a marriage can seem relatively trivial.

2. Lopsided parenting

Until parenthood the roles of wife and husband tend to be similar, but as couples become mothers and fathers their paths often diverge, accelerated by a crash course in practical tasks that involve mothers most at first, as mothers are glorified baby-support units. Meanwhile, fathers, and mothers, try to work out what fathers are for. The gulf in their experience was epitomized in the story told by Scottish television presenter Gail Porter about her pop star husband Dan Hipgrave. While Porter lay in agony in advanced labour, apparently Hipgrave showered, then started cooking himself a fry-up. When she begged him to drive her to hospital, she claims that he said, 'How about a bacon sandwich then?'

The division of parental labour can be stark, as summarized in the tale of a friend who had a five- and three-year-old to stay. When her newborn needed breast-feeding, she explained that baby wanted supper. The eldest shrugged. 'Mummy gives us boo-boo every morning.' My friend pictured them lining up for their breakfast boob. Later she asked if they shared a bedroom. 'No! We sleep with Mummy.'

My friend said, 'Not much room for Daddy.'

The eldest scoffed. 'Daddy has his own room.'

Lopsided parental burdens do not lead inexorably to separate beds, but usually they create lopsided parental expertise. Many fathers never catch up with the mothers' childcare skills, and are content to settle for the status of semi-competent, deputy parent. They may not feel the need to reproach themselves, since they are falling in with the traditional patriarch's part, a cameo role in the soap opera of family life. Their part may even be more fun. Now that dads are less likely to be remote authoritarians, who helicopter into the family to lay down the law or dish out punishments, instead they get to play. 'I have the distinct impression,' said psychologist Oliver James in 2009, 'that mothers rarely engage in fantasy play with their children because they're so busy with the logistics. I look around me at Fundays and it's full of fathers.'

In the past, many workaholic men, who today might be

classed as bad fathers, turned their cameo family role into a star turn. Charles Dickens hosted parties for children's friends, performing self-taught magic tricks with a defunct music hall conjuror's kit, transforming bran into guinea pigs, and, one Boxing Day, emptying eggs, flour, butter, sugar and fruit into his hat, then producing a steaming plum pudding.

Today, semi-detached fathers are considered less accept-able, and mocking them is de rigueur. It is a cliché among mothers I know to mock their klutzy husbands. Perhaps this helps mothers to feel prouder of their own achieve-ments in what are often pretty menial tasks.

It is the quantity of dull work that distinguishes the quality of a mother's life from a father's. A 2000 survey of 348 East and West German couples with children, married less than ten years, found in both countries that women did 34 hours' childcare a week, with Eastern men putting in 11 hours, and Western, 9. Extra domestic toil comes with the motherhood package too. Since the 1980s, married mothers' contribution to housework has fallen far less steeply than that of childless wives. Settling for less seems to be compulsory. 'When my husband comes home,' joked the comedian Roseanne Barr, 'if the kids are still alive, I figure I've done my job.'

Dividing parental labour has numerous advantages. In the short run, if one spouse stays home to look after chil-dren this can be cheaper than both working and paying someone else to do it, and more fun. It can also be more efficient to specialize in particular areas rather than try to split childcare, with parents doing everything equally, but nothing especially well, and both also thereby losing out on career progress. On the downside, a career break can be a disadvantage to a stay-home parent if ever they wish to return to paid employment. Misery beckons if a couple have unresolved differences of opinion about who should work and who tend baby, or cannot make up their minds what they want. (Many non-working mothers regard working mums as reproaches, and vice versa.) And the scope for arguments about money his huge.

There are mothers who prefer not to shoulder the main burden of childcare, and fathers who wish to do more, but they must swim against the abiding cultural prejudice, in which stay-at-home fathers are often portrayed as feckless. Divorce laws also tend to assume that child is more hers than his. As a result, children weaken a woman's bargaining power in marriage. If a mother wants the father of her children to do more, she also knows that if she fights too hard and they end up divorced, custody arrangements will almost certainly lumber her with a yet greater share of solo childcare.

Is it any wonder that once spouses become parents, often a sense of inequality emerges, a perception that one spouse is not pulling their weight. In one study fathers reported spending 18 per cent longer with their children than the mothers reported them doing. Whoever is right does not matter so much as the difference of opinion that causes trouble.

3. Worry

'Children today are tyrants. They contradict their parents, gobble their food, and tyrannize their teachers.' So said the philosopher Socrates in fifth-century BC Athens, at the dawn of civilization. Clearly, children have always been uncivilized. Civilizing them is the parents' job. Hence to have a child is to fall prey to lifelong anxiety about failure to meet this task. Ironically, the more conscientious and expert a parent you are, the greater your fears can be. According to studies, the more news media you digest, the more anxious you will be about your children (no surprises there). Wealth and success are no cushion. Oscar-winning film director Sam Mendes said, 'Having kids makes you fearful – it increases your level of vulnerability about a thousand per cent.'

On top of health and safety concerns, parents endure the logistical horrors of ferrying their tribe around and of paying for them. And long after a child is a teenager sleeping twelve maddening hours a day, sleep may remain an irregular acquaintance to its parents, since the worry synapses laid down in the parental brain tend to remain in a state of high alert until death or senility. A conscience never signs off. 'The children have been in my mind since the moment they were born,' said mother of six Alice Walpole in 2009, British consul-general in Basra, southern Iraq, whom you would imagine had plenty else to think about.

4. Exhaustion

Enough said? In her memoir of motherhood, *A Life's Work*, Rachel Cusk describes her relationship to her daughter's 'pure and pearly being' as 'that of a kidney. I process it's waste'. Unfortunately, waste management is an all-night task. After one insomniac marathon tending their unsleeping babe, the next morning the child set between their bodies 'like some triumphal mini-Napoleon, waving her rattle in victory'. The tiredness that ensued from such shenanigans, came as a 'physical shock'.

> In the morning I would sit up in bed, the room listing drunkenly about me, and would put a hand to my face, checking for some evidence of disfigurement: an eyebrow, perhaps, slipped down my cheek, a deranged ear cluttering my forehead, a seam at the back of my skull gaping open . . . I began to speak with a curious lisp, and would put a hand to my mouth several times a day to check that my tongue was not lolling out of it.

5. Rivals

'Insanity is hereditary,' quipped Ronald Reagan, 'you catch it from your kids.' The US President thought that his daughter Patti was 'nuts' and called his son Mike 'a really disturbed young man'. However, Reagan may have been motivated by sibling rivalry (his diaries refer to wife Nancy as 'Mommy'). As to have a child is to introduce a witness into your marriage, this witness can become a rival if one parent forms an alliance with a child, using them as an instrument of opposition to their spouse. This happened with all but one of Charles Dickens's children, who connived with a campaign to blacken their mother's name after Dickens fell for a younger woman, but tried to blame his wife for the marriage's breakdown, claiming that she had neglected the family.

6. Choice v. Necessity

Before a child, a couple's decisions are led by inclination and opportunity. With children, time previously considered free evaporates and many decisions that once were choices are driven by necessity. As life grows more complicated and the children grow older, a couple also have more to negotiate, and argue over. All of which may create the impression that your spouse has turned into a fractious, penny-pinching child who in no way resembles the person that you married.

Some parents are blackmailed into a whole new lifestyle, like my friends, who were eager to send their daughter to a Church of England primary school, but too honest to lie to the vicar and pretend they believed in God. The vicar appreciated their honesty, and offered to recommend their girl if they underwent intensive religious indoctrination. The family now attend church each Sunday, help at Sunday school, clean loos, serve coffee and arrange flowers. Four family activities and five years' church attendance are the minimum requirements before they can apply for a place at the Church of England secondary school.

7. Censors

With a child in the room, you can never be fully yourself, since you must also play the part of parent. Arguing is hard if conducted in parental double-speak, to ensure the little ones are not traumatized; so is talking dirty. Thus children introduce censorship into marriage. Which is a pity, as having children also means that you have plenty more to talk about.

8. Redefinition of love

To love a child awakens something wonderful, but its unconditionality imposes new conditions on parents' love for one another, as each expects the other to pull their weight.

The intensity of parental love is also apt to make the love of a wife for her husband, or he for her, seem pale by comparison. If either spouse feels neglected, misunderstandings can mushroom. Displaced husbands often gripe that their wife only wants sex to conceive and is treating them like a sperm donor. And if the sex falls off, they also lose one of the greatest pleasures of marriage – a pleasure that helps to defuse conflict.

If a husband or wife seems jealous, or seeks attentions reminiscent of pre-parental days, back when massaging oil into bodies had nothing to do with nappy rash, their spouse may feel blamed and defensive – which also sends a libido plummeting. My friend described how her husband never thanked her for pulling through with their two demanding kids. Yet she felt equally outraged when her husband got angry and 'behaved like a child'. Where in the past she would bill, coo and metaphorically mop his brow, now she had no patience or time for such tenderness, since she was doing them all day with her kids. Their problem was that she both expected greater acknowledgement of the new services that she was providing, and simultaneously withdrew her old services and regarded them as infantile. Both he and she wanted to be mollycoddled, and to be the child for a change. In short, so the high demands of parenthood mean that parents expect more love of each other just as they have least to spare.

*

When couples struggle to adjust to having children, some conclude that the test of parenthood has exposed innate flaws in their marriage. But it is more likely that the flaws are stresses on the axle of wedlock, due to the overload of new demands. If couples miscommunicate and their lives diverge so much that their children become their only common interest, their marriage is in trouble. If they fail to see how they reached this point, and start to believe that their marriage is doomed, then it is.

So the core challenge of parenthood is one at the heart of the art of marriage, for every couple, whether they have seven children or none: to keep reminding each other that at the beginning, middle and end, they are in this together. Sympathy gives a couple a centre of gravity, and it is this, as much as sex, that they will miss, if all the attention goes on baby.

In any event, as children grow up, parents need to make ever greater leaps of imagination to see each other's point of view – and to spend time together, away from the children, as they did in their footloose days. Those bedevilled by feelings of inadequacy should take comfort from a three-year study of 134 new mothers which found that 'mothers who were more satisfied with work or school choices were more likely to be chronically stressed'. Happiest were the laidback, who still enjoyed spontaneity, and intimacy with their children's father.

The secret of contented parents is not to care less, then, but to enjoy everything more, be aware of the pitfalls, and question all that goddamned angst.

WHAT ARE WE WORRYING ABOUT?
CHILDREN AS ASSET OR LIABILITY

Do we love children more than previous generations? No. But it helps for us to see them as beyond precious, as they have never been so expensive.

Once children were clearly an asset. The more you had, the more hands you had to tend your land, and the greater your network of supportive kin. Medical advances now allow us to plan our families, and ensure that many more infants reach adulthood. It is unfortunate that children have never been less cost-effective. Assessing their price, in terms of wages missed, and expenses for food, shelter, childcare and education, is difficult. But the loss of earnings of a mother of two has been estimated to be equivalent to the cost of a detached family home (£135,000 in the 1980s, a finding that had gone up in line with the housing market when the comparison was made again in 2003). The costs of child-rearing are rising too. Being a good provider is not good enough to protect your brood, nor is getting rich, according to one economist: 'Affluence, marital breakdown, and mental disorder have risen together, especially since the 1970s.' Parents must keep a weather eye on their children's diet, drug use and psychological state, their social skills, as well as get them to school on time and into higher education. All these and more are vital, if you take advice-mongers to heart.

Parental anxiety is not new. Painter John Constable adored his wife, so tried to be stoical despite money worries: 'I am reading a book on education for the advantage of my children, & I am perfectly satisfied with my four without wishing for any more.' At child six he sighed, 'I am willing to think of them as bless-ings. Only, that I am now satisfied and think my quiver full enough.' But if you are unhappily married, it is harder to bear. Dickens, out of love with his wife, was understandably less than pleased to meet baby five. 'I decline (on principle) to look at the latter object.'

If we are more sentimental about children, it is thanks to industrialization, which meant that we could afford not to send children to work. This created a new social problem: to work out what to do with children. To solve it, mass education began, and we started studying children too, with Charles Darwin the tenderest observer, comparing the devel-opment of his daughter Annie with an orang-utan at London Zoo. Inevitably, this raised child awareness and increased our self-consciousness about child-rearing. Now we have mothers such as ace former Microsoft director Melinda Gates, who approached motherhood in the same way that she might a start-up company. She and husband Bill hold six-monthly strategy meetings to decide family goals and holidays. She then produces a written report.

If child welfare is of paramount importance, why are children today so unfree, so monitored, so tested? Why are parents urged to work when few workplaces offer crèches, leaving parents to writhe in guilt about children and careers? Not to mention urged by our newspapers to lie awake at night for fear of paedophile bogeymen who patrol playgrounds and snatch sleeping babes from cots. This seems a distraction from, even a distortion of, our profoundly child-hostile culture.

The suggestion that modern life is inhospitable to parenthood is borne out in declining birth rates. Between the 1970s and 1990s, childlessness rose in the US by two-thirds. Birth rates in Western Europe fell too, but were propped up by immigration. So though many believe, with evolutionary scientist Richard Dawkins, that humanity is ruled by a 'selfish gene', the evidence indicates that growing numbers of the best-educated, best-placed would-be parents in the world are following a self-centred path. Some wait too long to 'afford' children, others never get around to wanting them, or are so tortured by the pros and cons of deciding to change their lives irrevocably that instead of making a decision they hope for an 'accident' that never arrives. Some prefer to be childless and lead a life that the greatest evolutionary scientist, Darwin, likened disparagingly to that of 'neuter bees'.

There are many reasons not to breed, but if it is to pursue a career, the choice is predicated on the idea that children are handicaps to one. Our workcentric world makes them so.

Children need not wreck careers. They can be a compelling motivation. For fathers, studies find salaries rise (10 per cent for baby one, 5 per cent for baby two, flatlining at baby three). But while historically the higher a man's status, the more children he had, for women, the more educated, the less likely they were to breed. It is no coincidence that rising childlessness has accompanied the entry of greater numbers of women into higher education and paid employment. Motherhood costs women more than fatherhood costs men, especially if they are ambivalent about it. If they wait to breed until they are higher up a notional career ladder, whether they are mother or father, to quit a corner office to pick up Lego may feel a bitter demotion. One mother felt an exile in motherhood, akin to a Polish professor who had emigrated to America only to find himself behind the wheel of a yellow cab: 'I used to be so gung-ho at work. But I just decided I had to put that aside while my kids are young. It was much harder than I thought, though, especially when I'm walking in the supermarket and other people think I'm just a housewife. I want to shout at them, "I have an M.B.A.! I have an M.B.A.!"'

Indeed, much child-related anxiety is self-centred, an expression of fear of the selfless love that parenthood asks. Comedian Sharon Horgan skewered this narcissism, with bitter irony:

The crèche starts in my house next week. Part of the point of going to the trouble of being in this parent-run co-operative . . . is to alleviate the guilt, of course. I do feel guilty every single day. Every day. Because my daughter likes being with me more than anyone else, obviously, on the planet; which is great, but then I cart her off somewhere, and I dump her there, and then I go home and I work on my career. And part of it's to give her a fantastic life, but a lot of it's for me to be happy and fulfilled and wealthy and so that people who I used to go to school with will see me on telly, as I said. So I joined this co-op, which makes you feel better about yourself; you provide wholesome lunches, and that makes you feel better about yourself; you can have a parent meeting every six weeks, and talk about your child's activities, and that makes you feel better about yourself.

It seems a convoluted bother. Can we not just do our best and feel okay? If relaxation is the best fertility treatment, the most effective contraceptive is to watch friends poring over school league tables, food labels, or hear them discuss Ritalin, or how their child was reported for bullying after telling another seven-year-old in the playground that, personally, she hated the colour pink.

Yes. Taste: it is the new thought crime. You heard it here first.

3.   HOW TO PARENT TO PROTECT YOUR MARRIAGE

So how can you parent to improve a marriage? The answer seems to be, by being a good spouse.

Contemporary experts find that two dimensions matter in parenting: control (or lack of it) and warmth (or lack of it). To parent well – defined as to aid a child's adjustment, development and wellbeing – requires support, supervision, discipline, cuddles and other forms of interest from parents. In this vision, the parents' task is that of benign custodians, to make the bars of their children's prison resemble trees along an avenue that leads, step by gentle step, up the hill to adult freedom.

If children mirror marriages, they can also distort them – and that includes making a marriage better. Hence all the research indicates that the best way to react to your children – the way that will transform your partnership positively – is to maintain a united front.

The more that parents pull in different directions, disagreeing over how to handle a child, the more parenting problems and rage they experience, found a three-year study of 516 American, two-parent, two-adolescent families. Co-parenting conflict had a worse impact on children even than a bad parental marriage, and also made that marriage worse, escalating any disputes between parents, as children grew into toxic adolescents — thereby pulling parents in different directions.

Parenting conflict will metastasize into hostility if one party is barely there, like scattergun dad and poet John Betjeman. In one of many such epistles, his wife Penelope railed at him:

> Wibz [their teenage daughter Candida] has been misbehaving in Florence and insulting the Contessa Marzotto . . . She seems now to have caused such disharmony in the Marzotto household that one almost suspects there is an evil influence at work within her and unless you as HEAD OF THE FAMILY, call her to task very severely next holidays, anything may happen. You are so weak you ALWAYS give in and start calling her WIBBLY WOBBLY and laughing when she is infernally rude to me.

Sibling rivalries, too, echo parental favouritism, and often parental intervention, far from a help, looks to children like taking sides. Instead parents do better to spend time with a squabbling brood, teaching them manners and how to see others' points of view – in other words, those peerless life and marriage skills, mindreading and good behaviour. By happy coincidence, the conditions for creating non-stressed parents are ideal for creating non-stressed children.

It helps to neutralize emotions to see disagreements over children as tactical failures, and to plan a parenting strategy and execute it together. Parents must back each other up, which will be easier if neither spouse has a monopoly on competence, and both have a clue how to change nappies or do algebra homework.

Couples who emerge strongest from their offspring's infancy are not those who talk everything through, discovered some astonished sociologists, but often those who avoid discussing problems (especially insolubles like exhaustion) and get on with it. Those who have fun – together, with and apart from the children – and who avoid overt selfishness fare better still. (Do not inform your wife, as did my friend in the first week of fatherhood, that you are going to book yourself into a hotel, because you are desperate for a kip.)

Mutual support evens out lopsided parental burdens, and this support is firmer if it is rooted in emotional commitment to children. Studies find that a father who wants a baby before pregnancy ends up more involved in playing and caring. However, any mother can boost her husband's emotional commitment to his marriage, and children, and fathers can do likewise.

Flatter each other and praise can be a self-fulfilling prophecy. Fathers who feel that their wives regard them as good fathers are more involved in child-related activities, and place greater importance on being a dad. Empowerment feeds responsibility. Interestingly, fathers who do jobs in which they are able to make their own decisions are also less apathetic at home. Therefore, frustrated mothers who dismiss their husbands as hopeless with the children should instead give them something to do, then leave them in peace to live up to the challenge.

Forgetting the little darlings from time to time helps. It seems natural to most parents I meet to frame their choices primarily in terms of their children's needs. Yet in the past wives and husbands came first. Even in patriarchal 1617, a bestselling marriage manual, the curiously titled *A Bride-Bush*, advised: 'A man must love his wife above all the creatures in the world . . . no neighbour, no kinsman, no parent, no child should be so neare and deare.' In the twentieth century Australian comedian Barry Humphries (better known as Dame Edna Everage, Housewife Superstar) recalls his mother telling him, 'Naturally I love your father most of all, then my mother and father and after that you and your sister, just the same.' Compare this with *Wife in the North*, Judith O'Reilly:

I had lain next to the six-year-old and said: 'You make me so proud and I love you so much. Do you know that?' And he said: 'No. How much do you love me?' And I said: 'I love you brighter than the stars.' He said: 'Do you love me more than Daddy?' I said: 'Yes. That's just the way it is.' He said: 'More than

Granny?' and I said yes and thought: 'Don't tell her, though.' 'More than television?' No contest. 'More than your make-up?' More than that even.

Whatever your priorities, place your marriage at the heart of parenthood and each will buttress the other. And to preserve the joy of the most natural thing in the world, it seems clear that parents need to simplify their children's world, not make them kings of it, and to give them two loving rulers to look up to. If there were any formula for success it would be to expect not success, but to be exhausted, to ask more of each other, to let things happen rather than control them, to listen, and to remember why you loved each other enough to sign up to the mission. High hopes can be self-fulfilling. It just takes the superhuman courage to be content with our lot.

Enjoy, while it lasts.

IN PRAISE OF THE STEPMOTHER, AND STEPFATHER

'Better a serpent than a stepmother!' cries the dying Alcestis in Euripedes' fifth-century BC tragedy, begging her husband not to take another wife. Her terrors reverberate in fairy tales of stepmothers who bake stepchildren in pies and feed them to unwitting fathers, or abandon them to the forest's wolves, like poor Hansel and Gretel. You might imagine some natural law dictated that all step-parents spell step-children's doom, and vice versa (in these tales, step-parents usually get their comeuppance). As stepparents only come into being as the result of death or divorce, naturally perceptions of them are often filtered through pain's dark glass. But given how many men and women have climbed the rickety stair of step-parentdom, it seems odd how few have spoken up for these interlopers. Why have they had such a bad press, and do they deserve it?

Let us spare a thought for those brave enough to assume the burdens of parenthood without any choice in the matter, or the instinctive love that makes it easier to tolerate mini-maniacs, who have sprung from your loins. To be a step-parent is to have a marriage that is lived, at least in part, on somebody else's terms. Those who have the courage to do so should be applauded, and encouraged, because being a good step-parent is harder than ever.

The step-parent's role has changed. Today, most are add-ons to family life, with a divorced ex lurking on the sidelines. By contrast, in the past, high rates of mortality meant that in a typical community in eastern France between the seventeenth and nine-teenth centuries, for instance, a third of marriages were remarriages, and most contracted within six months of the previous spouse's death.

Hamlet may have railed at his mother for marrying his fratricidal uncle with such unseemly haste that 'funeral baked meats' left from his father's wake were served at her wedding banquet, but for most widows and widowers, to delay re-marrying was to endanger a family's welfare. A wife or husband was vital to a domestic economy, so as a matter of child protection a widow or widower sought a new surrogate to step into the breach and tend the brood. The sainted Sir Thomas More so revered matrimony that he refused to petition the pope for the annulment of Henry VIII's union with Katherine of Aragon, yet took another, richer wife almost immediately after the death of his first.

The myth of evil step-parents haunts our beliefs about family life, in part because no child warms to someone for whom their parent's loss is a romantic opportunity. With the idealized dead parent an ever-present shadow, or an ex living nearby, and with the challenge of adapting to new family rules, to a stepchild, a stranger in their parent's bed will seem suspect, and an obvious target for the anger that accompanies grief. Likewise, if a step-parent doubts that their spouse married them for free babysitting, well may they resent their stepchildren too. Thomas More's second wife had to stomach the knowledge that her husband was so ashamed of his sensual weakness in remarrying that he wore a hair shirt to scourge his licentious flesh, and gave the task of washing this grisly garment to her stepdaughter. And if a step-parent has their own children, the relationship is riven with conflicts of interest that easily split families into factions.

Fears of step-parents illustrate the importance of good parenting to a child's destiny. Many folk tales focus on the primary task of a mother to find her daughter a spouse, such as 'The White Bride and the Black One', in which a stepmother tries to murder her stepdaughter on the way to her wedding and replace her with her own daughter. The dying Alcestis laments, 'What would be your fate, my daughter, what happiness would you find as you grew to womanhood, if your father took another wife? Might she not slander you in the flower of your youth to ruin your hope of marriage?' These may be fictions, but such scenarios played out in fact. The Ottoman Empire's imperial harem bristled with lethal stepmother and step-sibling rivalry, as wives competed for the sultan's favour, to get their son designated heir — out of love as much as ambition, since when a new sultan took over he was compelled by tradition to order the execution of all his male siblings to prevent civil war. The world's first female head of state, Hatshepsut, appointed co-pharaoh to Egypt in 1479 BC with her young stepson, Tuthmose III, promptly stole the throne for herself, shoring up her image of authority by wearing a false beard and men's clothes.

In other words, the myth of evil step-parents reflects how much it matters that a step-parent over-rides divided loyalties to put their stepchild's interests first as much for their marriage's sake as their own. Fairy tales were cautionary tales, popular not only because people recognised selfish neighbours in the wicked Queen of *Snow White,* but because they also served to remind step-parents of their duties. 'Every step-parent fears most,' wrote some-time stepmother, journalist Yvonne Roberts, 'that he or she truly is a monster.'

How to avoid this dire fate? If the chief problem for step-parents is a conflict of interest, the solution is to be more selfless. Up to a point. Contemporary suspicions of step-parents fixate on those who are too close to stepchildren as much as those too distant, with hair-raising statistics about the proba-bility that a stepfather will also be an abuser. The reverse is also possible.

Mario Vargas Llosa's fable, *In Praise of the Stepmother,* portrays a woman undone by the erotic attentions of her stepson, which is something of an old story. Æthelbald, son of Ethelwulf of Wessex, born 834, became king after making his father abdicate and mar-rying his stepmother Judith (the match was later annulled). The thirteenth-century infante don

Enrique de Castilla y León, fourth son of King
Fernando of Castile, launched a botched rebellion to
his brother's rule, then found refuge in Ponthieu in
the arms of his stepmother Jeanne de Dammartin, the
Dowager Queen. A liaison with less global but no less
torrid effects began when French novelist Colette, 47,
seduced her sixteen-year-old stepson after a friend
whom she had appointed to relieve the boy of his vir-
ginity failed in the task — but her motives were partly
vengeful, since the boy's father Henry was perennially
unfaithful. The affair lasted five years, ending not
long after Colette and Henry divorced. Such behaviour may sound grotesque, but boundaries between
non-blood relations are always fragile, and debatable.
British law took years to rule that a woman who wed her
dead sister's husband — a spinster aunt being the most
obvious mother substitute — was innocent of incest.

If the first rule of being a good step-parent is not to
fall in love, or hate, with your stepchildren, the second
is to find out what your role will be. This is more complicated than in the past, when most step-parents
'stepped' in to a ready-made parental part. Twenty-
first century step-parents are less often replacement
parents than bystanders, with no legal rights to their
stepchildren (unless they adopt), no defined duties,
and with another parent hovering, involved in major
decisions that do much to shape the course of the step-
parents' life. Far from starting with a clean slate, the

poor step-parent enters married life as a bit player in another family's story — one that already has an unhappy ending, for the stepchildren if no one else, and one which continues to be written. A top divorce lawyer whispers of numerous cases in court due to 'intervening stepchildren', who drive proceedings, determined that their geriatric dad should not leave the inheritance to a loathed stepmother.

There is much talk of 'blended families', but unless you fall into a food processer, there are bound to be lumps. Families don't blend, they graft people together. The following guidelines can help.

1. **Don't underestimate your influence.**

   How you relate to your stepchildren can make them easier to live with.A study of step-parent-stepchild relationships in 60 families with a 9- to 12-year-old stepchild found that positive relationships were associated with lower aggression and inhibition in all children, and higher self-esteem for girls.

2. **Don't play rivals.**

   A stepmother complained of her trying teenage stepdaughter, 'She only has to cry and he drops everything.' Ask yourself: if she was your daughters, wouldn't you?

3. **Reduce expectations.**

   Why should they like you, or listen to you? You

are not their mother or father, and they may yet hope for a reconciliation between their parents. Any hint that you are attempting to fill these shoes is an excuse for them to reject you. You need to earn authority in their eyes, just as you must gain each other's trust and affection. So leave the rod and staff to your spouse, until you know each other — but do not neglect to discuss the rules with your spouse, in private, to ensure that your voice is heard. If you and the ex have radically different routines, schedules, or ideas about good behaviour, it is unfair to impose your regime and expect the children to understand. Inevitably, a child inhabiting two households will also discover that manners and routines are subjective, not immutable laws. Adjusting to two ways of being a child is difficult — and the temptation to play parents off against each other hard to resist. Can you blame them?

If you are the dull weekday parent, there to ensure that they go to school, do their homework, sadly you cannot compete with the glamorous weekend parent who takes them to the zoo. Don't try to, and do not be too hard on yourself if you screw up, especially if you have no children of your own. Nobody becomes a loving, capable parent overnight; they learn in the bootcamp of baby rearing. But you could be honest with your stepchildren about your

shortcomings: let them help you to become the sort
of step-parent they can live with.

4. **Close your ears.**

   The ex may not set foot in your house, but his or
   her voice will be heard through your stepchildren. Are they to blame if they listen to their
   parent? Still, differences of opinion between
   you, your spouse and the ex should not be fought
   through the children.

5. **Remind your spouse that they are not your
   children.**

   'Any weekend with kids is hard work, but when
   his are staying with us, I'm giving myself double
   points for being good. But because they are his
   kids, he forgets how much harder it is for me,
   and doesn't make allowances,' complains one
   stepmother. So tell him.

6. **Watch yourself.**

   Children are witnesses. You cannot be fully
   yourself in front of them, so don't expect to be.

7. **Find a connection.**

   You have walked into another family's history. To
   stitch yourself into it, create rituals and find time
   to have fun with your stepchildren without their
   birth parent vying for attention. Once they accept
   that you are part of their lives, and have an idea
   of what you are good for, you may find that they
   start to do wonderful things for you too.

9

FOR LOVE OR MONEY

TURNING THE WHEELS OF WEDLOCK

My grandmother told me that it was rude to talk about money. But if money cannot buy love, sadly, no marriage can do without it, as this anxious father made clear to his daughter's suitor: 'Before your relations with Laura are definitely settled, I must be completely clear about your economic circumstances. You know that I have sacrificed my whole future to the revolutionary struggle. I do not regret it. Quite the contrary. If I had to start my life again, I would do the same. But I would not marry.' The author of this gold-digging letter was Karl Marx. If his desire for a well-off son-in-law appears at odds with his social principles, Marx appreciated better than most how capital can warp relationships.

Marriage is the best welfare plan that money cannot buy. Its economies of scale make us richer in the long run (as noted earlier, spinsters were 86 per cent poorer, and bachelors 61 per cent poorer than the married or widowed, in 1992's US Health and Retirement Study). But the uncomfortable truth remains that the richer we are, the longer we wait to get hitched, if at all. To those with deep pockets, wedlock looks less like a safe haven than a padlock. Does this mean we are more mercenary than we like to think, marrying less for love than creature comforts?

Perhaps. But there are other reasons why wealth might make us altar-shy. For a start, fear of loss. ('Ah yes, divorce,' said Robin Williams, 'from the Latin word meaning to rip out a man's genitals through his wallet.') Love also operates in a marketplace, so the greater a person's options, the choosier they will be. Maybe the rich also find it harder to fall in love, if they are too busy or their social status affords them few doses of human kindness if they move in a world where people carry their bags less to help out than in hope of receiving a tip. Certainly, if wealth makes the rich more self- or work-obsessed, and suspicious of others' motives in being nice to them, it may also be the case that the rich are less lovable too. One thing is certain. As film star Harrison Ford said, money does not solve problems, it creates new ones.

These are problems I could live with. But is it not odd that in an era of supposed financial equality, many couples are as coy as my grandmother, unwilling to discuss money, aside from the horrifying cost of weddings? They do so at their peril. Because work and money are more than occupations and preoccupations, they change our view of ourselves. When we marry, our view of work and money changes too. So the better we understand the strange ways in which work and money warp the human heart, the likelier that they will alter a marriage for the better.

GOLDDIGGERS

Marry for money, and you will pay for it. On the other hand, as an acquaintance was advised by her cynical aunt after a proposal from a rich suitor, if the marriage did not work out, at least the cash would 'butter the staircase down'.

An American bride caused scandal in the nineteenth century when the moment came in her wedding to vow to obey her husband. 'I will,' she said, 'if he does what he says he will do, financially.' But she was only pointing out that marriage is a covenant, and that few contracts are valid unless money changes hands.

Money has long helped both sexes to stick their courage to the conjugal sticking post. In 1639 moderately wealthy twenty-two-year-old Christopher Guise of Gloucester was unwilling to wed, 'having observed some young married couples to live in a very narrow compass'. By 1642 Guise decided that life might improve with a spouse after all – and with the handsome settlement that his father promised him if he wed – and promptly fell for an heiress: 'I was at last content to make all sure,' he wrote solemnly, 'at the loss of my loved liberty.' Seven weeks later he hit the jackpot when she died, leaving him everything.

Wealth can sweeten the bitterest pill, as Jane Austen implied in *Pride and Prejudice*, the most popular romantic novel in the English language.

'Will you tell me how long you have loved him?' asked Jane Bennet.

'It has been coming on so gradually, that I hardly know when it began,' replied Elizabeth. 'But I believe I must date it from my first seeing his beautiful grounds at Pemberley.'

Many a woman has converted her sexual currency into gold to improve her marital prospects. One young Neapolitan beauty was so eager to marry that she traded her virtue with the lothario Casanova, for which he paid two hundred scudi towards her dowry. Likewise, wives have long used their romantic wiles to seduce husbands into overlooking their extravagances. Eighteenth-century aristocrat Emily Fitzgerald, writes her biographer Stella Tillyard, manipulated her Irish husband, the Earl of Kildare by playing on his lust whenever her purse was empty, diverting his irritation into desire.

Money still changes hands in marriage. When Marie-Chantal Miller married the exiled heir to the Greek throne in 1995, her father, who made billions in duty-free retail, is rumoured to have handed over a $200 million dowry. And weddings have ever been fund-raising galas, from the pennies that grease the palm of whoever joins the bride and groom's hands at the ceremony, to the caterers at the reception afterwards, to the cornucopia of gifts to set up the bride and groom. In July 1166 Eleanor of Aquitaine's eleven-year-old, Lady Matilda, was escorted from England to her intended, Henry of Saxony, thirty-five, like a well-heeled hostage, her ransom, a £4,500 trousseau, worth a quarter of England's annual revenue. A more affordable tradition in Yorkshire was to precede the wedding with a 'bidding' or 'brideswain' in which the bride-to-be sat spinning in a cart that was pulled around the village. Neighbours tossed coins or loaded furniture and utensils into the cart.

Now at a traditional Greek wedding party, the happy couple dances while guests pin money to the bride's dress, but in most instances, the fund-raising aspect of nuptials is veiled. However, some take a sneaky approach to maximize their profits. In *The Liar* it is claimed that Conservative politician Jonathan Aitken and his first wife, Lolicia, set up a wedding list with a little-known silverware company,

hundreds of miles from their London home. Guests
were advised to call party planner Valerie Scott. If
they asked what was on the list for around £40,
Valerie was instructed to reply, 'Unfortunately
nothing at that price, but there is a beautiful tureen
at £50' – then ask for a cheque payable to the Aitken
wedding account, bank it and hand the Aitkens the
cash. Valerie saw very few of the presents.

1. WHY MONEY IS THE HARDEST WORD

Money and marriage have a long, treacherous history, one
that has done much to give marriage a bad name. Primarily
because in most cultures, for most of the centuries that marriage has existed, the prequel to a wedding was the negotiation
of a settlement in the preferred local currency, be it cash,
land or camels – either dowries (to lure grooms) or bride-
wealth (to bribe brides' fathers). Consequently, lovers who
could not meet their market rate were stranded. As Maria
Bicknell wrote to her impecunious suitor, the painter John
Constable: 'My Dear Sir, His [my father's] only objection
would be on the score of that necessary article Cash.' The
couple waited another seven years to marry.

   Dowries and bride-wealth payments seem about as romantic as today's divorce-anticipating prenuptial contracts. In
part they were designed to stop paupers from snaring posh
spouses, and they reek of child-selling too. 'We do not

marry,' lamented the heroine of the nineteenth-centrury Russian novel *Oblomov*, 'but we are given in marriage.' Some deals were blatantly commercial. In Cameroon's Bamileke tribe, a credit system, *nkap*, let poor grooms marry without down payment. In return, fathers-in-law were entitled to arrange the marriage of any grandchildren that resulted, bringing them extra social influence as well as bride-wealth too. And from the eleventh to the early twentieth centuries, poorer Britons could employ a cheap alternative to divorce, wife-selling. Eighteenth-century German traveller Johann von Archenholtz steamed up his pince-nez describing how, if 'a husband and wife find themselves heartily tired of each other' and 'the man has a mind to authenticate the intended separation by making it a matter of public notoriety . . . he puts a halter about her neck, and thereby leads her to the next market place and there puts her up to auction to be sold to the best bidder . . . By delivering up the end of the halter, [he] makes a formal and absolute surrender of his wife.' Wife auctions were rarely blind. 'The purchaser, always widower or youth,' wrote another observer, 'is ordinarily a connois-seur of the merchandise sold.' However, by selling his wife, a cuckold could regain some social standing, and another man, a bargain. According to the history of the King's Own Regiment, before leaving Hythe for Canterbury, Kent, in March 1805, the drummer went to market and for sixpence bought a labourer's wife of not more than twenty years of age and 'of a likely figure'.

While no money talk sounds romantic, the financial

concerns that dowries were designed to assuage were far from sinister, but practical. In an age before the welfare state, cash was indeed a necessary article, and to spell out how you would provide for your spouse a testament of your devotion, as well as an opportunity to think through your future together before taking an irrevocable step. This moment of reflection was helpful and so it would be for couples today.

Marriage settlements had the added benefit of sparing couples from negotiating their own financial affairs. Indeed, bossy fathers like Karl Marx demanded that grooms show them the money before handing over their daughters because women relied on men for their living, so once they were wed, husbands controlled the purse-strings. Although couples were often business partners and working-class women certainly worked, in England, legally a wife's goods were her husband's, not her own, and with earning power went the spending power. Even the home of Victorian domestic goddess Mrs Beeton was picked and furnished by Mr B., according to the custom of their day. In 1882 the Married Women's Property Act rebalanced British law, but around the world the legacy of skewed financial arrangements lingered in skewed social attitudes, with many consequences for marriage.

First, wives were thought financially irresponsible. 'When I bought my first car in the 1950s I had to have the credit agreement countersigned by my father and husband,' revealed Australian psychologist Dorothy Rowe – two men who had not a clue how to handle money. Women's earnings were also considered less important than men's, with female-friendly professions, like nursing and teaching, demanding that female employees resign on marriage. Nobel-winning scientist Maria Goeppert Mayer battled to teach at her husband's university, Columbia, after fleeing Nazi Germany, and was told she was lucky to put in a 40-hour week, unpaid. Only in 1973 did the British Foreign Office cease to demand that married women quit.

For girl power, most wives had to fall back on their powers of persuasion. Eric Hatch's *Spousery* (1956) promised to decipher 'the genus known as *Spousus Polaris* or, as the species is more familiarly known, The North American Fur-Bearing Spouse. In other words, the girl who likes the good things of life and generally gets them — by the simple expedient of prodding, steering, guiding, helping, restraining, et cetera, either the man of her choice, or . . . whichever she was able to hook'.

It sounds rather undignified. But people were sufficiently unselfconscious about this unhinged state of financial affairs that otherwise nice men, like my grandfather, could honestly think it no insult to sell what he regarded as 'his' family home and buy another, 100 miles away, without informing, let alone consulting his wife. Granny only rumbled him when she mistook an estate agent and buyer in her kitchen for unusually well-dressed burglars. No wonder that her generation preferred not to discuss the vulgar topic of money. Give it any thought and it would have been enough to keep a person single. (One reason among many why, historically, the better educated a woman, the lower her probability of sliding down the centre aisle and into this sticky situation.)

Now that careers are nigh a religion, and men and women have more work in common, and arguably more cash to splash, it might appear that financial arrangements in marriage should be freer than ever. Surely the taboo on discussing money would be over, given that couples marry later, when they are more financially responsible, and have more complex affairs to discuss.

But this is to forget that more choices mean more options to quarrel over. Hence a 2006 survey found that three-quarters of couples agree with my grandmother, that money is the hardest word to raise with a spouse. In a 2007 YouGov poll of twenty issues that couples argue about, money came top with a mighty 40 per cent ('partner's insensitivity' came second at 25 per cent).

So what exactly is our problem?

2.   HOW WE ARE ALL OLD-FASHIONED ABOUT WORK AND MONEY

There are two types of work in a marriage: the paid stuff that pays for your life, and the unpaid stuff that holds your life together. But there are further distinctions between these two types of work that have had far-reaching effects on how couples operate.

As we have seen, money is magic. Its alchemy not only transmutes each salaried hour of labour into anything else that money can buy, but also transforms our emotions. Nobel-winning economist Amartya Sen observed that countries where women had recently joined the workforce had seen an accompanying shift in cultural attitudes, bringing women greater social status. Not because paid work is worthier than caring for children or tending a home, but because societies value people by their spending power. Since we give extra credit to the rich, money's possessors also accrue unearned extra doses of self-esteem, as anyone who met an investment banker prior to 2008 may know. So the spouse who earns the most has advantages over their less-remunerated partner, regardless of who puts most hours of work, paid or unpaid, into the marriage. The advantages that money brings have made work a more attractive prospect to many wives than staying at home − supposing that they had a choice in the matter.

So forget wandering eyes: your greatest love rival begins with the letter C and rhymes with arrears. It is that strange vampire, a career. And if one is bad, two can murder a marriage.

Tragedies used to disdain ambition as folly (check out Macbeth and his lady's work-life balance), yet success-chasing has long been applauded. In 1887 Welsh politician Lloyd George warned his fiancée, Margaret Owen: 'My supreme idea is to get on. To this idea, I shall sacrifice everything − except, I trust, honesty. I am prepared to thrust even love itself under the wheels of my Juggernaut if it obstructs the way.' Did she give him the heave-ho? No. She was impressed, and in time he became British Prime Minister, yet felt it no shame to rely on women – any women – to button his shirt, tie his laces and warm his bed.

In today's buyer's labour market, ambition is less an option than a necessity, and yields one product in abundance: workaholics. Workaholism is a disease. It yields misery, sleep deprivation and broken marriages, not to mention dwindling returns for employers. The Human Rights Commission should produce a report on the poor business sense, inhumanity and cost of antidepressants of a work-fixated culture, and the wisdom of compelling parents to work full-time. (Unlike in Sweden where the government promotes the ideal of one and a half jobs between two and, in recognition of the fact that parenthood often costs mothers more than fathers, also offers a total parental allowance of 480 days' paid leave when a child is born or adopted – measures that may explain why in Sweden, 79 per cent of women are gainfully employed, which is among the highest in the world).

The unkindest aspect of a society led by aspiration is that the choices that money is supposed to buy us often turn out to be fictional. Indeed, an irony of women's liberation into the workplace is that family life has grown less free as a result. Going to work is not, for most middle-class couples, a lifestyle choice but compulsory, since a direct consequence of rising wealth in two-earner households has been to drive up both prices and social aspirations. What our grandparents saw as luxuries today seem essential, and with increased competition for limited desirable resources, such as professional jobs, places at good schools, or houses with gardens, it takes two wages to afford what previous generations considered to be an average middle-class lifestyle, paid for by one working husband. Therefore our chance of giving our children the sort of opportunities that our parents gave us seems remote (unless we work in finance). We run faster, but still we slip behind. What is worse, the more we earn, the less time we have to spend on marriage and family, though they may well be our avowed motive for all this work.

The status-chasing game is a zero sum, because gains are cancelled out by equal losses. There is a yet greater cost to marriage, if our growing investment in our careers increases our expectations of each other, in direct proportion to our declining investment in each other. If we toil so hard that we rarely meet, then instead of a better life we gain dividends in disappointment and a family life conducted by e-mail. Especially if we come to feel that we would rather stay at home with our children but cannot afford it, then blame our spouse for not earning enough. Should we both flog our guts out, and so both feel that when we come home we are entitled to sit back and soak up a little extra love from our equally overwrought spouse, the consequences can be catastrophic.

In a world plagued by affluence, exalted expectations

make less sense, yet seem all too common. A study followed 1,704 couples over two decades and concluded that the richer you are, the likelier it is that you will divorce. Earning the same as your spouse is worse. Couples at greatest risk of splitting have low to average levels of marital contentment, with wives earning 50 to 60 per cent of the family income. It is possible that such couples give up because they have little to lose, financially, from calling it quits, but more probable that they buckled under other strains. Because when it comes to winning our daily bread, social attitudes are out of step with our economic situation. At heart, most nourish expectations that are far more traditional than our present lifestyles will allow.

A survey of twenty-one countries compared assumptions about whether husbands were the chief family breadwinner with the reality of how money was earned. In all cases, men and women overestimated husbands' contributions to the family purse, the gulf between belief and reality being greatest in Italy.

Sadly, there is plentiful evidence that men feel emasculated if they earn less than their wives, or do women's work. Wives who out-earn traditionally minded husbands are at greater risk of domestic violence. And any husbands reluctant to pick up a dustpan and brush may be right to feel that their unpaid domestic work boosts their wife. A 2008 study found that every hour of a husband's housework per week added $56 to his wife's annual salary.

As explained elsewhere, the everyday outcome of mixed

financial fortunes in families is often that whichever half of the couple does most paid work sees their salaried hours as worth more than their spouse's unpaid domestic hours. Many a husband who does nothing at home protests to his also working wife, 'But I pay the rent.' And their spouse will be the more upset by this attitude if they, too, underrate their own family efforts as low-status drudgery. Numerous wives who work also create a rod for their own backs because they are reluctant to relinquish their status as domestic overseer. In consequence, they denigrate their husbands' domestic efforts.

'However hard Ross works around the house – cleaning windows, hoovering floors – he can never reach my impossibly high standards,' said one wife of her stay-home husband. Of course her standards were impossible: in her mind, the only person fit to do these jobs was herself. To compound their misery, her husband also felt he 'ought to be the one making the money and treating me', so refused to spend money, 'because he doesn't feel it is "his" money, it's mine'.

Why could this couple not adapt their emotions to fit their financial situation? Because work and money are about power and pride, and our feelings about them shift with our priorities. Today, as much as in Mrs Beeton's day, men and women have very different working priorities. When we marry, it is as if we step into a time machine, and walk out with the family values of another age, since if you scratch the surface of the most modern and enlightened couple, you may find that both wife and husband expect him to provide.

To illustrate the point, in 2005 709 young adults were asked what they valued most in work – its intrinsic rewards (interest, challenges, responsibilities) or its extrinsic rewards (pay, job security, prestige). The singletons valued intrinsic rewards most. But young husbands were far more motivated by money and power than their wives. If couples were also parents their feelings about work were further polarized. While cash became a greater priority for fathers, reflecting their sense of duty to provide, married mothers did not care more about their salary. By contrast, single mothers suddenly cared a lot more, because, rightly, they saw themselves as breadwinners.

Can marriage sustain two bloodsucking careers? Many of the most liberated, privileged working wives decide that the answer is no. A 2006 American investigation into the 'hidden brain drain' of female talent from business found that one in three women with MBAs opted to work part-time, as opposed to one in twenty men with the same qualification. Thirty-eight per cent of these women had rejected a promotion or intentionally taken a position with lower pay. To only 15 per cent was 'power' a top priority in a job; the rest put intrinsic rewards first. They wanted flexible hours, to 'be themselves' or to work with people they admired. If there was a glass ceiling, then, it was in their minds.

We should not be surprised, therefore, that if work and domestic priorities clash, couples usually respond differently. A wife is likelier to decrease her hours at work, and likelier than her husband to alter her work patterns to fit her spouse's or take on a greater share of the domestic burden if he is putting in longer hours, or simply earning more than her. Not only will she mop up the extra, but generally she will not mind doing so – unless she is forced to change her working patterns by upping her office hours. Unlike husbands, who will countenance reducing their working hours only if the conflict originates at work. Even then, when men face frequent work-home conflict, most attempt to solve the problem by increasing their work hours. In only one situation do men feel entitled to reduce their time at work: when they are being paid more.

Under pressure, it seems that women regard the home as their refuge and first responsibility, whereas men, given the choice, incline to see providing as their main job, and their refuge. In other words, work and money mean very different things to men and women, in different phases of life.

This divergent outlook is not inscribed in our DNA; it does not come to us naturally so much as culturally. If we grew up with a stay-at-home mother, then, if push comes to shove, more likely than not we will feel that a mother's place is at home, as that is how it was for us. But ask someone raised in Eastern Europe, where mothers worked, and the answer will be different. (A cultural bias which is echoed in the finding that couples surveyed in Russia, the Czech Republic and Estonia are more likely than those in the US to report that husbands did at least half the housework.) Ask a child of a working mother if he believes that mothers should stay at home and he will say no, studies find – so long as his mother has been positive about going out to work, and not let stress or distress colour her child's perceptions of her choices.

To make matters more fraught, many of us entertain conflicting ideals too. Lucky me, I love work. For now, it loves me back. So I long to earn from writing until the day I die – an occupation that demands silence and uninterrupted solitude – but would also yearn to be footsteps away from my child, because that is where my mother was for me.

For all of us today, the commonest desires of work often seem to be ill-sorted with reality. We talk of careers in a merciless job market where long hours are praised as commitment, yet employees' loyalty is rarely rewarded by job security. We are like Russian dolls, possessed of many dreams, many long past their use-by date, dreams that do not fit neatly inside each other. The worst way to respond to these pressures is to hold responsible the person with whom we share our life if our impossible ideals cannot be met.

GREAT DOUBLE ACTS?

An alternative to work-home rivalry is to make home into work, together, and say hello to a whole new world of woe.

When Ernest Hemingway fell out of love with his

wife, war reporter Martha Gellhorn, he went out of his
way to destroy her livelihood too. He stole her job at
Collier's magazine, and with it, her front-line reporting
accreditation, gaining himself a plum view of the
D-Day landings in an attack transport off the Normandy
coast. When Gellhorn heard of the landings, she
smuggled herself on to a hospital ship, hid in a lavatory, travelling through mined waters under heavy
shellfire, to slip ashore with the stretcher-bearers,
becoming the first American journalist to land on
European soil. Enraged, Hemingway insisted that her
scoop was buried at the back of *Collier's* and until his
dying day, claimed that she had made the story up.

Sometimes conjugal co-work leads to an identity
merger. Magnum photographer Robert Capa was
the fictional invention of Gerda Pohorylle and
André Friedmann, a couple who figured their pic-
tures would command higher prices under an
American name. Only later did Friedmann assume
the moniker Capa, while his wife became Gerda
Taro. But Taro, unlike Capa, is forgotten.

Mrs Vladimir Nabokov's biographer described
'the ultimate portmanteau couple': 'Most people
never saw him without her. Not only were they
inseparable but their sentences fused, on the page
and in person.' Vera's role in Vladimir's prodigious
literary output was both supporting (she learned
Italian in eighteen months, to vet the translation of

Lolita) and creative. Nabokov explained: 'She sits down at her typewriter and I, I dictate, I dictate off the cards to her, making some changes and very often, very often, discussing this or that. She might say, "Oh, you can't say that, you can't say that." "Well, let's see, perhaps I can change it."'

For most couples, the roles of spouse and colleague jar. Actress Helen Mirren recalled: 'It was lovely to go home at night and be with my husband [director Taylor Hackford. But] . . . my husband in work mode is not the easiest . . . I would get upset if he was shouting – not at me, but at someone else . . . I would find myself rushing around trying to mop after him.'

To F. Scott Fitzgerald, wife Zelda was more than a muse. He sent her a draft of *This Side of Paradise*, commenting that 'the heroine does resemble you in more ways than four'. Unsurprisingly, as the book cited her letters, diaries and conversation word for word. Fitzgerald also truffled through his wife's journal for his later work. 'Mr Fitzgerald,' said Zelda, 'seems to believe that plagiarism begins at home.' But she was inspired to write her own semi-autobiographical work, *Save Me the Waltz* (1932). Her husband gave this measured response in a marriage guidance session: she was 'a third-rate writer and a third-rate ballet-dancer' who had stolen his 'material' (he was referring to scenes Zelda had based on her time in an asylum).

'Is that your material?' she replied.

'Everything we have done is mine.'

Even couples who successfully combine work and marriage can find their relationship is the price they pay for success. 'I was really happy in the early days of starting the business, no matter how hard,' said Chinese paper magnate Zhang Yin. She and her husband 'worked hard together', but he had time to cook for her. The last time he did so was 1991. By 2006 she was China's richest person, yet the greatest luxury she could imagine was to find her husband is 'on the same flight'.

If a spouse is a colleague, or work begins at home, it is vital to know when to knock off. 'We have a rule,' said Tom Chapman, co-owner of Matches fashion boutiques with his wife Ruth. 'We don't talk shop after 8 p.m., otherwise I'll be up all night worrying.' Otherwise, what made Ruth an exceptional colleague – the fact that 'notices everything, every little detail' – became hell in her as his wife.

3. HOW TO STRAIN THE PAINS OF WORK AND MONEY

Since work and money are management issues, coloured by our individual desires and insecurities, there is no one-size-fits-all answer to the stress they impose on marriage. But some tactics always cause trouble.

The Russian count and novelist, Leo Tolstoy, ever
insightful in his masterwork of wedded woe, *Anna Karenina*,
squandered decades on warring with his wife over money,
which, as only a millionaire can, he considered a meaningless hindrance to true happiness. In 1895, aged sixty-seven,
he finally renounced his property, but was prevailed on to
sign his estate over to the countess. A flavour of their
marriage is given in this 1881 letter:

> My heart's love; do not be angry, but I can attach no
> importance to these monetary affairs. Surely they
> are not important events, as for instance, sickness,
> marriage, birth, death, acquired knowledge, good
> or bad actions, pleasant or unpleasant habits of
> those dear and near to us, but they are our forms,
> arrangements, which we have arranged thus, but
> could have arranged in a thousand different ways. I
> know that what I am here saying is often unbelievably
> tiresome to you and to the children (I believe that
> this is sufficiently well known), but I must always
> repeat, that all our happiness or unhappiness does
> not depend one's hair's breadth, whether we make
> money or spend it, but only on what we are our-
> selves.
>
> Let [our son] Kostja inherit a million – will he
> become thereby happier? . . . Languages, diplo-
> mas, the world, but in particular, money, have had
> no part in our happiness and unhappiness.

Therefore the question as to how much we spend cannot interest me; if one attaches particular importance to it, it pushes the chief thing out of sight.

If money had no part in their misery, why did he write the letter?

Sadly, those who are not millionaires must sell some hours they might rather spend with their family. There is little point railing against this. But preparation is possible. Here are six common scenarios in which ill-considered assumptions about work and money can whittle away marriage, and some tactics to avoid them.

1. My Paid Hour of Work is Worth More Than Your Unpaid Hour

Often a spouse sees their hours of paid work as a form of domestic labour, and at home contributes nothing. It is worse if both halves of a couple work hard, expect extra support from their equally depleted spouse, and feel entitled to put their feet up while the other irons, cooks, spoons food and homework into little mouths and minds . . .

The remedy is to count each other's hours of marital work, paid and unpaid, and rectify the balance.

2.   I am Your Benefactor

Some earners enjoy controlling their spouses via their
purse-strings. Long have wives lamented their husbands'
penny-pinching. In the early fifteenth century, young
Norfolk bride Margaret Paston wrote to her husband in a
panicky stream of consciousness: 'I suppose I must borrow
money in short time, but if you come soon, So God help me,
I have but four shillings, and I owe near as much money.'
Thus a spouse who works, unpaid, in the home while their
other half goes to work and earns hard cash may feel obliged
to wheedle and whine for non-domestic luxuries, like my
friend, who in order to acquire extra funds to buy a pair of
boots, found herself employing tactics identical to those she
once used 'to winkle pocket money out of Dad'.

The solution is to be generous, and approach a union as
one of financial equals.

3.   Your Love of Work Means that You Don't Love Me

'My jailer is named Arthur Miller. Every morning he goes
into that goddamn study of his . . . I mean, what the f*** is
he doing there?' asked Marilyn Monroe, suffering momen-
tary amnesia about her husband's writing career.

When a spouse's commitment to work stirs marital
trouble, and that spouse responds by spending more time
at work, the suspicion that they are having an affair, if only

with their spreadsheets, will grow. Even if that spouse is working harder out of a misguided sense that this will magically heal their marriage.

The solution is to appreciate the value that your spouse vests in work. If they take pride in what is for you a means to an end, your priorities are not irreconcilable; rather, one of you can get off from doing so much dull work. What coupling could be more complementary?

Since work priorities change as we age, at some point most couples have clashing feelings about work and money. But if they cannot reconcile their views, they can respect them, like the future Mrs Darwin, who was sanguine at the prospect of a family life subjugated to her fiancé Charles's scientific study: 'I believe from your account of your own mind that you will only consider me as a specimen of the genus (I don't know which, simian I believe). You will be forming theories about me and if I am cross or out of temper you will only consider "What does that prove". Which will be a very grand and philosophical way of considering it.' At that time, Emma could not guess that Darwin's life's work would worm away at the foundations of her cherished Christian faith, but to her credit she continued to support him nonetheless.

Spouses who celebrate our achievements outside marriage can be forgiven many shortcomings. When homosexual economist John Maynard Keynes married a Russian ballerina, Lydia Lopokova, his friends, Bloomsbury's literary snobs, were baffled. Lydia had roamed London with a shopping basket on her head, and attended Glyndebourne Opera Festival in her dressing gown. Yet how could he resist? 'When I read what you write,' Lydia confided, 'somehow I feel bigger than I am.'

4.   Money Causes Arguments so Let's Not Talk about It

Ignore money worries and resentment festers, fuelling arguments. It is tempting to duck the subject, however, because so many emotions are wrapped around money. If a couple has wildly different attitudes to spending, their differences will seem more alarming, still since our attitudes to money reflect our attitudes to planning and risk – characteristics that have the greatest influence on the management challenge that is marriage.

Anthropologist Helen Fisher's study of personality types found that planners and risk-takers make particularly incompatible couples; unsurprisingly, they struggle to plot a mutually pleasing course through life. By extension, to savers, a lavish spouse can seem lacking in commitment, when their liberality may stem from no worse than naivety.

Ideally, couples need to find a method for managing finances that both can stomach, and one that builds their confidence in each other. Analysis requires a cool head. One approach is to ringfence time, say ten minutes a week, when money and work can be discussed without prejudice or distracting children at the table, before you are arguing over a red bill notice. Try the Just-in-time Worrying System. It is simple to use: write down any concern that arises during the week, add it to the agenda, then forget it. Admittedly, in emergencies an occasional extraordinary meeting may be needed. But set aside anxiety until a moment when you can actually do something to resolve it, like make a decision, and you should feel calmer.

5. What is Yours is Not Mine

Some couples imagine that if they keep their finances separate, money cannot drive them apart. This is illogical.

If trust is the fundamental quality that keeps us believing in our marriage, it seems unwise to introduce mistrust. But fears of divorce, and being taken to the cleaners via the courthouse, lead many not to pool their assets. Divorcees report learning that not only has their spouse squirrelled away assets, but also lied throughout the marriage about their salary and bonuses. In this climate, well-intentioned friends advise newlyweds, 'Keep your money private – then you have some leverage.'

Can marriage be a shared experience if there are two financial worlds within it? Whoever has less will feel, relatively, that they are living in hardship. Split domestic expenses 50-50 and extra, tedious discussion about minor expenditure becomes necessary – creating conflict. If, as is usually the case, a couple's wages are not 50-50 but one spouse out-earns the other, they can end up leading semi-detached lifestyles — creating jealousy. Novelist Ann Hood watched her husband spend thousands on solo mountain-climbing expeditions while she took out loans to pay her half of bills: 'These quiet resentments, this push and pull of money — how to get it, how to spend it, how to share it — grew more tense over time.' Finally, she had a windfall but did not call her husband; she rang Mother.

A proprietorial attitude to spending also has the unfortunate consequence of commodifying exchanges between a couple, leading to transactional thinking, such as, I bought the takeaway; you owe me a night out. This robs a relationship of the spontaneity and gratitude that makes love live. Which is why, if pooling incomes is unconscionable to you, being open about finances, and your feelings about them, is essential.

6. You Always Bring Work Home

It is difficult to prevent the flow of work stress into other parts of life. However, studies find that it impinges on marriage only if couples permit it to put them in a bad mood, and then let the bad mood linger. Ironically, it is closer couples who are most dogged by work stress at home. So when work gets you down, it may be best to keep your distance from your spouse until you cool off.

*

The price and value of work and money to a marriage are not fixed. If budgeting makes sense, there are other measures couples can take to shield their marriage from the attrition of forced labour, if they look for ways to maximize their happiness.

Where do you place greatest emphasis, seek most fulfilment? It is possible that you are looking in the wrong direction. A fascinating paper discovered that couples who took lessons that they had learned at home and applied these lessons at work, fared better than couples who were inclined to bring their working methods to bear at home. In other words, trying to tame a tricky boss in the same way as you do your demanding wife will make you happier than approaching your wife as if she were a tricky employee, or your baby as a project. This same paper also found that couples who feel that what they do at work makes them 'more interesting' at home, or who imagine that work helps them to deal with family problems, have higher odds of problem drinking. I imagine their poor, bored spouses do too.

Prioritizing your private life enriches in a way that impersonal work transactions cannot. While work and money have a financial bottom line, if love is our bottom line, we prosper. Put our needs first, create our own set of values, and we can train ourselves to want less: not to gaze at those overpriced goods, not to window-shop others' lifestyles, not to live life from the outside in.

No marriage need fall hostage to a job. Slavica, ex-wife

of Formula One supremo Bernie Ecclestone, sloped off when finally she accepted that the seventy-eight-year-old would never renounce his first love, business. Asked if he would retire, he replied, 'Never, never, never,' adopting a similar approach to holidays. 'The first day I won't be going into work, is the day they will be lowering me into my grave.' This was Ecclestone's choice. Of course, there is only so much that anyone can do to control our financial choices. All things are unequal, in work, as life, so unpalatable decisions must be faced. To sweeten them, we must value each other's sacrifices, and accept that we will be wrong, some of the time.

'I've spent a huge chunk of our marriage trying to convince him to do something more sensible to change the world, like be a head teacher or write books,' said Michelle Obama of her husband.

It is not clear if she was joking. But be fair: she had a point, didn't she?

10

A GOOD ARGUMENT

WHY HUSBANDS SHOULD ROW

One night, after drinking heavily at a party thrown at his New York home to launch his campaign to become the city's mayor, American novelist Norman Mailer stabbed his second wife, Adele, in the chest with a pen-knife, narrowly missing her heart. He commemorated the act with a poem, 'Rainy Afternoon with the Wife'. The chorus states:

> So long
>> as
>> you
>> use
>> a knife,

there's

some
love
left.

Not quite enough love. Almost five decades later, Mailer died in the tranquil company of wife six, Norris Church.

Whatever prompted Mailer's attack, it is an extreme example of a husband taking an indirect route to express his feelings. The least pacific of men like arguing with their wife. Research in cultures as disparate as Brazil, Italy, Taiwan and the US find that demand-withdraw communication (the posh term for nagging) damages couples, and more often than not it is a wife demanding and a husband withdrawing.

Numerous solutions have been deployed to avert marital disputes. Surely it was for the avoidance of debate that in Japan and China 'talks too much' was one of seven traditional reasons for which a man could divorce a wife. This ensured against the likes of Penelope Betjeman, the trying wife to the equally trying poet laureate, John. Her simple method for silencing her husband grew to be so much her catchphrase that for the first year of her employment, their German housekeeper thought that John's name was 'Shut up'.

Some couples recruit third parties to settle their differences. In ancient India, if the *Kama Sutra* can be trusted, special men were employed as intercessors, to pacify quarrelsome women: 'A Pithamardia . . . a man without wealth, alone in the world, who comes from a good country, and who is skilled in all the arts; and by teaching these arts is received in the company of citizens.' In Uganda's Bakiga tribe, marriage guidance was doled out by older clan members, whose judgements were binding. Not coincidentally, the Bakiga had high divorce rates.

In the Lutheran village courts of eighteenth-century Germany, husbands who felt let down by their wives — for failing to lead the horse that pulled their plough as the husband followed, or by spending time helping to farm the in-laws' land instead of their own — could prosecute them for dereliction of duty. Very many wives who were considered scolds found themselves treated to ridicule — to mock plays before the village, parodying the way they nagged their husbands, or to 'rough music', when young men banged drums and blew horns outside their homes. Society considered it everybody's business to keep unruly wives in line — with the aid of cruel implements such as scolds' bridles, painful metal headpieces that held women's tongues for them.

Be that as it may, avoiding arguments does a marriage no favours. Although couples row when their marriages are failing, research suggests that arguments are not symptoms of bad marriages; on the contrary, it is destructive arguments that bring couples down. Rowing well is the best remedy, since withdrawing is itself grounds for a row, as it looks like disrespect.

But destructive though it may be, the push-me-pull-you, nagging dynamic exerts a strong pull. Husbands are inclined to stonewall in arguments for three reasons.

First, marriage analysts believe that much nagging is about one spouse (usually her) seeking greater closeness, and the other (usually him) seeking greater independence. And while women are culturally conditioned to take the emotional temperature of relationships, men are conditioned to avoid displays.

Second, wives often have more to nag about than do husbands. In traditional set-ups, most of a man's marital contribution takes place away from home, at his paid employment. Therefore he has far fewer issues that he needs to raise with his wife. However, if the wife's marital contribution is largely domestic, and she is overloaded, then her actions will impinge on her husband directly, and she will want him to enter into her dilemmas, or better still, to help – which of course gives him a further incentive not to listen.

Third, in conflict situations, men under fire surge with stress hormones, and it takes them longer than women to cool off. Given how unpleasant the consequences of rage and violence can be it is little wonder if men do their best not to be riled, get drawn into an argument, and go off on one. Whereas women, who are more relaxed in arguments, have a natural advantage over men, and may underestimate the strength of men's rage, as well as how long men's anger can ferment in silence. So we do husbands a disservice to accuse them of being more emotionally distant than women. If husbands are significantly more vulnerable to mood swings than women, to ignore a prating wife may not bespeak indifference, but a genuine desire to keep the peace and protect a relationship rather than turn into the Incredible Hulk. After all, their wives would not like them when they are angry. That said, if women's cool wits give a tactical advantage in arguments, husbands may also duck out for fear that their wives will outwit them.

I sympathize. After all, if you want to win a point, an argument is a risky way to set about it. As the anonymous scribe of 1658's charm manual, *Mysteries of Love & Eloquence*, confided: 'without blushing . . . I have known a wench of 14 . . . put to the *non plus* a Gallant of thirty . . . I have heard such a Lass defeat a Gentleman of some years standing at the Inns of Court.'

1. THE VIRTUES OF TONGUE-LASHING

Sadly, husbands must argue, if only because silencing a spouse cannot guarantee their compliance. Charles Chabot's 1827 *Conjugal Grammar: General Principles Through Which Wives Can Be Trained to be at Your Beck and Call and Rendered as Gentle as Lambs* numbered among women's defects their 'love of liberty'. Yet even Chabot counselled against wife-beating: 'Once the quarrel has begun and the husband has used force to reduce his wife to silence, can he hope to live with her from then on in harmony? – No. Can he hope that she will remain faithful to him? – No. Can he hope that she will not betray him again? – NO.' Not to argue can signal that a marriage is crumbling. When actress Jane Fonda told her atheist entrepreneur husband Ted Turner that she was a born-again Christian, he was flummoxed: 'I had not an inkling. I thought this was surely something we would discuss because it's going to alter our entire lives together.'

It is the nature of marriage, and dialogue, to spur couples into opposing positions. Sometimes this gives rows exhilarating destructive momentum, or leads us to say things that we do not mean. There have been times I did not know my views on a subject until I found myself disagreeing with my husband — then wondered, guiltily, if I thought these things at all.

Every argument has one virtue: like a volcano, it releases pressure. Some rows are cathartic, others make fine foreplay. Many also uncover a point of conflict, clarifying feelings about issues, and communicating them unambiguously to a spouse. This service can be particularly useful to men. While wives tell researchers of their disappointment in marriage, husbands talk not of their own but of their wives' disappointment. This oblique, not to say obtuse, approach to expressing their emotions is even more disturbing when you learn that it is husbands' sorrows, not wives', that have the strongest influence on a marriage's success.

In 2000 the US National Survey of Families and Households found that aside from poverty and hardship, what increased a couple's odds of divorce was not the wife's but the husband's dissatisfactions, and whether he was attractive enough to have a romantic alternative. Yet if a husband was generally happily married, this could entirely compensate for his dissatisfaction in other areas, such as work. The ghastly conclusion that one is forced to reach is that our grandmothers were right to fuss over their men. Keeping a husband happy is central to the success of a marriage. For this to happen, however, husbands must somehow articulate their needs.

So if he picks a fight, you could say that, in his clumsy way, he is sending a powerful message that he cares and wants his marriage to improve. As a biographer said of poets Robert and Elizabeth Barrett Browning, 'one sign of the warmth of feeling' between them 'was the warmth of their disagreements', on everything from seances to her opium addiction to their adolescent son Pen's luscious shoulder-length ringlets. Elizabeth complained to her sister, 'Robert wants to make the child like a boy, he says (because he is a man).' After she died, Robert's first act was to lop off the boy's ringlets.

If a husband knows how to argue well, his marriage will improve. Marriage expert John Gottman concluded from his extensive studies of newlyweds that those who started their marriage refusing to tolerate 'negativity – those who insisted on gently confronting each other when, say, the other was contemptuous or defensive – wound up happy and satisfied years later'.

In marriage, many things are worth fighting for, and any row can deepen a relationship, if handled with care. Think of

Samuel Pepys, who on the night of 12 January 1669 'observed my wife mighty dull, and I myself was not mighty fond', after a contretemps earlier that day, provoked by her anger that he had been off on office business – or so Pepys thought. Instead of asking her what was wrong, he went to bed, drawing the curtains against the cold winter's night, and Elizabeth sat by the fire, glowering, as he begged her to join him. After two silent hours, suddenly she 'fell out into a fury', accusing him of cavorting with another woman. 'I did, as I might truly, deny it, and was mightily troubled, but all would not serve. At last, about one o'clock, she come to my side of the bed, and drew my curtaine open, and with the tongs red hot at the ends, made as if she did design to pinch me with them.' He jumped up in horror and forced her to beat a retreat. Then 'little and, little, very sillily, I let all the discourse fall' until he had heard Elizabeth out, then they 'lay well all night, and long in bed talking together, with much pleasure'.

2. HOW TO ROW WELL

In any bust-up, two matters are under dispute: first, your respect for one another's right to have a different point of view, and second, the headline issue that the row is officially about. Seek to win an argument and you are trying to impose your point of view, as much as to reach the right solution, thereby weakening your marriage. Since 69 per cent of marital rows are over insoluble differences, neither can win, so a domineering approach is also often doomed.

The safe goal is to dismount your high horse and seek a win-win solution. By this light, a good argument respects each side's point of view, does not escalate tension and reaches a conclusion that injures neither. To row productively, one must first diagnose what is at issue, then air your views without interrupting, then clarify and summarize each other's positions to ensure that points are understood. Then grope for a solution.

An argument may concern the subject under discussion, or stem from an underlying issue. In marriage, there is usually at least one further subtext. For instance, early in a relationship, we are not only getting to know each other, but working out if we can trust each other, so if we see our beloved flirt, or catch them telling a lie, a humungous row can blow up. If our reaction seems overblown, the extra emotion is not about the flirt or the little white lie, but the underlying fear that this person we adore may not after all be someone to trust with our life. This is why one in five arguments between newlyweds are more explosive than the issue triggering them would seem to merit. They are tugs-of-war in which the ground rules of the relationship are redrawn, or misunderstood. Often these are rules that both parties would struggle to state explicitly, but which immediately become apparent when one feels that a line has been crossed. If some arguments are purposeful, to do with solving problems, others are excuses to vent;

emotional workouts similar to how cats sharpen their claws on chair legs. The unfortunate husband (or metaphorical chair leg) simply happened to be in the wrong place at the wrong time.

Common fuses to marital fireworks include:

- Work pressures and conflicts
- Personal criticisms
- Housework
- Inattentiveness
- Money
- Being crotchety
- Leisure
- Children
- Lack of time together

Having identified the nub of the matter, the next step is to make a case for it. In this, our argument tactics can help or hinder. There are six tactics, some more inflammatory than others. Here they are, in rising order of their capacity to irk a provoked spouse:

Pass: Ignore the complaint
Refocus: Change the topic under dispute
Mitigate: The plaintiff reduces the intensity of their complaint
Respond: The accused acknowledges the merit of the complaint

Not respond: The accused denies the complaint's merit

Escalate: The complaint intensifies, hostility rises

While none of these moves is exactly constructive, research finds that couples who hedge, fudge, dodge or flat-out fib can have perfectly happy marriages. Only two argument tactics have seriously detrimental consequences to marriage: ignoring a spouse's concerns, or the drip-drip of contempt. Both are acid to a couple's bond, because they ignore the fundamental conjugal premise: that the other person matters.

'*Plus on juge, moins on aime,*' remarked Balzac, summarizing the way criticism not only distances but can also kill love. A dispiriting example of contempt grinding affections comes in George Eliot's *Middlemarch*, as the idealistic heroine Dorothea learns that she does not enjoy the 'superior instruction' of her elderly, dry-as-dust husband, Mr Casaubon, nearly as much as she had anticipated: 'If she spoke with any keenness of interest to Mr Casaubon, he heard her with an air of patience as if she had given a quotation . . . and sometimes mentioned curtly what ancient sects or personages had held similar ideas, as if there were too much of that sort in stock already; at other times he would inform her that she was mistaken, and reassert what her remark had questioned.'

So pitch your moves intelligently. Note that some approaches assert ('I want', 'No we don't' or 'I think'), some concede ('Okay', 'Whatever you want'), and others dissipate the me versus you tension ('By the way', 'What's on telly?', 'Is it cold in here?', 'I heard it was going to be sunny', 'I was wondering . . .'). Self-assertion and self-abnegation have their uses. Invite a spouse to express their view, rather than coerce them to accept yours, and you can use listening to steer conversation where you would rather go. Tactical questions plant the seed of an idea. Summarize what your spouse said, but make it sound more like what you think, and they may shift their position towards yours without realizing.

If a spouse goes on the offensive, defensiveness is self-defeating. There are five ways to drain the negative energy in an argument:

1. **Chill**: If your inner voice is screaming, 'She is so rude', 'He hates me' or 'Why am I always bullied?', take a row-break. Irish novelist Maeve Binchy and her husband have a rule. When upset, they may sulk for ten minutes, slam doors, bang saucepans, and so on. Then the rage must be over.

2. **Make nice**: Help a spouse speak, show you are listening, and have respect for their opinion (it is not necessary to agree to appear supportive – try 'I understand'). Highlight issues that you can agree on, build consensus, flatter them, and do not mock, criticize, tell your spouse what they are really thinking, or hop from topic to topic, hoping to find the moral high ground by itemizing all the bad things they

have ever done, or all the good that you have done them. (For one wife, enumerating her husband's failings became something of a memory game, played whenever she felt that he was stepping out of line. As the litany of his crimes grew, he found he was no longer in a position to say whether he was guilty or not, having forgotten most of his alleged abuses. In the end, he concluded that he would always be labouring in debt to his supposed misdemeanours, so bailed out of the marriage.)

When raising your points, try to distinguish between complaint, criticism and contempt. Complaints are specific statements of how you feel, limited to one situation. Criticisms are more general and include a portion of blame (words like 'You always' or 'You never'). Contempt loads insult on to a criticism.

3. Focus on solutions: Often we get upset if we feel that we have not been heard, then lose sight of our interests and fail to conclude the argument. So if a discussion is about a decision, try to approach it as a business task, aiming to find a position both can live with. Draw up an agenda, seek consensus and explore solutions, then trade points.

4. Create incentives: Bully a spouse and they have only one way to save face: to defy you. To give them a motive to comply, market your preferences to appeal to their self-interest instead. There are three ways to do so: refer to the consequences ('If you do/don't . . .'); invoke their sense of duty ('Please do X for me/for us/because I . . .'); or appeal to their greed or vanity ('You only want that rotisserie for their birthday barbecue . . .').

5. Care less: Eddie Elcott, married sixty-three years, advised couples to 'play the role of the other person. Mentally stand in their shoes'. If you 'keep things in their proper perspective – ask yourself: if my wife were gone, would I really care about this? – you'll find that in this frame of mind, most things are petty'.

The wisest argument is the one that we have with ourselves before opening our mouth, when we ask, 'Does it matter?' Then think up another way than arguing to get what we want – ideally, something that we both want. But if a bust-up is truly unavoidable, the artfullest tactic is surprise.

Two little words. Repeat after me: 'Yes, dear.'

11

THE A TO Z OF
MARRIAGE

ANNIVERSARIES, BIRTHDAYS AND SPECIAL
OCCASIONS

One sunny morning in 1950, film director Billy
Wilder sat at breakfast, reading the *Hollywood Reporter*.
His wife Audrey came in. 'Do you know what day it is?'

'June 30th,' he said.

'It's our wedding anniversary.'

He looked up. 'Please – not while I'm eating.'

Unless you can summon quips like that, it is best to
remember special occasions, or your spouse will hold it
against you. What is more, you are missing a trick. Research
finds that happy memories heat desires. Set aside a few

hours to recall, in a suitably romantic location, in alcohol-softened focus, the fond illusions that once brought you two misfits together, and you will be rewarded in the bedroom.

If ever you screw up a special occasion, take comfort in the following tales of spousal sabotage. Drop one into conversation, if a darling needs to be diverted from a rant.

Imagine if your spouse forgot your birthday, not even a card, the day after your honeymoon. Then in mitigation, told you off for whining, because the honeymoon – dubbed by him, a 'hell-y-moon', for reasons too grim to recall – was your 'gift'. Naming no names, dear.

But cards can insult too. Entrepreneur Lord Sugar forgot his wife's birthday. His daughter nipped out, bought a card, left it in a pile of documents. He signed it, 'Best wishes, Alan Sugar.'

Other husbands go overboard. Take Barbara Amiel's $62,870 sixtieth birthday party, two-thirds of which was billed to her hubby's media company. But Conrad Black, never knowingly understated, was generous in his speech: 'The little woman's body is agile and youthful. I've seen her naked and it's all natural. She looks better with her clothes off than on . . . The little woman is perfect, vertically and horizontally.'

BATHING

In *Marnie* a frustrated husband repeats Michael Caine's quip that separate bathrooms save marriages.

Sharing means enforced surveillance, distressing if you live with a hygiene freak, but worse with a slob. The spattered loo, the feminine products, the yours-is-mine appropriation of flannel or worse. Who wants to awake to find a memento of their spouse's supper, peeping shyly from the bristles of their toothbrush?

Others argue that too much personal space weakens partnerships. To strengthen them, someone invented the TwoDaLoo, billed as 'a Supertoilet That Saves Rocky Marriages and the Planet'. The TwoDaLoo is the world's first double-yolker throne. Built on similar principles to the tandem bicycle, the TwoDaLoo has two seats and one cistern, which is shared like a loving cup. Apparently 36 per cent of us pee in front of our partner, claim manufacturers — a great chance for 'relationship therapy': 'At your most relaxed, that is the best time for you to communicate with your partner, discuss your concerns, and learn from them to grow as a couple . . . because it saves water by using one flush for two, you can fight global warming and divorce at the same time.' In 2007 it retailed at $1,400. Deluxe models' features include a TV and an iPod dock, presumably for couples bored of talking.

Our love of bathrooms is expanding, and so are bathrooms. Their average size tripled in America between

1994 and 2004. And it has to be said that hygiene can be sexy. Émile Zola's 1885 novel, *Germinal*, describes a wife washing her miner husband's blackened body from a day in the coal pit: 'She had gone down from his back to his buttocks and, warming up to the job, she pushed ahead into the cracks and did not leave a single part of his body untouched, making it shine like her three saucepans on spring-cleaning Sundays . . . The bath always ended up like this . . . it was the time when all the chaps in the village took their fun and more children were planted than anyone wanted.'

But do yourselves a favour and reach a truce over leaving the seat up or down, rolling versus squishing the toothpaste tube, or leaving the cap off. If enraged, remember that these minor irritants are what you would miss if your beloved was gone. Welsh poet Dannie Abse, bereft of his wife, lamented the 'malice of ordinary things' like an 'unused toothbrush'.

CELEBRATIONS

'It was awful when we phoned England and heard all the crackers being pulled,' said author Zoë Heller of the days when her husband banned Christmas (carols are now permitted from 15 December). By contrast, exhausting chef Gordon Ramsay did a double shift, claiming not to have missed a Christmas lunch at his restaurant in Claridge's

hotel for seven years. First, Ramsay gobbled brunch there
with his family, then he packed them off and oversaw lunch
service, before charging home, hot and fragrant in his
chef's jacket, to dish up the family repast. Ramsay enumer-
ated these feats as soldiers offer biographies of their battle
scars. (Since 2008 he has slacked off to pull crackers with
David and Victoria Beckham.)

There are less arduous approaches to annual festivals,
but opting out is not an option. Whatever your religious
disposition, these beanos are in our blood. They tug at the
roots of the fantasy that we can defy the years' passage with
cosy old cyclical time, and remake the magic of childhood,
by force of will, tinsel, turkey, alcohol, make-believe, indi-
gestion and Alka Seltzer alone.

Why then do we dread family feasts? Do we fear they will
pickle us in the sour vinegar of our teenage years, back
when we last lived with our families, but did not want to?
Or is the hangover of a more recent vintage? After all, by
the time we take that first dry bite of turkey, we have
endured the conjugated jamborees in the build-up to such
seasons. The enforced merriment of office parties, enforced
expenditure on cards for people we never see, and the
endless, endless shopping.

Or is the problem that we make a crisis out of seasonal
drama? Roasting poultry in an oven's monastic calm is not
difficult, yet many couples, especially wives, approach feast
days as a chance to display in vivid Technicolor that mad
modern fairy tale, 'Having It All'. Meanwhile, any spouse

who is not signed up to this vision will growl and count the costs, or buy the wrong presents, or choose a crap Christmas tree. One man calls 'a Wii with a few games, some school things and stocking-stuffers' 'plenty' — but his wife 'buys everything the kids want'.

If sugar-crazed children, relations and untethered friends are obstacles to festive merriment, so is the desire to match a wipe-clean family vision, as seen on TV, in magazines and books. Cooks and lifestyle gurus who unsettle us by urging us to do new things may have the best intentions, but they are also smiling burglars, come to rob us of confidence and our family culture.

Relax, remake traditions, graft yours on to your spouse's, and the seasons' rituals can bring many happy returns. Provided that we do not take them too seriously, or foist them on to others.

A friend, a widow, dreads the annual Noël with her daughter's in-laws, which she likens to 'a Punch and Judy show without the crocodile, but with lots of sausages' (naturally, she is vegetarian). She says yes to stop her daughter feeling guilty about her being alone. The in-laws play 'Mine Host', saying how 'brave' she is to live alone, and how her daughter worries about her 'coping'. If she says she likes solitude, they get cross. And for three days, when her hosts are not bullying her, my friend watches them squawk and snipe, then hugs herself in gratitude on her solitary train ride home.

CLOTHES

Paul Newman once confided: 'Do you know what my definition of marriage is? When we get in the elevator
together, my wife checks my fly without even looking.'
Other couples cherish dressing up for a sense of occasion.
Which seems wise. We must wear clothes, so why not wear
them well?

The cliché is that the married, once their mate is
hooked, let themselves go. But not every effort is appreciated. Pity penniless Renée-Pélagie, wife to the Marquis de
Sade, whose sufferings included his eloping with her sister.
Four and a half years she battled to visit Sade in gaol, where
he languished for torturing prostitutes, then saved to go
'dressed to kill in a décolleté white dress, her hair curled in
the latest style'. Did he notice? Indeed; Renée-Pélagie
received a passionate letter:

> Would you go do your Lenten duties in that moun-
> tebank's or quack doctor's garment? You wouldn't,
> would you? Well, the same sense of reverence that
> informs your Lenten duties should inspire your
> visits here; grief and sorrow should produce, in your
> case, what piety and divine respect produce in other
> souls . . . If you're a decent woman, you must solely
> please me, and the only way you'll please me is
> through the greatest decorum . . . In sum, I demand
> that you come . . . coiffed with a very large bonnet

. . . without the smallest hint of curl in your hair, a
chignon and no braids; your throat must be extraor-
dinarily concealed.

It is hard to get excited about a spouse's wardrobe if it is
stuffed with costumes you cannot afford, for a lifestyle
beyond your reach. Shopping for them is a double torture
if you are the watching spouse, running out of ways to say a
bottom or belly does not look big. Slow dressers madden
too, although when Pattie Boyd, wife to rock star Eric
Clapton, got into a tizz before a party, she came downstairs,
expecting an earful, but he said, '"Listen to this!" In the
time I had taken to get ready he had written "Wonderful
Tonight".'

To avert fights you could, as art historian Roy Strong
did for thirty-two years, choose your spouse's outfits and
lay them out each morning. But this is time-consuming.
Madonna once sang of dressing up a man in her love,
which is probably the thing to aim at: praise what you like,
meet lapses with silence. Never flatter a spouse and we
forfeit any right of protest if they wear trousers with elas-
ticated waistbands, or boob tubes, or nipple-high pants.

DANCING

Aside from bruises, broken toes and public humiliation,
what is not to like? Dance is intimate, rhythmic, synchro-

nizing, and tango aficionados' risk of Alzheimer's disease is 75 per cent lower. So pretend that no one is watching.

DRINK

Alcohol has a bad name, but as many marriages have been saved as destroyed by the demon, drink. Without it we would miss scenes like this, between writer Brian Thompson's cockney grandparents:

> Once in a while he [Jockie] came home late and, as he put it, aeriated. On one of these occasions, he staggered in, a canvas news-seller's bag on his shoulder.
>
> 'Yes,' Queenie yelled. 'And now you want your dinner, do you?'
>
> She opened the oven and drew out a plate to which his scrag end and spuds stuck in carbonised lumps. She threw the sizzling mess the length of the passage and Jockie, swaying gently in the shop, opened the neck of the bag. His dinner disappeared inside as if directed by radar. With perfect timing, he hung the bag on the tyre rack and advanced on us with his arms out, like Captain Cook greeting the natives.
>
> 'What was that you just said, my beloved?'

Pub, inn, bar and tavern were male preserves long before the invention of darts and pay-per-view sport TV. In the early Roman Republic a husband could divorce a wife for sipping wine. Drink's time-honoured role in marital strife is captured in this seventeenth-century poem in which spendthrift chastises his prating wife:

> Go wash your dishes, or go spin,
>> and do not talk to me,
> Ile play, or ramble where I please,
>> and ne're be ruled by thee . . .
> When I do please to work, ile work,
>> when I do please ile play,
> And to the Ale-house I will go
>> To drive sad care away.

Alcohol drives away care in more ways than one. My friend's lonely mother describes her husband's sprees as 'a party every night, but I'm not invited'. 'The sound of a sozzled spouse,' wrote Jemima Lewis, 'scraping away at the front door, trying in vain to direct his key into the lock, can make a woman's blood boil.' Perhaps in anticipation of subsequent misdirected fumbles?

Different constitutions divide couples too. Journalist Cosmo Landesman, a conscientious lark, watched in awe as ex-wife Julie Burchill came alive at night: 'She'd put paper in her . . . typewriter, alcohol in her blood and cocaine up her nose. Then it would start: she'd sip and tap . . . sip and tap . . . sip and tap . . . tap and tap-tap-tap-tap till she had liftoff.' And 'it was perfectly formed copy'! Burchill's third husband lives alone, for the sake of his liver.

Hopefully few wives today would be moved to write, as one did to 1970s Transport Minister Barbara Castle on the introduction of the breathalyzer: 'Thank you for giving my husband back to me. He used to go to the public house alone. Now he takes me with him to drive him home.' But, drinking apart does not inevitably damage marriage. However much or little you imbibe, you can alter your approach to help your marriage. A study of different drinking patterns found that alcohol's impact on married bliss depends on three factors: companionship, location and volume. Light drinking out of the home, mostly apart — with friends, colleagues, family — indicates a healthy, happy marriage. As does light drinking, together, at home. Heavy drinking together at home is fine too, aside from the health consequences. Problems come if couples drink heavily outside the home, together or apart, then get into scrapes, or stumble into bed with somebody else.

Drink is invariably contentious if one is having fun, but not the other. So whether your tipple comes in a thimble or a Methuselah, try to keep up with your beloved. Couples who drink the same amount are more affectionate. Even if they down buckets of the stuff, they also have more sex than sober or mismatched counterparts, brewer's droop not-withstanding.

ENTERTAINMENT

The battle of the television remote control used to be the testing ground for domestic supremacy. It can also be used as a tactic for diplomacy. If she wants to see a romcom, but he a Nam movie, both should consider that a gracious concession can win extra points, which can be redeemed against any other trade-off, from where you eat after the movie to whose turn it is to take out the rubbish tomorrow.

FOOD

Gordon Ramsay's preoccupation with food may be explained by the high standards of his difficult father. Ramsay's mother recalled: 'He loved liver and tripe and mince and onions, but everything had to be separate on the plate. If they touched each other then he'd throw the whole thing against the wall.' Aside from pleasure, peace and quiet, it is worth getting eating and feeding right as it symbolizes love, so may be painfully eloquent about the state of a relationship. As a 1940s soldier found, returning after 'six years of longing' to a key under the doormat and a cat that 'couldn't wait to get outside for a wee'. A note in the kitchen read: 'Help yourself to cocoa and sardines.'

Food is about power. It has a nasty tendency to bring out honesty too. None can disguise a look of disgust. To add to the pain, any problems with food magnify because they arise every day. And the intimate associations of food are such that among the Yao of Nyasaland a man could charge his wife with adultery on the sole evidence that she had cooked for another man. An anthropologist explained: 'His rights to his wife's cooking go with his rights of sexual access to her.'

According to a 1998 survey in the BBC's *Good Food* magazine, 90 per cent of women prepared supper every night for their partners. Some must enjoy their dominance. Vera Nabokov relished editing her novelist husband Vladimir's dinners as much as his writing, cutting them into bite-sized chunks. Historically, women's feelings about food are more contorted than men's, so a further plague of food on marriage is diets. Once restaurants gave women menus without prices, so that only men knew what they spent. Will a similar policy come in for calories, with menus giving the dietary low-down to women?

Husbands complain that wives 'share' puddings, or order salad, only to snaffle their carbonara. Is this worse than a spouse with intolerances? Foodie Rachel Cooke married 'the world's second-fussiest eater'. 'He doesn't like fruit (except kiwis) or vegetables (except potatoes), and he won't eat any "dirty food", the concept of which is too complicated to explain here – though I can tell you that stew is dirty food, whereas Thai green curry is not.' The world's fussiest eater was his father, who held that lemons smell of disinfectant. But neither is in the league of billionaire financier Warren Buffett, whose diet is limited to burgers, fries and Cherry Coke. (No leafy vegetable may graze that burger). If he feels fat, he halves his calorie intake to 1,000 a day by not drinking the Coke, then grows dehydrated.

Food grows contentious if one party takes no active role in its production, yet reserves the right to an opinion. Comedian Emma Kennedy recalled the balmy first night of fourteen days' camping in 1970s France. Her mother, a non-cook, sighed as families around them tucked in.

> 'Look over there,' said my mother with a nudge. 'They're eating mussels. On a campsite. Incredible. What are we having for dinner, Tony?'
>
> 'Spam,' said Dad.
>
> 'Do you not think we deserve a treat?' asked Mum.
>
> 'Well, all right then, we'll have corned beef. Everyone likes corned beef.'
>
> 'I don't.'

This was a budget holiday. The family was restricted to the money in her husband's pocket. But he had brought little, as a friend had told him that French food was extortionate, inedible and often featured dead horse. To forestall disaster, he had therefore stockpiled Spam, corned beef and pickled onions.

If you are an opinionated non-cook, use praise creatively. But avoid reflex flattery. Call each meal the 'tastiest ever' or, like my Great-uncle Bill, 'Very nice indeed', and soon you will sound like a comedian in need of a new catchphrase.

GAMES

Games are good for venting stress, and indulging in vicarious marital warfare. But I watched a couple separate over the theft of a blank letter tile in a game of Scrabble. Prince Andrew offered a revealing insight into the British royal family's Christmas: 'We're not allowed to play Monopoly at home. It gets too vicious.' Solo games are risky too, especially those conducted on-line in alternative realities. In 2007 a couple who had met on the net divorced after the husband committed virtual adultery in fantasy world Second Life, with the avatar of another woman whom he had not physically met.

GARDENING

Gardening is dirt at its best. Light exercise, self-forgetfulness, creativity and fecundity — all seduce those fortunate enough to possess their own patch of earth. Like food, gardening offers a reassuring illusion of control, with the added comforts of cyclical time; of watching trees

bud, blossom scatter, leaves fall, swallows quit their summer's lease, and so on, *ad* bucolic *infinitum*. Unless, that is,
you slack off, in which case gardens are no end of
trouble.

Earth can grip the soul when all else fails you, which may
be problematic. As Monty and Sarah Don's jewellery business sank in recession, they moved to a derelict farm, and
he became a man obsessed. When Sarah said he was
'married' to the garden, he was so far gone in his infatuation that he mistook her accusation for a compliment.
Other spouses struggle to propagate a gardening habit in
their other half, like enterprising wartime housewife Nella
Last:

> After tea, my husband said, 'I'm going to do a bit of
> gardening — I've my onion bed to make.' He spoke so
> importantly that I chuckled to myself. I've sung the
> praises of my little useful garden so much all winter —
> and let him see how clever I thought he was to rear a
> whole row of leeks, when more experienced garden-
> ers' leeks failed in the drought of last spring. He is
> planning and talking of what he will plant — so much
> better than when I'd to coax and bully him to get a few
> cabbages! I hate asking and asking, and I dare not dig
> in the garden if my husband says not — he is so keen on
> his roses. The real joke is, though, that with not being
> used to gardening, he would very carefully plant them
> and prune them but nothing else, and I had to get up

early and hoe and weed and spray. I heard him say he 'never had that trouble', when neighbours talked of thistles or greenfly, and that his soil kept light and friable! A neighbour split, and he then found gardening was an all-the-year-round job, not just a spasm now and again, and was not so keen.

So ask yourself this: do lawns exist (a) to make us feel guilty about not mowing? (b) to offer the balm of a somnambulist, repetitive task? (c) to idle on? Take your pick, then consider a patio.

GIFTS

In forty years' marriage, my friend's father, a successful businessman with an allergy to shopping, gave his wife not one present. He adored her, and their lively sex life was a fact of which their children would prefer to have known less. Yet the gift embargo lasted until their youngest son (thirty) called it a disgrace. You may think that the husband is amazing, but his wife's self-possession is what impresses me. Mind you, she had secured a joint bank account.

The Roman historian Titus Livy wrote: 'A woman's mind is affected by the meanest gifts' – meaning, it costs little to buy female favour, but as this happily married couple shows, feelings about presents are fluid, and always an index of a relationship's insecurities.

'The manner of giving is worth more than the gift,' claimed Pierre Corneille – in a play entitled *The Liar*. In reality, gifts cause upset because in theory they are supposed to embody the giver's esteem for the recipient. In practice, they often say more about the giver's budget, the relative length of queues in Harrods and Superdrug, or our family's gifts etiquette. Hence a litmus test of new in-laws at Christmas is how they read local custom. My first time, all gifts 'for me', in thrice-recycled paper, were 'for me and him'. The highlight? A wooden spoon. Was I gracious? As if. But I have since learned that so deep is my mother-in-law's aversion to receiving gifts, that to her something useful, costing pennies, is the best gift imaginable.

For many, gifts are tokens in a love story. The homespun can speak to hearts for years to come. Screenwriter Jimmy McGovern treasures a thirty-seven-year-old jumper knitted by his wife: 'She's attempted to throw it out but I always retrieve it.' Although originality is great if you know what your spouse wants better than they do, clichéd gifts (chocolates, scent, flowers) do not linger in clutter, and have the virtue of being in no way practical. Lynn Darling almost left a husband for whom she had wrecked her career (he was already wed) on their first Valentine's, on opening a bag tied with a bow to find two towels. 'I cried . . . I was furious; the towels were a metaphor . . . The reasoning must have been something like this: I have staked everything on this man, and he is not what I thought.' Fortunately her hysteria abated. From then on he gave her bath towels every year, and every time she laughed. (Towels became 'part of our mythology'.)

If unfortunate gifts ripen life's comedy, my favourites link for ever with the comments they prompted. My grand-mother, seeing the birthday roller-blades, enquired, 'Are you trying to catch her or chase her away?'

When choosing a gift, see it as a votive offering, a deposit at a shrine: your aim is to incline your household god to smile on you. To prove that your god is powerful, then, a gift must be of sufficient magnitude. But do not expect it to be returned. American doctor Richard Batista donated a kidney to his wife. When she filed for divorce, he demanded $1.5 million in lieu of his pound of flesh.

GROOMING

We could all enjoy hair more. If not as much as Elvis Presley, who not only tinted his barnet black, but wife Priscilla's too. '"You have blue eyes, Cilla, like mine. Black hair will make your eyes stand out more,"' she reported him saying. 'He made a lot of sense to me.'

Grooming is a sensual pursuit that has only recently been privatized to the solitude of the bathroom at home. Late into the Middle Ages, delousing was a social activity, ideal for gossip. Indeed, evolutionary anthropologist Robin Dunbar has argued that grooming not only helped groups of primates to stick together, but also inadvertently spurred the evolution of language, enabling early humans to keep in touch once tribes grew too large for them to backscratch one another personally. It is impossible to verify Dunbar's speculation, but gossip certainly grooms friendships. Sadly, grooming is losing its social aspect, and its sensual side. In the seventeenth century, combing hair was an accepted erotic pastime. (Picture mermaids singing and stroking their locks.) These days, we call them hair fetishists. Why?

HABITS, DIRTY

Habits are not static. They migrate, because humans mimic each other. So if a spouse picks and chews, either you will want to hit them, or find yourself picking and chewing too.

Like its companion antisocial activities — pocket billiards, biting nails, burping, farting — we tend to be particularly annoyed by spouses' nose-picking. Not because it is not fun but because it is fun *only for one*. It is also a poor spectator sport. To do it shows a lover how relaxed you are in their company, which is nice as far as it goes. But in a bad mood, the sight of that unselfconscious finger, winkling its furry cavity, may be an unwelcome invasion of privacy, or even suggest that its owner does not care if you do not fancy them, since they no longer fancy you.

What better image is there of stale, nuptial despair? In

Richard Yates's novel, *Revolutionary Road*, a wife urges her
man to quit his job and move to Paris. In her vision, she is
a Nato secretary, while he 'finds himself':

> 'You'll be reading and taking long walks and think-
> ing. You'll have time . . .'
>
> And that, he knew as he chuckled and shook his
> head, was what he'd been afraid she would say. He
> had a quick disquieting vision of her coming home
> from a day at the office – wearing a Parisian tailored
> suit, briskly pulling off her gloves – coming home
> and finding him hunched in an egg-stained bath-
> robe, on an unmade bed, picking his nose.

HOLIDAYS

Holidays are for remembering why you married each other,
then wondering what on earth possessed you. Although the
untrammelled doing of nothing, or hiking up hills, or whatever, may be bliss, holidays are also marital booby traps.

They unmask tyrants. When Charles Dickens decided to
travel to America, his wife's objections – six months apart
from several small children, two long, terrifying voyages –
were swept aside on the tide of Dickens's enthusiasm. 'It
must be a source of happiness to her,' he commanded,
while confiding in a letter to a friend that Kate was not
exactly Phileas Fogg material: 'She falls into, or out of,

every coach or boat we enter; scrapes the skin off her legs; brings great sores and swellings on her feet; chips large fragments out of her ankle-bones; and makes herself blue with bruises.' To nurse Kate through chronic seasickness — to which Dickens, naturally, was immune — he treated her to cheering bouts on his accordion.

An away-break need not be a Dickensian melodrama to unsettle a couple. Although holidays are atypical situations, unmoored from the reality of conjugal life, we vest huge significance in them. If we cannot be happy together on vacation, the twisted logic goes, then 'we' as a couple must be up the Swannee. This logic seems the more ridiculous because holidays are rigged not to be factories of fun.

There are those hours to kill — doing what? Working up a sun-lounger sweat? Exposing yourselves like flashers to improving sights of cultural interest (interesting to a culture about which you know little or care less)? Hurling your person down snowy hills? Being whisked at horrifying speed over water? Or, as has been known, building dry-stone walls? With nothing 'real' to worry about, the slightest decision (room service or buffet?) may grow fraught.

Now add children to the mix. All day they must be entertained, contained and drained of surplus energy. If in everyday life one of you spends more time looking after the children, on holiday, very soon your contrasting parenting skills will be painfully apparent. Any conflict over childcare routines or manners, which are usually thrown up only on weekends and evenings at home, will play out all day long.

Those expecting a family holiday to be relaxing may therefore be disappointed. And this is not accounting for the constant screams for ice cream, or all that kiddy paraphernalia, those favourite toys, buckets, spades to cart around and mislay, or the susceptibility of small people's stomachs to play up at the first sight of foreign food.

These pressures need not in themselves ruin a holiday, but the enforced intimacy might. For some reason, although me-time and that mythic entity, 'personal space', are cherished in normal life as necessary periods to detox from the family, to want time away from a spouse on holiday is considered odd. Perhaps this is because many couples feel obliged to reconstitute that old honeymoon feeling. Yet if things feel remotely stale between you on holiday, the tension will intensify if you have to lounge on the beach, watching other couples flirt and swill Sangria.

If comparing your relationship to loved-up strangers' is unflattering, holidaying with friends seems unwise. Yet some couples welcome the distraction. Just as a family Christmas with annoying supernumerary relations can bring a nuclear family together, couples may be united in adversity against annoying friends on holiday. Seeing others squabble can be fun too: 'It gives me and my husband something to bond about, and the kids, other children to play with. We go to bed at the end of an evening and gossip about everyone and feel gloriously smug. And we all have other people to spend time with, which takes the pressure off.'

On shared holidays, without separate accommodation, the trouble is that it soon becomes apparent how minutely our living arrangements are custom-fit to us. Clashing routines or parenting styles (with biting brats or parents who applaud each poo on a living room floor) cause 10 per cent of shared holidays to end in violence, usually between mothers. This is not helped by the fact that 75 per cent of husbands secretly fancy their wife's best friend. Allegedly. No wonder Relate, the counselling service, reports surging demand in September, after the long summer break. Problems arise from failure to plan, discuss expectations or compromise.

If sharing your holiday can be unflattering to a marriage, so can some destinations. I know two couples who will not visit Venice, for fear that their marriage would not live up to the romantic backdrop. But greater disappointment may come from a comparison in your head: the contrast between the holiday that you spent months anticipating, and the one that you got.

Even a successful getaway can turn into a guilt trip, if it holds out an ideal that is unachievable in normal life. Breakfast TV presenter Fiona Phillips quit her gruelling job after twelve years, after an unprecedented five weeks away with her young family. Only towards the end did Phillips finally unwind, recovered from the accumulated exhaustion of a decade's early starts and sleep deprivation. Her husband chose this moment to turn to her and say, 'It's so nice to have you back.' She went back to work and resigned. (Interestingly, her husband was also her TV show's editor. His work-life balance must have improved no end.)

What to do? Philosopher Alain de Botton suggests that hotels should open 'temples to disappointment' where travellers could unburden to 'a sympathetic priestly type'. Until this catches on, dampen expectations. Accept that we work hard, so vest greater hopes in holidays, but are out of practice at being together. If a row brews, reflect that so few holiday choices matter, who cares if we eat chips every night? The dull rule of normality is suspended, so why not give up, give in and relax? Or, if you can, why not go alone? Joan Burstein of Browns boutiques, married for over six decades, took up to three weeks off. 'That, for me, is a new life blood. I can do what I like, I'm not always compromising. Then I appreciate him more.'

IDLING

Actress Emily Mortimer finds herself 'incapable of lying in'. Her failure to laze is 'a real problem. My husband often says he can hear my eyes opening at about 6.30 in the morning and I'm instantly wide awake'. Hard as she tries, 'I inevitably disappoint my husband and fall fast asleep on the sofa at about nine. So much of my life is taken up by me pretending to him that I'm not falling asleep.'

Ms Mortimer is a mother, which may explain everything.

I have no wish to torture those who can only fantasize about a protracted doze that ends in waking to silence, or to the smell of toast on a tray by the bed. I will say that couples have every incentive to synchronize their body clocks. The alternative can be decades of long, boring evenings, watching skeins of drool abseil from an open mouth, as a spouse dissolves on the sofa. The drooler's punishment is decades of lies about 'resting' their eyelids.

JOKES

An essential marital shock-absorber is the in-joke. All marriages are sitcoms, so all of us need catchphrases. Develop a few stock lines, code-names for dreadful relations perhaps, and a selection of funny stories, beginning with the words 'Remember when . . .' Then when you run out of things to say or need to change the subject, or deflect a tirade, you can detonate the grumpster out of a sulk with an in-joke.

KISSING

It is claimed that husbands who kiss their wives before leaving home in the morning live five years longer than those who do not. I cannot verify this claim, but would you not rather be safe than sorry?

LOVE LETTERS

Ambrose Bierce defined 'love' as 'a temporary insanity curable by marriage'. But a little insanity is a fine thing in marriage. To top up the supply we have love letters.

When did you last receive one? Was it not pleasant? Why not write one now? You need not be a quill master. Be inspired by socially autistic, Nobel-winning quantum physicist Paul Dirac. So minimal were his communications that his colleagues were moved to name the smallest possible particle of speech required to maintain a conversation a 'Dirac' (rate: one word per hour). Yet in 1935, the chatterbox managed to hook gossipy Hungarian Manci Wigner with weekly love letters from Princeton to Budapest.

The correspondence started badly: 'I cannot write such nice letters to you,' he confided, 'perhaps because my feelings are so weak and my life is mainly concerned with facts.' He corrected her English and wrote of a photo, 'I do not like this picture of you much. The eyes look sad and do not go with the smiling mouth.' Undeterred, Manci accused him of being evasive. So he re-read her letters, numbered them, and tabulated precise answers to every question that he had ignored:

Letter No.	Question	Answer
5	What makes me (Manci) so sad?	You have not enough interests.

5	Whom else could I love?	You should not expect me to answer this question. You would say I was cruel if I tried.
5	You know that I would like to see you very much?	Yes, but I cannot help it.
6.	Do you know how I feel like?	Not very well. You change so quickly.
6.	Were there any feelings for me?	Yes, some.

Their back and forth reads like an experiment in programming a robot in human feeling. Manci did her best, at one point accusing Dirac of deserving a second Nobel in cruelty. He replied that it would be wrong to pretend that he was in love with her. Still, the questions and answers continued. Had he played ping-pong with pretty girls? 'With one pretty girl.' Did he flirt? 'No. She was too young (15). But you ought not to mind if I did. Should I not make the most of what you have taught me?' In time Manci's romantic training was such a success that eventually he could write: 'You are the only girl for me . . . You have made a wonderful alteration in my life. You have made me human.' In 1937 they married.

If you write love letters, do not be selfish, like Colombian novelist Gabriel García Márquez, who refused to let romance mar his literary reputation. In 1958 he wed Mercedes Barcha, whom he scarcely knew, after wooing her by pen (he vowed to marry her when they met, twenty years before, aged nine and ten). On honeymoon he took her to bed with three packs of cigarettes, an ashtray apiece, and outlined his plans for what would be his two great novels. She agreed to support him. In gratitude, Márquez paid her to burn his love letters, on the grounds that they would be a literary embarrassment: 'It's like being caught in your underwear.' Strangely, he was quite happy to be snapped in his long johns, among fans dressed in white tie, before receiving his 1982 Nobel Prize.

MUSIC

If you can play it, fantastic. If you can duet, to die for. If you must resort to an iPod, do. So often about love (40 per cent of pop songs), music is perfect for creating moods, if you are in the same mood. English cricketer Andrew Flintoff operated a zero-tolerance policy when motoring with his missus. 'When Rachael tries to put one of her CDs on, I tell her she has until the count of five to take it out or it goes out the window. Steve Harmison was amazed, when we gave him a lift once, all those CDs flying out of the window.'

NO

A word that has wide uses, but is rarely endearing to spouses. Interestingly, studies find that few refusals actually contain the word no.

ORNITHOLOGY

Entirely suspicious if it is a spouse's solitary pursuit. However, birdwatching together is admirable.

PETS

Few love triangles are richer in comedy than those featuring befurred four-footed friends. Like children, pets can unite couples or wage war on their union. Some are traitors. In a surprise encounter at the Russian court, Catherine the Great's dog barked ferociously at Count Horn until it spotted her lover, Count Poniatowski. 'I thought he was going to go mad with joy,' the empress wrote of her pet's ecstasy. '[Count Horn] pulled Count Poniatowski by the coat and said to him: "My friend, there can be nothing more treacherous than a small dog; the first thing I used to do with a woman I loved was to be sure and give her one, and through them I learned if someone was more favoured than myself. It is an infallible test."'

Before ruling out a pet and its inconvenient hairs, ailments, aromas and odoriferous effluvia, hear that purr, picture that wagging flag of greeting. A pet is cheaper than gym membership and patting it releases oxytocin, lowering blood pressure. All this, before you consider a critter's attractive looks, amusing personality and extensive lap-, heart- and foot-warming abilities.

Note: Pets can assist spurned spouses. Model Marie Helvin tolerated a decade's unremitting infidelity by photographer David Bailey, but was tested by his seventy-strong flock of free-range pet parrots which roosted willy-nilly, 'shitting here, there and everywhere'. His rabbits were little better, but after catching him with a love rival, Helvin added pellets of bunny poo to Bailey's nightly bowl of peanuts and felt better.

QUIZ

Quizzing and interrogating a spouse opens emotional quagmires. Pub quizzes, on the other hand, are fine, unless you lose.

RITUALS

What makes a cup of coffee your cup of coffee? When it is drunk from your favourite cup. Ask James Frey, the writer whose memoir caused a storm, when it was revealed to contain semi-fictional passages. With his sacred coffee cup, Frey uses his creativity to make his antisocial morning demeanour seem almost a tribute to his warm family feeling: 'My wife always laughs that she doesn't like to talk to me before I've had a cup of coffee. She and my daughter went to one of those places where kids can colour their own cups and plates and she made it for me. I don't drink coffee out of anything else.'

Psychologists find that if you make tea in a certain way, then drink it from your favourite cup, it truly tastes better. Only to you, of course, but then you are the one who matters.

Rituals imbue experience with greater value and pleasure. When we repeat actions, our brains form neural pathways, and the more we repeat that action, the better it feels, lighting up cerebral circuits like a Christmas tree. A similar glow ignites our brain cells when we pray, if we pray often enough. This is because repetition strengthens the neural pathway, adding resonance and comforting recognition, enhanced by anticipation, which also ups the release of dopamine.

So all couples do well to form shared rituals, to become more conscious, ceremonial, instead of falling into habit. A meal can be an occasion, as can a regular Sunday jog. You may look smug bastards, but happy, smug bastards.

SHED, THE

The shed is to man what a kennel is to dog. It need not be a wooden hut; a caravan, or even a loft or basement hide-away will do. The point of the shed is its separation from the family domain. Not just a sanctuary, to qualify as a shed a space must also serve as a field of operations.

In the past, possibilities of shed industry have been taken far. Roald Dahl, Philip Pullman and Daphne du Maurier wrote bestsellers in theirs. Rob Beattie's *101 Things to Do in a Shed* suggests brewing ale, mummifying fishes, or making paper, kaleidoscopes, telescopes, stilts, bird-scarers, documents of ancient appearance and worm hotels. Yes, in a shed, man becomes Renaissance man: equal parts inventor, forger and Enid Blyton hero. If this sounds like bullshit, it is apt, as the original sheds were outdoor privies.

If you envy your spouse their shed, get your own. Before considering a shared shed, remember devoted wife Marie Curie. Her husband, Pierre, an obsessive fellow scientist, resented any moment away from the laboratory. So however exhausted Marie was after cooking, cleaning, or making her children clothes, if Pierre was in a bait, she threw off his sulk by suggesting that they go back to 'the miserable old shed'. Curie's rewards were a Nobel Prize and eventual death by radiation poisoning.

SHOPPING

Shopping became a semi-professional female sport when women ceased to make items because it was cheaper to buy them. However, making things is satisfying, so when women stopped doing so, they had extra time in which to feel unsatisfied with their lot in life. To stop them going back to their soothing knitting, lovely tranquillizers like Valium and Mogadon were invented. Wily merchants and admen also upgraded the status of shopping. With the myth-making powers of marketing, shopping was rebranded. It bought you more than stuff; that brand of shampoo, that pair of high heels, brought a lift in spirits, and pride.

Men have been slower to swallow this ethos as they have real sports. Husbands who loathe shopping also fear that the siren call of a ringing shop till will turn their darling into an empo-rium whore. Some have heard of shopping's tragic heroine, Jackie Onassis, who makes husbands quake more than Bluebeard's legend ever did any bride. The widowed Jackie Kennedy's marriage to shipping magnate Aristotle was arranged with a detailed contract, including clauses specify-ing the number of nights the couple should spend together, and moneys to be rendered in lieu of Jackie's wifely services. But she was not satisfied with her life or allowance, so passed many days apart from Onassis in New York, undertaking a high-end version of supermarket sweep, as she used Onassis's name to loot Fifth Avenue stores of thousands of dollars' worth of clothes, then re-sold them at a hefty discount to second-hand outlets and pocketed the cash. Onassis filed for divorce, but died before they went to court.

To sell shopping as a fun activity, never claim that it will 'only take a few minutes'. Immediately your spouse will sniff a lie. You are also sending the message that this activity is something bad, to be over with quickly. To convince of a purchase's wisdom, instead focus on what it can do for them. Describe how that mechanical ham-slicer will enrich their life. Try to create a sense of urgency, suggesting that they act now or regret for ever: 'Oh look, a special offer!'

If you struggle to convince your spouse that shopping is good for both of you, mention that scientists have found a little improvidence is prudent. Researchers at Columbia and Harvard discovered that those who splurge are happier than scrimpers and savers. 'People feel guilty about hedonism right afterwards; over time that guilt dissipates.' But never splash out and 'what builds up is this wistful feeling of missing out on life's pleasures'. After all, make each choice on the basis that one day it will rain, and life passes in the shade. But spend, and if you are motivated to work to pay for it, the hamster wheel of existence will feel like it is heading somewhere.

SPIRIT

Politics causes arguments, yet political beliefs are not a burning issue in marriage, whether a couple agrees or differs. Studies find that the only category of spouse to be influenced by their other half's voting preference is an unemployed man whose wife works (he actively disregards her opinion).

But politics have some correlation with marital success. There is evidence that political tribes fall into general trends of conduct, with right-wing couples tending to last longer, and to sleep around less than leftie liberals. Or rather, this is what they piously tell researchers.

Religious beliefs have a greater impact on marriage, which is not surprising as marriage is an act of faith between two people often pledged in the name of God. Religious couples also have to jump through more hoops to reach the altar than those entering civil unions, which helps to stiffen resolve, and encourages reflection. Occasionally couples break laws to marry outside their creed, at their peril in Malaysia, where under sharia law a woman who marries a Muslim without converting to Islam, and then bears her husband's children, condemns her husband to gaol.

Those disposed to believe in God of one kind or another are also more inclined to keep faith with wedding vows. True believers' marriages often last longer than atheists', the degree of success varying by religion. (Episcopalians hang in there longer than Catholics.)

SPORT

Sport is an informal means of marital apartheid, a licence for abdicating from long Saturday afternoons of child entertaining, or for dispatching son and father to the park for quality time while a wife catches up with some quality lazing. Supporting a sports team is for many husbands a cheap alternative to joining a gentleman's club where women are banned. So spare a thought for those socially handicapped husbands who cannot synthesize a credible sporting passion, or vouch allegiance to a tribe, be it Red Sox, Team Honda, Dynamo Kiev, or Real Madrid.

TECHNOLOGY

'Men don't care what's on TV,' said Jerry Seinfeld. 'They only care what else is on TV.'

Once, whoever held that little black remote-control box ruled the roost. Today this issue seems dated. Now gadgets are pluralistic portals to other worlds, technology has introduced an unwelcome multitude of third parties, and acres of solitude, into marriage. Communication tools bring us together but as often drive us apart. I know a wife who is lost to the joys of on-line chess. Indeed, most Britons spend more time at a computer than with their spouse, and increasingly throughout the developed world, the barrier between public and private space is gone. Nowhere is inaccessible, and for many, working days have no beginning or end.

Technology does not just devour time and attention. Every computer is a shopaholic's or gambler's wet dream.

Anyone with access to the world-wide web and a credit card, laptop or iPhone, has their very own pixellated harem, obedient and accessible at the touch of a button, 24/7. And opportunities for unexplained absences multiply, thanks to the adulterer's best friend, the mobile phone. Marriage guidance counsellors also talk in hushed tones of an epidemic in on-line porn addiction, a form of virtual adultery that afflicts the majority of couples in sex therapy. If furtive cyber-lechery is rude, so too are the casual insults of an iPhone or BlackBerry addict, who is always present, but never entirely there.

With these tools a spouse need no longer sneak around to get up to things without you knowing, so technology also introduces the temptation to spy on each other's text messages, phone bills, Google searches. It also means that you may struggle to get away from each other should you want to. Tony Blair's first gift from his wife on leaving political office in 2007 was a BlackBerry. Until that day he had sent not one e-mail. But once started, he could not stop, to the chagrin of family and colleagues, who now received regular bulletins.

It is always worth asking whether our modern conveniences are truly convenient. To prevent gizmos from perforating your union, you might follow Wendi Deng, who handles all her media magnate husband Rupert Murdoch's e-mails personally. I would not. But you might.

TOYS

In *Biting the Dust*, historian Margaret Horsfield observed that women with 'overbearingly fastidious husbands' found that their husbands' cleaning fetish seldom encompassed anything so convenient as a whole household. Instead they fixated on specifics: 'A prized object like a car, a motorbike, a bicycle, a boat, a computer, a collection of CDs even, [will] regularly receive scrupulous attention.' As their wife looked on and sighed.

Toys are extensions of the ego. The advantage of obsessing over the state of your car, rather than the state of your home, is obvious. If you are in a family, full of small people and high-octane egos, to identify your personal toy, and protect it, can help preserve sanity and define the borders of where your family ends and you begin. A toy need not be a car. For instance, historian Antonia Fraser carved out a space for herself by creating mystique about the closed dressing room door. If it was shut, her numerous children were given to understand that they should not knock. They did not, and Fraser wrote a bestselling series of biographies.

UNIVERSE

Feeling down? Look up at the stars and gain a sense of proportion.

VICE

Very like virtue in its benefits, but with the additional penalty of a hangover. Still, who wants to die without something to regret? For vices to enhance rather than impair a union, try to ensure that yours are compatible.

WEEKENDS

Weekends are sacred, but often not as nice as they should be, with those tugs of war over shared time, me-time, chore-time. Rival priorities can be dangerous, as Sophie Radice demonstrates:

I wake up on a Saturday morning with my mind focused on a weekend list of things to do. Not just domestic things — such as washing, shopping for food, cleaning the bathroom — but serious stuff, put off for weeks, months even . . . By the time my husband comes downstairs at 11 a.m. I have already been up for three hours, walked the dogs, gone to the market and started throwing things around the garden. He, tired from a busy week and our late night with friends, slowly cooks bacon and eggs, and announces that he is going to double-dig the allotment today. An ugly row ensues — with me wanting us to do things together and him wanting to recharge, even if that means spending little time with me or the children. He tells me I'm 'Miss Perfect' and I tell him he is a 'selfish pig'. He wins, on the grounds that the allotment is a virtuous activity.

To me, a well-balanced weekend is spliced with as much vice as virtue and spontaneity. Why cannot you simply 'announce' like Sophie Radice's husband what you are doing? Free time is supposed to be free. To me the joy of living in a world of opportunity is that you can elect to do nothing, and enjoy it. But as novelist Rachel Cusk observed, 'What the outside world refers to as "the weekend" is a round trip to the ninth circle of hell for parents. Weekends are when children don't go to school . . . You are woken on a Saturday morning at six or seven o'clock by people getting into your bed. They cry or shout loudly in your ear. They kick you in the stomach, in the face.' Which is never fun, and less still with a Friday night hangover.

X FACTOR, THE

An ex-spouse is more than a hangover that will not go away. As far as the ex is concerned, certain rights and responsibilities continue, predating and therefore superseding any new marital contract made with their replacement. To marry a divorcee, then, is to marry their ex too.

You need not hang out with your ex, or your spouse's,

for them to impinge on your lives like a particularly demanding embodiment of the ghost of Christmas past, such as bedevils the miser Scrooge in Dickens's *A Christmas Carol*. Even if the ex is lovely, you need not be pennywise to find yourself counting their cost. Your pain can be measured in the sum that evaporates from your bank account every month, or the humiliating monthly stipend by which an ex subsidizes you, in the ex's big house versus your poky flat, in the holidays that you cannot quite afford, or the new clothes that the ex's children wear while yours are stuck in their hand-me-downs, or the weekends that you can never call your own, because while the ex is prompt enough at dropping off their offspring, they are mysteriously unreliable when it comes to collecting them.

None of these factors in your marriage is your choice, but all have an impact, testing diplomacy and draining patience that might be better deployed on your spouse. What is more, you will feel that your forbearance deserves extra indulgences that your spouse may not be aware of, since for them this complicated state of affairs is normal.

The presence of an ex in a marriage means that each spouse has different loyalties from the start, thereby making the central marital task — to reconcile your differences — harder. The worst of it is, the spouse who used to be married to the ex may find the ex hardest to cope with, compelling the new spouse to play diplomat.

However charming an ex-wife or ex-husband, the fact that they attempted to scale the marital edifice with you or your spouse and fell off renders them an unwelcome reminder that marriage may not necessarily be for life. Retrospective jealousy, unresolved anger, fear of betrayal may linger to taint your present love. What if your ex left you, or your spouse's ex ran off with the milkman, then regretted it? Who can ever be entirely sure an ex is finished business? Numerous divorcees remarry, finding nobody to suit them as well as their ex.

Inevitably, an ex's continued unsolicited opinions, scheduling crises and unending flow of wants and needs, are testing. That the ex must be deferred to regarding the upbringing of stepchildren stops the new spouse from being number one too. If an ex is unhappy, or holds their replacement responsible for the end of their marriage, the hurdles will keep on coming.

So it is in everyone's interests to court the ex. However dastardly the ex factor in your marriage, it is worth recalling that were they less noxious, they might not be the ex – and you might be alone.

YES

'Just say yes, it saves time,' as the caterer advised my father in the run-up to my wedding. This advice serves marriage well.

ZONING OUT

When your beloved's jowls slacken and their eyes film, as they slip into screensaver mode, why not let them grab a few Zzzs? This is a perfect opportunity to ask them questions and secure consent to contentious proposals, like that holiday with your parents.

THE LONG AND WINDING ROAD

If marriage was a business, every quarter we would audit its costs and benefits.

List the inconveniences of marriage: the lack of thanks, the heavy hints, the hecatombs of laundry, the spilled milk, the coffee rings, the burned toast. The occasions when a spouse is embarrassing, the familiar chuckle before they launch into an anecdote you have heard a dozen times, their nod and smile as you itemize all that you have done and all that ungrateful they have not.

Now imagine life without the grit of these irritations. Hear the silence of a night bereft of the sound of them asleep. Picture the unwrinkled sheets, the uncrushed pillow, the pristine bath, the no-stolen socks. The nobody to drop you off at work, the solitary dinner, the absence of an ear to hear you moan, the missing pair of hands to heft that chest of drawers, the bottle of wine for one, the lack of a shoulder to dribble on while drifting off after another tiring day, the lack of a warm, soft body in bed, to have and to hold.

At the end of this audit, should the annoyances exceed the joys, or after a particularly gruelling Christmas, it may be tempting to wish that, as in the past, a marriage could be terminated if a wife lost her wedding ring. In the nineteenth century, at a Court-leet dinner in Exeter, after the roast beef, a plum pudding was brought to the table, and found to contain a wedding ring. When the elderly host was told, he began hopping about the room to the astonishment of his guests. The old man thought that his wife, having lost the hymenal lock, left him free to marry again. But the veteran ceased to caper when he found he was mistaken, remarked an observer, 'and must, in spite of this, cleave to his old rib still.'

Before giving up, or sharing your inventory of irritations with your beloved, reflect on the toxic spouses: Empress Theodora of Byzantium, said to cavort with whores and do unspeakable things with horses before the general populace at the Circus, to the ignominy of her husband Justinian; Mary, Queen of Scots, whose overbearing second husband, Henry Stuart, Lord Darnley, was dispatched by strangulation and an explosion; or icy husband Edward II of England, whose infatuation with his Ganymede, Piers

Gaveston, led to the insurrection of his people and Edward's death at the sharp end of a red-hot poker, up his royal behind.

Then recall the devoted ones: Queen Victoria and her German consort, Albert of Saxony, whose rule of the British Empire was so joint a partnership that his and her writing desks can still be found, side by side, at their summer retreat, Osborne House, on the Isle of Wight; the Denis and Margaret Thatchers; the Eva and Juan Perons; the Johnny Depps and Vanessa Paradis.

Ask, if you changed your darling, would they be the person you fell in love with? Would life improve? If so, do what you must do.

To cleave to the long and winding road of marriage, American statesman Benjamin Franklin commended the great political imperative, caution: 'Keep your eyes wide open before marriage, and half-shut afterwards.' However, seek better things ahead on the obstacle race of marriage and it is easier to achieve the everyday heroism that elevates this relationship above all others.

Unlike our parents, or our children, we choose our spouse. In so doing, we stake a claim that in this person we have found somebody to complete our world. To make this wish come true, we must compromise to uphold the greater interests of our marriage. In return, we change our lives, seize our destiny, and are elevated into less selfish people, strengthened by our connection with this person who elected to complete their world with us.

To marry is not only the greatest compliment that you can pay someone, but also liberally repaid by the extended possibilities of living in partnership. The value that a loving wife or husband brings to our days is intensified by shared goals, pleasures and memories. To stay side by side without running aground, to keep true to the course, is more than a moral victory, but a sweet one. It proves that what we set out to do in life, we will. With a little help from our spouse.

> 'Marriage, which has been the bourne of so many narratives, is still a great beginning, as it was to Adam and Eve, who kept their honeymoon in Eden, but had their first little one among the thorns and thistles of the wilderness. It is still the beginning of the home epic.'

When George Eliot wrote these words in her novel, *Middlemarch*, she was pointing out that although in fiction many stories terminate at the altar, in reality this is the point at which the hard facts of life begin. Each couple embarking on marriage's timeless story can decide how they want it to end, but neither can control how it will be written, which is what keeps marriage interesting.

Matrimony survived for thousands of years because it adapted, and the happiest couples are adaptable, changing to fit each other, and to suit themselves. Anyone expecting love to make them feel young may find in a spouse's wrinkling face evidence to the contrary. But those who wish to transcend time can find no better proof than in a pair of eyes that have witnessed so much of what we have witnessed, seen us at our worst, yet still seek the best in us.

Marry and we draw a line around our relationship. Whatever our efforts, our gains, losses and longings, if we hold this line we have made something more of the passage of our days, something that nobody else can touch, and that only we can share. A marriage.

AFTER WORDS

The couple sit on the park bench, side by side, with the blank inward gaze of commuters in a crowded train, as if asleep with their eyes open. This is how it was when their children were young; through sheer placidity they seemed to erase the bustle and noise around them. Now that their children are gone and growing old themselves, to anyone who glances at the couple they resemble commuters less than inmates of an asylum.

If pressure once held them together, today silence acts as a seal, shielding them from the world, seemingly invisible to each other. Yet they are conspicuous to romantics: testaments to desiccation that make the young shudder and promise that they may scream, they may holler, but never will they be that way. Cynics wonder if the couple swore a Trappist vow, and if this is a good idea. Or is one waiting for the other to say sorry for something unforgivable? Can they remember who did what?

If the couple senses our fears, neither face will betray it. Marriage is a secret, but they will never tell. They are the mutes in the teashop. The pair whose halting choreography in the supermarket follows the beat of a slower age. On the park bench they watch and wait, departing at a summons that they alone hear.

They have seen and said and done it all, many times before, and continue with the defiance of defeat. Or perhaps theirs is a private language, of gesture, duty, pledges fulfilled, and their silence merely the dogged glue of days, compact of trust and layered memory, ready to ignite at a glance, the touch of a hand, the scrape of a boot, a closing door.

ACKNOWLEDGEMENTS

First thanks to my agent, Eugenie Furniss, for her unflagging inspiration and insights, and Rowan Lawton and Claudia Croft at William Morris Endeavour. I am also grateful to Eleanor Birne for commissioning me, Helen Hawksfield for her sharp editing and smooth steerage, and Nikki Barrow, Victoria Murray-Browne, Roland Philipps, James Spackman, Caroline Westmore, Morag Lyall and Margaret Gilbey at John Murray.

Many people have trusted me with their secrets, friends and strangers. You know who you are, but you may prefer to remain nameless. Thank you all, my lovelies. Anonymity is not an option for everyone, however. Deepest gratitude to my in-laws; my parents, Vivian and Stephen Blyth (my model married couple); my sisters, Heidi Morin and Jenny Blyth, and my husband, Sebastian Shakespeare, who is the last word.

SELECTED BIBLIOGRAPHY

Abse, Dannie, *The Presence*, London, Hutchinson, 2007

Ackroyd, Peter, *Blake*, London, Sinclair-Stevenson, 1995

Apter, Terri, *What Do You Want From Me?*, London, W.W. Norton, 2009

Beagan, Brenda, Chapman, Gwen E., D'Sylva, Andrea, and Raewyn Bassett, B., '"It's Just Easier for Me to Do It": Rationalising the Family Division of Foodwork', *Sociology*, 42, August 2008

Beecher Stowe, Harriet, and Beecher, Catharine, *The American Woman's Home*, New York, J.B. Ford and Co., 1869

Belot, Michèle, and Francesconi, Marco, *Can Anyone Be 'The*

One'?, London, Centre for Economic Policy Research, 2006

Boggs, Mathew, and Miller, Jason, *Project Everlasting*, New York, Simon and Schuster, 2007

Bond, Michael, 'The Three Degrees of Contagion', *New Scientist*, 3 January 2009

Brian, Denis, *The Curies*, Chichester, John Wiley, 2005

Brindle, Stephen, *Brunel*, London, Weidenfeld & Nicolson, 2005

Broad, Richard, and Fleming, Suzie, eds., *Nella Last's War*, London, Profile Books, 2006

Brooks, Geraldine, *Nine Parts of Desire: The Hidden World of Islamic Women*, London, Hamish Hamilton, 1995

Bruner Eales, Anne, *Army Wives on the American Frontier*, Boulder, Johnson Books, 1996

Bryant, Chalandra M., Conger, R.D., and Meehan, Jennifer M., 'The Influence of In-Laws on Change in Marital Success', *Journal of Marriage and the Family*, 63, August 2001

Cameron, Deborah, *The Myth of Mars and Venus*, Oxford, OUP, 2007

Casanova, Giacomo, *The Story of My Life*, London, Penguin, 2001

Castor, Helen, *Blood and Roses*, London, Faber and Faber, 2004

Chasman, Deborah, and Jhee, Catherine, eds., *Here Lies My Heart*, Boston, Beacon Press, 1999

Cockrell, Stacie, O'Neill, Cathy, and Stone, Julia, *Baby-Proofing Your Marriage*, London, Collins, 2007

Crawford, Duane W., Houts, Renate M., Huston, Ted L., and George, Laura J., 'Compatibility, Leisure and Satisfaction in Marital Relationships', *Journal of Marriage and the Family*, 64, May 2002

Crawley, Ernest, *The Mystic Rose*, London, Spring Books, 1965

Cressy, David, *Birth, Marriage, and Death*, Oxford, OUP, 1997

Csikszentmihalyi, Mihaly, *Flow*, New York, Harper & Row, 1990

Cusk, Rachel, *A Life's Work: On Becoming a Mother*, London, Fourth Estate, 2001

Davenport-Hines, Richard, *Ettie*, London, Weidenfeld & Nicolson, 2008

de la Tour du Pin, Lucie, *Memoirs of Madame de la Tour du Pin*, London, Harvill Press, 1969

Dempsey, Ken, *Inequalities in Marriage: Australia and Beyond*, Oxford, OUP, 1997

Didion, Joan, *The Year of Magical Thinking*, London, Fourth Estate, 2005

Dillner, Luisa, *The Complete Book of Mothers-in-Law*, London, Faber & Faber, 2008

Druckerman, Pamela, *Lust in Translation*, New York, Penguin Press, 2007

Duby, Georges, *The Knight, the Lady and the Priest*, London, Peregrine Books, 1985

du Plessix Gray, Francine, *At Home with the Marquis de Sade*, London, Chatto & Windus, 1999

Ehrenreich, Barbara, and English, Deirdre, *For Her Own Good*, London, Pluto Press, 1979

Eisenach, Emlyn, *Husbands, Wives, and Concubines*, Kirksville, Truman State University Press, 2004

Elliott, Sinikka, and Umberson, Debra, 'The Performance of Desire: Gender and Sexual Negotiation in Long-Term Marriages', *Journal of Marriage and the Family*, 70, May 2008

Erickson, R.J., 'Why Emotion Work Matters: Sex, Gender, and the Division of Household Labour', *Journal of Marriage and the Family*, 67, 2005

Fallaci, Oriana, *The Egotists*, Chicago, H. Regnery Co., 1968

Feinstein, Anthony, *Journalists Under Fire*, Baltimore, Johns Hopkins University Press, 2006

Fisher, Helen, *Why We Love*, New York, Henry Holt, 2004

——*Why Him? Why Her?*, New York, Henry Holt, 2009

Flett, Kathryn, *The Heart-Shaped Bullet*, London, Picador, 1999

Fox, James, *White Mischief*, London, Penguin, 1984

Fromm, Erich, *The Art of Loving*, London, Thorsons, 1995

Funt, Marilyn, *Are You Anybody?*, New York, Dial Press, 1979

G__, Vicomtesse de, *The Art of Being Loved by One's Husband*, 1823

Gabor, Andrea, *Einstein's Wife*, New York, Penguin Books, 2005

Garfield, Simon, ed., *Our Hidden Lives*, London, Ebury Press, 2004

Gatrell, Caroline, *Hard Labour*, Maidenhead, Open University Press, 2005

Gay, Peter, *The Tender Passion*, Oxford, OUP, 1986

Gladwell, Malcolm, *The Tipping Point*, London, Abacus, 2001

Gottman, John, *Why Marriages Succeed or Fail*, London, Bloomsbury, 1997

Greer, Germaine, *Sex & Destiny*, London, Secker & Warburg, 1984

——*The Whole Woman*, London, Doubleday, 1999

Hahn, Emily, and Hatch, Eric, *Spousery*, New York, Franklin Watts, 1956

Harding, Luke, *The Liar: The Fall of Jonathan Aitken*, London, Penguin, 1997

Hardy, Rev. E.J., *How to Be Happy Though Married*, London, T.F. Unwin, 1885

Healey, Edna, *Wives of Fame*, London, New English Library, 1986

Helms-Erikson, Heather, 'Marital Quality Ten Years After the Transition to Parenthood: Implications of the Timing of Parenthood and the Division of Housework', *Journal of Marriage and the Family*, 63, November 2001

Herman, Eleanor, *Sex with the Queen*, London, Harper Perennial, 2007

Hewlett, Sylvia Ann, *Off-Ramps and On-Ramps*, Boston, Harvard Business School Press, 2007

Heymann, C. David, *A Woman Named Jackie*, London, Mandarin, 1995

Hickman, Katie, *Courtesans*, London, HarperCollins, 2003

Hilton, Lisa, *Queens Consort: England's Medieval Queens*, London, Weidenfeld & Nicolson, 2008

Horsfield, Margaret, *Biting the Dust*, London, Fourth Estate, 1997

Hufton, Olwen, *The Prospect Before Her*, London, HarperCollins, 1995

Hughes, Kathryn, *The Short Life & Long Times of Mrs Beeton*, London, Harper Perennial, 2006

Hughes, Ted, *Birthday Letters*, London, Faber & Faber, 1998

Jackson, Rosie, *Frieda Lawrence*, London, Pandora, 1994

James, Oliver, *They F*** You Up*, London, Bloomsbury, 2002

Jenkins, Dafydd, and Owen, Morfydd E., eds., *The Welsh Law of Women*, Cardiff, University of Wales Press, 1980

Kahr, Brett, *Sex and the Psyche*, London, Allen Lane, 2007

Kerenyi, C., *Zeus and Hera*, London, Routledge & Kegan Paul, 1975

Kierkegaard, Sören, *Either/Or*, tr. Swenson, D.F. and L.M, and Lowrie, W., Oxford, OUP, 1944

Kluwer, Esther S., Hessinkand, José A.M., and van de Ulvert, Evert, 'The Division of Labour Across the Transition to Parenthood', *Journal of Marriage and the Family*, 64, 2002

Laird, James D., and Strout, Sarah, 'Emotional Behaviours

as Emotional Stimuli', in *Handbook of Emotion Elicitation and Assessment*, ed. Coan, James A., and Allen, John J.B., Oxford, OUP, 2007

Layard, Richard, *Happiness*, London, Penguin, 2005

Levine, Janice R., and Markman, Howard J., eds., *Why Do Fools Fall In Love?*, San Francisco, Jossey-Bass, 2001

Lewis, Gwyneth, *Two in a Boat*, London, Fourth Estate, 2005

Liu, Chien, 'A Theory of Marital Sexual Life', *Journal of Marriage and the Family*, 62, May 2000

Lovell, Mary S., *The Sound of Wings*, London, Century, 1989, *Bess of Hardwick*, London, Little Brown, 2005

MacCarthy, Fiona, *Byron*, London, John Murray, 2002

Magner, James A., *The Art of Happy Marriage*, New York, Guild Press, 1947

Mailer, Norman, *Deaths for Ladies and Other Disasters*, New York, G.P. Putnam's Sons, 1962

Mainardi, Patricia, *Husbands, Wives and Lovers*, New Haven, Yale, 2003

Mais, S.P.B., *This Delicious Madness*, London, Leslie Frewin, 1968

Markham, Gervase, *The English Housewife*, ed. Best, R., and Kingston, Michale, Montreal, McGill-Queen's University Press, 1986

Martin, Andrew, *How to Get Things Really Flat*, London, Short Books, 2008

Maushart, Susan, *Wifework*, London, Bloomsbury, 2002

McCarthy, Conor, ed., *Love, Sex and Marriage in the Middle Ages*, London, Routledge, 2004

Menefee, Samuel Pyeatt, *Wives for Sale*, Oxford, Blackwell, 1981

Monson, Karen, *Alma Mahler*, London, Collins, 1984

Morgan, Marabel, *The Total Woman*, New Jersey, F.H. Revell, 1973

Morris, Jan, *Fisher's Face*, London, Viking, 1995

Neville-Sington, Pamela, *Robert Browning*, London, Weidenfeld & Nicolson, 2004

Nock, Steven L., *Marriage in Men's Lives*, Oxford, OUP, 1998

Nyborg, Helmuth, *Hormones, Sex, and Society*, Connecticut, Praegur, 1994

Offer, Avner, *The Challenge of Affluence*, Oxford, OUP, 2006

O'Reilly, Judith, *Wife in the North*, London, Penguin, 2008

Otisa, Kifo M., *Culture and Customs of Uganda*, Oxford, Greenwood, 2006

Perel, Esther, *Mating in Captivity*, London, Hodder, 2007

Pinker, Susan, *The Sexual Paradox*, New York, Scribner, 2008

Presley, Priscilla Beaulieu, *Elvis and Me*, London, Arrow, 1986

Pritchard, Edward Evan Evans, *Marriage and Kinship Among the Nuer*, Oxford, Clarendon Press, 1951

Roberts, Linda J., 'Fire and Ice in Marital Communication: Hostile and Distancing Behaviours as Predictors of Marital Distress', *Journal of Marriage and the Family*, 62, August 2000

Roberts, Linda J., and Leonard, Kenneth E., 'An Empirical Typology of Drinking Partnerships and their Relationship to Marital Functioning and Drinking Consequences', *Journal of Marriage and the Family*, 60, May 1998

Roiphe, Katie, *Uncommon Arrangements*, New York, Dial Press, 2007

Rose, Phyllis, *Parallel Lives*, London, Chatto & Windus, 1984

Russell Hochschild, Arlie, *The Time Bind*, New York, Metropolitan Books, 1997, with Machung, Anne, *The Second Shift*, London, Piatkus, 1989

Schiff, Stacy, *Véra (Mrs. Vladimir Nabokov)*, London, Picador, 1999

Sen, Amartya, *Development as Freedom*, Oxford, OUP, 1999

Simpson, John, *A Mad World, My Masters*, London, Macmillan, 2000

Smith, Virginia, *Clean,* Oxford, OUP, 2007

Squire, Susan, *I Don't: A Contrarian History of Marriage*, New York, Bloomsbury, 2008

Stone, Lawrence, *The Family, Sex and Marriage*, London, Peregrine, 1982

——*Uncertain Unions and Broken Lives*, Oxford, OUP, 1995

Surtees, Virginia, *Jane Welsh Carlyle*, Wilton, Michael Russell, 1986

Thomas, Caitlin, *Leftover Life to Kill*, London, Putnam, 1957

Thompson, Brian, *Keeping Mum*, London, Atlantic Books, 2006

Thurman, Judith, *Secrets of the Flesh: A Life of Colette*, London, Bloomsbury, 1999

Timmer, Susan G., and Veroff, Joseph, 'Family Ties and the Discontinuity of Divorce in Black and White Newlywed Couples', *Journal of Marriage and the Family*, 62, May 2000

Tomalin, Claire, *The Invisible Woman*, London, Penguin, 1991

Tusser, Thomas, *A Hundred Good Points of Husbandry*, London, The Company of Stationers, 1638

Vangelisti, Anita L., and Perlman, Daniel, eds., *The Cambridge Handbook of Personal Relationships*, Cambridge, CUP, 2006

Vatsayana, *Kama Sutra*, tr. Burton, Sir Richard, and Arbuthnot, F.F., London, Luxor Press, 1963

Vaughan, Diane, *Uncoupling*, London, Mandarin, 1993

Vecchio, Silvana, 'The Good Wife', *A History of Women in the West*, vol 2, ed. Duby, Georges, and Perrot, Michelle, tr. Goldhammer, Arthur, Cambridge, Belknap Press, 1992

Waite, Linda J., and Gallagher, Maggie, *The Case for Marriage*, New York, Doubleday, 2001

Warhurst, Chris, Eikhof, Doris Ruth, and Haunschild, Axel, eds., *Work Less, Live More?*, London, Palgrave Macmillan, 2008

Weiner Davis, Michele, *The Sex-Starved Marriage*, London, Simon & Schuster, 2004

Weir, Alison, *Eleanor of Aquitaine*, London, Pimlico, 2000

Westermarck, E.A., *The History of Human Marriage*, vol 2, London, Macmillan, 1925

Wexler, Joan, and Steidl, John, 'Marriage and the Capacity to be Alone', *Psychiatry*, 41, February 1978

Whately, William, *A Bride-bush*, London, 1617

Wilson, A.N., *Betjeman*, London, Hutchinson, 2006

Wulff, Helena, ed., *The Emotions: A Cultural Reader*, Oxford, Berg, 2007

Yates, Richard, *Revolutionary Road*, London, New English Library, 1964

Young, Michael, and Willmott, Peter, *Family and Kinship in East London*, London, Penguin, 2007

Zuckerman, Marvin, *Behavioral Expressions and Biosocial Bases of Sensation Seeking*, Cambridge, Cambridge University Press, 2004